SHAPING YOUR CAREER

SHAPING YOUR CAREER

A Guide for Early Career Faculty

Don Haviland, Anna M. Ortiz, and Laura Henriques

Foreword by Ann E. Austin

STERLING, VIRGINIA

Published by Stylus Publishing, LLC.
22883 Quicksilver Drive
Sterling, Virginia 20166-2102

Library of Congress Cataloging-in-Publication-Data
Names: Haviland, Don, 1968-, author. |
Ortiz, Anna Marie, 1963-author. |
Henriques, Laura, 1963- author. |
Title: Shaping your career : a guide for early career faculty /
Don Haviland,
Anna M. Ortiz, and Laura Henriques ; foreword by Ann E. Austin.
Description: First edition. |
Sterling, Virginia : Stylus Publishing, LLC, [2017] |
Includes bibliographical references.
Identifiers: LCCN 2017014321 (print) |
LCCN 2017039332 (ebook) |
ISBN 9781620364451 (Library networkable e-edition) |
ISBN 9781620364468 (Consumer e-edition) |
ISBN 9781620364444 (pbk. : alk. paper) |
ISBN 9781620364437 (cloth : alk. paper)
Subjects: LCSH: College teachers--Vocational guidance--
United States.
Classification: LCC LB1778.2 (ebook) |
LCC LB1778.2 .H38 2017 (print) |
DDC 378.1/25023--dc23
LC record available at https://lccn.loc.gov/2017014321

13-digit ISBN: 978-1-62036-443-7 (cloth)
13-digit ISBN: 978-1-62036-444-4 (paperback)
13-digit ISBN: 978-1-62036-445-1 (library networkable e-edition)
13-digit ISBN: 978-1-62036-446-8 (consumer e-edition)

Printed in the United States of America

Bulk Purchases

Quantity discounts are available for use in workshops and for
staff development.
Call 1-800-232-0223

First Edition, 2017

CONTENTS

Faculty members constitute the essential core of American higher education. They teach students; design curriculum; conduct research; and use their expertise to interact with and contribute to local, national and international communities. Faculty work is complex and multifaceted, and those who serve in the role sometimes find it challenging to help others understand the full array of diverse responsibilities and tasks with which they engage. Over the years, various images of faculty work and faculty life have emerged. Movies, books, and the popular press have often portrayed faculty members in stereotypical ways, sometimes suggesting academics are removed from the stresses in the workplace experienced by much of the population, that their days are unpressured and largely consumed with quiet time for reflection, and that they can spend most of their time following their own interests. In contrast to these popularized descriptions, the scholarly literature examining faculty work over the past few decades has often emphasized the multiple demands on faculty members, particularly highlighting the concerns of many faculty that preparation for work in the academy does not always address the full range of professorial work, that expectations for success are often unclear, and that finding balance between personal and professional responsibilities can be challenging. Often this body of scholarly literature has been designed to call the attention of institutional leaders to strategies for more fully supporting their faculty colleagues.

Recognizing the ways in which academic work is often portrayed, this book, *Shaping Your Career*, steps into the dialogue about the academic profession with fresh perspectives and inspiring ideas for those considering professorial work, those recently starting careers as faculty members, and those in established faculty roles or institutional leadership roles who have the responsibility to guide the next generation of academics who will be the heart of American higher education.

Don Haviland, Anna M. Ortiz, and Laura Henriques are clear about the purpose of their work. They recognize that the academic landscape is changing in significant ways that are reflected in who constitutes the professoriate; what work they do; and what factors impact the nature of their work, their workplaces, and their lives. Of particular note, for example, is that the student body is becoming more diverse, a trend that is encouraging in regard to broadening opportunities for more people and contributing to an educated populace and workforce, yet one that requires faculty members to be prepared to teach in new and varied ways in order to respond to diverse student needs. The fiscal contexts at the state and national levels impose pressures on higher education institutions, leading to calls for greater accountability and more expectations that faculty members find ways to enhance institutional revenue. And, of great import in terms of the nature of faculty work, academic appointment types are diversifying, with a significant increase in recent years in the proportion of academics in non-tenure-track and part-time positions.

The authors of this book offer a vision of faculty work that recognizes these changes and challenges and embraces the full diversity of faculty demographics and faculty appointment types. In providing this practical handbook to guide those new to the professoriate, they are informed by deep knowledge of the research and literature on academic work and careers, which they weave skillfully throughout the book in ways that shape their recommendations, as well as by the extensive personal experiences they have each had in their own careers. They honor the needs of each individual academic reading their advice, while also acknowledging and urging consideration of and respect for the missions, history, and commitments of the range of institutions in which today's faculty members serve. Most important of all—and particularly noteworthy—is their ability to hold idealism and practicality in balance, and, in fact, to show how vision and hope for what the faculty career can be should be held up alongside practical wisdom that responds to the demands, challenges, and responsibilities that comprise the daily work of most academics.

The book is filled with detailed, reasoned, and useful advice, informed by research and experience, about how to construct a productive and enriching academic career. Woven throughout are three key themes that constitute the essence of this book and, I believe, provide very wise and worthy guidelines for aspiring, new, and established academics. First, recognize that your identity and values should guide all that you do as a faculty member. You have the agency and the responsibility to self-author the career that you would like and that you can uniquely fulfill. Take control of your work and your career and recognize that you have the responsibility to develop good habits to connect your research, teaching, and outreach to your professional commitments and values and to see your career as a journey where components are connected by the identity that you create. Second, collegiality and trust are essential to accomplishing work within the academy and to creating meaningful careers. Be interested in the priorities, work, and commitments of others; be willing to invest in the academic community; and realize that excellent academic work—in a department, in outreach activities, in research—is often an ensemble affair, requiring the contributions and the give and take of colleagues who value the particular contributions each brings to the task. Third, understand the nuances of the context in which you work. Institutional types vary, and, within similar types, each institution has a unique culture. Your responsibility, if the work is to be both productive and satisfying, is to develop an understanding of your particular institution and find ways to connect your values, interests, and commitments to the mission, culture, and expectations of that specific context.

I have served as a faculty member for more than three decades. For me, the career has been wonderfully stimulating, challenging, enriching, and rewarding. This book rings true in describing what makes an academic career so meaningful, even while acknowledging the issues and challenges that sometimes occur. It holds up a vision of what the career can be, while also explaining squarely that the academic, herself or himself, must take responsibility for creating the hoped-for career and for helping the academy fulfill its responsibilities to its students and the society—as well as to the faculty whose work carries it forward into the future.

Ann E. Austin
Michigan State University

ACKNOWLEDGMENTS

A project like this simply does not happen without the work, guidance, support, and encouragement of many others, and we are indebted to them for the roles they have played in making this book possible.

As this book was being conceived, we reached out to several individuals who were leading the Preparing Future Faculty programs on their campuses. Ilene Alexander (University of Minnesota), Gwendolyn Bethea (Howard University), and Shamini Dias (Claremont Graduate University) generously helped us think through the needs and interests of new and future faculty members. We hope we have honored their good advice.

Our current and former graduate students also played a key role in making this book possible. Andrew Kretz, Diliana Peregrina-Kretz, Elizabeth Nuñez, and Carolyn Sevilla all patiently transcribed hours of interviews or reviewed those transcriptions for accuracy. Dinesa Thomas-Whitman then waded through these extensive data, coding the interviews to help us narrow down the quotes from early career faculty that you will see in the chapters that follow. Jenny Jacobs has been invaluable in helping us get this book over the finish line, sitting through meetings, doing initial formatting, organizing references, editing, and basically managing three busy faculty members to help us finish this book. We are grateful to you all.

We were also fortunate to work with a graphic designer, Thomas Anderson (www.thomasanderson.net), who gave the images you will see in this book a much more professional feel. He grasped our needs and used his design skills to far surpass anything we could have accomplished on our own. Thank you!

Our editor, John von Knorring, has been a guide and partner in this work. In the early stages he helped us think about the ideal coauthoring team and identify missing content. Reviewing early drafts, he nudged us to refine our thinking, add some new elements, and make what we feel are smart choices (we hope you agree). Throughout he pushed, prodded, and challenged, even as he encouraged and motivated us. Such is a fine and difficult balance to strike and reflects his skill as an editor. This work is better for his guidance.

As you read the book, you will see quotes from early career faculty about their experiences and advice. These professors were part of a longitudinal study on the experiences of pretenure faculty (see Appendix A). We are indebted to them for sharing their experiences, challenges, and hopes with such honesty and openness. We learned from their experiences and their wisdom and we hope you will also.

Finally, to our families and partners. You have been patient with us as we have been writing and had to meet deadlines. And most of all, you have cheered us on and supported us. To Amy and Al, thank you for your love and support.

If you have picked up this book, you are likely an early career faculty member looking for tips for success, a doctoral student wanting to know more about faculty life, a mid-career faculty member considering the next step in your career, or an administrator or faculty development specialist wanting to support your pretenure faculty. Whether you fit one of these descriptions or are someone completely different, welcome!

We wrote this book for many reasons. First, there is ample evidence that graduate school does an incomplete (even inadequate) job of preparing doctoral students for the full range of faculty roles and the varied institutions in which they will find themselves working (Gaff, Pruitt-Logan, & Weibl, 2000; Golde & Dore, 2001; Rice, Sorcinelli, & Austin, 2000). The abilities to understand and navigate institutional context, identify and manage politics, develop positive professional relationships, and align individual goals with institutional expectations are critical to faculty success but are seldom covered in graduate school.

Second, and closely related, early career faculty members often struggle with a host of issues as they transition into their roles. They face varied and conflicting demands on their time: courses with multiple preparations that take more time than anticipated, committee work, advising, and often the need to develop a research agenda (Gaugler, 2004; Murray, 2000). As a result, many early career faculty members struggle with time management, making career choices, and balancing work-family responsibilities (Boice, 2000; Gaugler, 2004; Solem & Foote, 2006).

Third, external forces (accountability, technology, the decline of tenure-track lines) are reshaping faculty work (Gappa, Austin, & Trice, 2007; Matveev, 2007; O'Meara, Terosky, & Neumann, 2008). Faculty are increasingly asked to work across disciplines, be more collaborative, and be responsive to market as well as governmental expectations to keep their institutions and academic programs competitive. These external forces shape the expectations held by our students, institutions, and other stakeholders, and knowing how to navigate those expectations is critical to success and very challenging.

However, most of all, we wrote this book because we *love* what we do. Among us, we have more than 50 years of experience as faculty members, and none of us can imagine a better or more fulfilling career. We have benefited from rich interactions with students and colleagues, learned new ideas and skills along the way, and (we hope!) contributed to our institutions and the profession. To be sure, our work is among the most challenging things we have ever done, but it is also among the most rewarding.

Our careers have become richer and more successful as we have learned to take an active role in shaping them ourselves. With time, experience, and reflection, we each came to think more deeply about how we want to spend our time, what we could best contribute, and the kind of professor we wished to be. As we did so, we took control of our careers, making it easier to manage our time, navigate institutional politics, and learn and grow ourselves.

Fundamentally, we wrote this book to help others succeed in and appreciate a faculty career as much as we do. In this book we draw on our own experiences, but we draw on other resources as well. We share lessons, insights, and strategies from early career faculty collected as part of a longitudinal study of pretenure faculty. We also draw on literature from higher education about faculty work and careers, mentoring, and institutional climate to provide critical context for faculty careers. We hope that you find this useful. Enjoy!

Purpose of This Book

The purpose of this book is to facilitate the success of all faculty members, particularly early career faculty members. For us, this task breaks down into four main goals. We want to

1. provide you with resources, tips, and strategies that you can use to develop a strong, healthy career as a faculty member;
2. empower you to take ownership for and be an active agent in shaping your faculty career;
3. provide advice and strategies to help women and members of traditionally underrepresented racial and ethnic groups (minoritized faculty[1]) navigate institutional structures that affect these faculty members differently; and
4. contribute to a changed narrative around faculty work and offer concrete strategies for faculty to grow and succeed.

Our first goal for this book is to make more transparent the tools, strategies, and approaches you can use to navigate your faculty career. Think of these things, if you will, as trade secrets—lessons from other faculty to help you succeed. While you will surely make mistakes along the way, we hope these nuggets allow you to make *new* mistakes rather than the same mistakes that others before you have made.

A second closely related and no less important goal is to empower you to be an active agent in shaping your career. A substantial body of research (e.g., Helms, 2010; Rice, Sorcinelli, & Austin, 2000) has pointed to the shock that new faculty experience at the isolating nature of faculty work; while a challenge in itself, this isolation also means that early career faculty typically are unaware that their peers face similar challenges and frustrations. It is easy to feel like you are going through these challenges alone. The results of this feeling can include a sense that there is something wrong with you because others appear to be thriving while you are not, and even a decision to not ask for help or raise questions lest you look bad in the eyes of your peers or senior colleagues. These feelings happen to most new faculty but can be especially pronounced for those in the minority (e.g., women and those from traditionally underrepresented groups).

The very challenges we have discussed already (e.g., difficult transitions, varied and competing time demands, institutional politics) can make you feel like you are merely responding to situations rather than actually steering your career. Especially early in your career, when you are seeking to establish yourself and build your reputation, it can feel like you must say yes to any opportunity. We have felt these pressures ourselves and seen our colleagues struggle with them as well. However, even *new* faculty have choices and options. Moreover, as you move forward in your faculty career, you will continue to find that the nature of your work will change, as will your own priorities, goals, and interests. The same skills and knowledge that will help you shape your faculty career early in the process will be useful throughout your career.

Thus, in this book we seek to empower you by normalizing the new faculty experience, naming and making explicit the challenges early career faculty face, and identifying the different dimensions of institutional culture and the political environments that affect faculty work. We hope that the stories, tips, ideas, and information we share will also empower you from the onset of your career and lead you to feel that you can reach out to others for help and support, and that you can drive your own career rather than respond to the needs, interests, and agendas of others.

Third, and closely related to our goals of empowering you to navigate your career, our goal for this book is particularly to help women and members of other traditionally underrepresented groups succeed as faculty. If the curriculum of a faculty career can be obtuse for most early career faculty, it is often particularly so for scholars from these specific groups, who face a variety of unique challenges for their success, including limited access to mentoring and less integration into the faculty community (Boice, 1993). We hope to speak specifically to challenges those of you from these groups might encounter (from your institutions, colleagues, students, etc.) and identify strategies you can use to facilitate your professional success and personal well-being.

Our fourth goal, and related to the goals just described, is to contribute to a new perspective on faculty work. O'Meara, Terosky, and Neumann (2008) have observed that much of the existing literature on faculty work takes what might be considered a negative or deficit perspective on faculty careers. Far from appearing as autonomous professionals actively shaping their careers, faculty are often depicted as beset by numerous challenges, responding to external pressures, and victims of larger organizational and social structures. There are indeed forces that influence our work and careers as faculty. However, O'Meara and colleagues (2008) offer a different vision, one in which the faculty career is defined by growth and development, in which faculty are agents in their careers. This vision undergirds our book. We aspire to contribute to that emerging vision of faculty work through the stories we share (stories of our own, of our colleagues, and of participants in our interviews) as well as by offering tools for reflection and strategies to shape your career to operationalize the concepts that O'Meara and colleagues (2008) laid out so nicely.

Audience

Who then is this book for? We hope that multiple audiences find value in this work. Primarily, we have written the book for early career faculty members at four-year institutions. Why not also address faculty careers at community colleges? While we wish we could do so, those institutions are much different from four-year institutions in their missions and the nature of faculty work, and we did not feel we could do a credible job of addressing faculty careers across such a broad spectrum of institutional types.

One of the leaders in the faculty development field, Robert Boice (1992), coined the term *quick starters* to describe new faculty who were able to step into their positions and thrive early in their careers. He identified four main attributes or behaviors of these successful faculty members (we identify the relevant chapters in this book in parentheses after each attribute):

  1. *Involvement.* Quick starters are actively engaged with others in their work. Quick starters seek advice and guidance from colleagues, work

collaboratively on projects, discuss teaching, and build relationships with students (Chapters 4–8).

2. *Regimen.* Quick starters are less concerned with *time* management and more focused on *task* management. They focus for appropriate but brief amounts of time on a given task, do not feel rushed, and talk less about how busy they are (Chapters 4, 6, 8, and 10).

3. *Social networking.* Quick starters build relationships with colleagues that provide them with the learning, support, and mentoring to help them succeed as early career faculty (Chapters 3–4).

4. *Self-management.* Quick starters make use of a tacit knowledge and understanding of themselves that allows them to find balance in their work and relationships and take creative risks (Chapters 4, 10, and 13).

While Boice (1992) was describing individuals who seemed to have figured out much of faculty life on their own, our intention is give early career faculty members who read this book the tools and tips needed to get off to a quick start in their career. All faculty members can be quick starters. This goal makes this book particularly useful for faculty who are in the first stage of their careers.

Given our focus on empowering faculty to be active agents in shaping their careers, we also hope the book is useful for full-time faculty at all career stages and at multiple institutional types. Perhaps associate and full professors can find value for themselves in the reflection and planning strategies we outline in the book or use these strategies while mentoring more junior faculty. In addition, we recognize that the tenure-track professor is no longer the normative model in colleges and universities. Full-time non-tenure-track faculty, a group whose work increasingly resembles that of tenure-track faculty (Hollenshead et al., 2007; Kezar & Maxey, 2013; Kezar & Sam, 2011), should also be able to find ideas and strategies they can put to use in authoring their careers, as should clinical and research faculty. While we have written this book primarily with faculty at four-year institutions in mind, we recognize the wide variety of institutions within this category, and we try to speak to this variation where relevant for a given topic (e.g., service).

Graduate students who are preparing for careers as professors can also find value in these pages, because the content will help them start preparing for and thinking about their career *now.* The habits of being a successful professor begin in graduate school and extend far beyond the research and writing skills that are part of the formal curriculum. The questions posed and information shared in this book can help you make informed decisions about what kind of faculty member you wish to be. Would you prefer to be at a research university, a comprehensive institution, a liberal arts college, or a community college? What types of students do you want to work with, and what does that mean for you as a scholar? Similarly, the tools and strategies for reflecting on and authoring your career, as well as the more operational tips related to teaching, research, and balance, can be used even before that career officially begins to create habits and practices that will facilitate your success.

Finally, we expect the book to be useful for department chairs, deans, and faculty developers, to whom we devote a chapter. These individuals can be critical in shaping the successes and challenges that pretenure faculty members experience. Moreover, what is a success or a challenge looks different for each faculty member and varies by gender, race, and ethnicity. Our hope is that by openly discussing these issues within a framework of faculty growth we provide departmental and institutional leaders with fresh perspectives and resources with which to support not just early career faculty but all faculty from all backgrounds.

The Faculty Growth Perspective

O'Meara and colleagues (2008) offer a concept of professional growth that provides a positive, agentic view of faculty lives and careers. As we said earlier, we have sought to craft a book that reaches beyond a narrative of faculty constrained by challenging times or a mere how-to; our intent here is to empower and energize. The growth framework of O'Meara and colleagues (2008) helps us achieve this goal, and we weave it (together with other models or frameworks as relevant) throughout the book. Specifically, O'Meara and colleagues (2008) propose four dimensions or aspects of faculty growth:

1. *Learning.* Faculty are learners. Fundamentally, it is what we do. We are trained to identify new problems, learn about them, and craft new solutions and understandings. This learning is ongoing and key to our growth as professors. We are not expected to know it all in our roles, but rather to grow into those roles and change and grow throughout our careers.

2. *Agency.* Agency is the ability to act with intention, which for faculty means the opportunity to influence our professional contexts and experiences in ways that influence our learning, our work, and our professional identity. Rather than being passive recipients in our contexts, we can shape our environments. Agency, or at least its impact, is not absolute. Our ability to influence our environment varies by career stage, employment category, and our multiple social identities

(e.g., race, gender, and sexual orientation). However, we always have some level of agency.

3. *Professional relationships.* Much faculty work is ultimately social. We interact daily with colleagues, students, administrators, staff, community members, and numerous others, and these relationships inspire, challenge, invigorate, and enhance us. They are key to our professional growth and identity.

4. *Commitments.* As faculty we have made commitments to our field and to our institutions. But other commitments remain to be explored. We can choose how to invest our time and energy in a range of endeavors, such as teaching, community engagement, or research and creative activities. To the degree we are intentional about making those commitments, they can both reflect and inform our professional identity.

This framework is particularly useful for giving faculty an empowering way of thinking about their careers. Making the framework explicit gives you a structure through which to consider your professional choices. Thus, we come back to these concepts throughout the book, particularly in Chapter 13.

This Book's Structure

This book is intended to provide you with a broad context for faculty work, specific tips and strategies for success in the main components of faculty work (teaching, research, and service), and the opportunity for reflection to guide your faculty career. It is organized to help you situate yourself and your faculty career in the context of higher education while giving you concrete tips, resources, and vignettes that you can use to succeed.

The book has an hourglass shape. In Part One, Chapters 1 through 4, we provide the broad contextual background for faculty work. In Chapter 1 we examine the nature of faculty work, differences in institutional types, and the forces shaping the environment in which faculty operate. In Chapter 2 we explore the faculty career and provide a big-picture perspective of how your career might unfold while giving you some of the foundational pieces for developing your own career plan. In Chapter 3 we look at institutional climate and culture as critical elements in your faculty experience and review ways to assess and work within the climate and culture at your institution. In Chapter 4 we explore the idea of professional relationships. While faculty work is often thought of as solitary, it involves relationships with a wide range of people; developing and maintaining these relationships is critical to your success.

In Part Two, Chapters 5 through 8, we move to the middle of the hour-glass and narrow our focus by looking in detail at issues and strategies related to the specific components of faculty work. In Chapter 5 we review issues related to teaching and advising and highlight resources you can use to become even more effective as an instructor. In Chapters 6 and 7 we discuss issues related to scholarship and external funding. Specifically, in Chapter 6 we explore how to build and maintain a successful scholarly program, and in Chapter 7 we discuss externally funded research programs. Finally, in Chapter 8, we discuss faculty service, including how to think strategically about service opportunities. We want to offer an important caveat: This book is focused on how to be a faculty member, not necessarily how to teach or do research. There are many good resources that we offer for these activities. Our focus in these chapters is to give you basic how-tos while addressing trends and contexts (e.g., the growth of active learning) that might influence how you think about your work and professional identity.

In Part Three, Chapters 9 through 13, we once again broaden our focus. In Chapter 9, we address the question of promotion and tenure, providing tools for thinking about the process right from the start of your career in a way that fits with your professional identity. In Chapter 10 we tackle the difficult but important topic of how to find balance and practice effective time management; these are core elements of a successful career and often a significant challenge. Having a clear and sound professional identity can make managing your time and finding balance easier. In Chapter 11 we pose scenarios and explore some of the difficult dilemmas (e.g., considering leaving your job, negotiating) you may confront in your career. In Chapter 12 we speak specifically to chairs, deans, and institutional leaders and highlight our suggestions for ways to support faculty members from all backgrounds. In Chapter 13 we share some final words and reflections on developing, refining, and maintaining your professional growth and identity.

We have also woven throughout this book, as appropriate, views of other personal or institutional dimensions that can affect the faculty experience. For example, as we have noted previously, your experience as a professor looks very different depending on whether you are at a research university or a liberal arts college; each setting provides many options for your professional identity, but the expectations of each environment also constrain options. Similarly, disciplinary differences matter. The work life of a professor in theater or other arts looks very different from that of a chemist. Faculty work may also be influenced by whether you work in an environment that utilizes collective bargaining. Last but by no means least, our various identities as individuals greatly influence how we approach our work as faculty and how others approach us in our roles. Our race, ethnicity, gender, and sexual orientation all influence our professional goals and priorities, the agency that might be available to us and ways in which we can exercise it, and our relationships with students and colleges. Together with the professional growth framework of O'Meara and colleagues (2008), we use these institutional and personal characteristics to guide our discussion of how to shape your faculty career and professional identity.

The book includes three different types of inset boxes. The first type is labeled *Words From Early Career Faculty*. These inset boxes (shaded with no border) include vignettes or quotes from a six-year, longitudinal study of nine pretenure faculty (see Appendix A for more detail on the study). These quotes are used to frame problems, suggest possible solutions or strategies, and illustrate key points. They come from real faculty facing real challenges and finding real solutions; therefore, we hope, they support our goal of normalizing many of the things you may be feeling as a new faculty member. The second type of inset (bordered with no shading), *Resources for Success*, provides books, websites, blogs, and other resources that may be helpful to you in specific tasks (e.g., teaching) or in learning about faculty work more generally. The third type of inset (shaded with a border), *Strategies for Success*, is designed to summarize key ideas from a section or offer concise tips for success in the topic at hand.

At the end of most chapters we provide exercises and/or goal-setting activities. These reflect our belief that faculty can and always are growing in their roles; as a result, the book has a decidedly developmental feel to it. In Chapters 3 to 10, we provide *Exercises* (a mix of reflective questions and activities) designed to help you gather information or understanding about your faculty career. In Chapters 4, 5, 6, and 8, we also provide *Goal-Setting Activities*, which are designed to help you create plans of action related to the chapter topic to shape your faculty career. Beyond just giving you tips and tools, we give you resources you can use in the future to continue authoring your own success.

Concluding Thoughts

As we said at the start of this introduction, we love the work we do as faculty members. It is rewarding, challenging, and meaningful work on an almost daily basis. But the work and career can be a bit opaque at times, and each of us struggled early in our careers to figure out the rules of the game, how best to spend our time, and the kind of faculty members we wanted to be. We have written this book in an effort to make the nuances of faculty life more transparent and to empower you to become the professor you want to and can become. We hope you find the book useful as you embark on your professional journey.

Note

1. We have adopted the term *minoritized faculty* consciously to represent members of social identity groups that have consistently been underrepresented among faculty ranks.

PART ONE

UNDERSTANDING YOUR CAREER IN CONTEXT

I

THE FACULTY ROLE

Whether you are currently a faculty member or a graduate student who wants to be a faculty member, you likely know that this is a dynamic time in higher education. As we discuss later, students are coming to higher education with new expectations, different needs, and different goals than in the past. The nature of the faculty and of faculty work are changing, as technology plays a greater role, budgets are constrained, and pressures for accountability and efficiency grow (Gappa et al., 2007). The structure of the faculty as a body is also changing, with new categories of faculty employment (e.g., clinical, full-time non-tenure-track) that have implications for the makeup of faculty work and the faculty's influence in higher education. Many of these changes are good; some probably are not; and for others, the jury is still out.

Still, we believe a faculty career continues to be an immensely rewarding and positive experience. Faculty work comes with many roles and duties; we teach, advise, serve on campus committees and in the community, take on leadership roles, engage in scholarship and other creative activities, and act as consultants—to name just a few. And we get to *choose* when, how, and the extent to which we do many of these things. Certainly not all of these roles and responsibilities are optional, but some are, as is the emphasis we give to each. Because of the autonomy faculty members have, we can shape the nature of our work, learn, grow, change, and take on new challenges along the way. Moreover, we can develop our own professional identities all while contributing to our students, disciplines, and institutions. We can *author* the kind of faculty career we want to have.

Having this kind of faculty career requires taking an intentional, proactive role in imagining and becoming the kind of faculty member you want to be. In this chapter we provide you with a broad overview of today's faculty and the context in which they work. Understanding your institutional context, as well as the context of higher education more generally, is a critical part of being a proactive, successful faculty member yourself.

The Faculty

As you embark on defining and shaping your identity as a faculty member, consider the characteristics and structure of today's faculty. The composition of the faculty is changing in terms of gender, race, ethnicity, and categories of employment. Faculty also work in a wide range of institutional types. These changes in the faculty's makeup as well as the nature of the institutions in which they work have important implications for what is expected of early career faculty and the interactions you will have with your faculty colleagues.

What Does the Faculty "Look" Like?

Today's faculty looks different from the faculty of past decades in many ways. Consider, for example, its gender diversity. In just 10 years (2003 to 2013), the percentage of women who are part of the faculty grew from 43.4% to 48.8%, a gain of almost 5% (NCES, 2015a, Table 315.10). While these gains are not evenly distributed across all fields, disciplines, or institutional types, this sign is positive for higher education overall.

Gains in the racial and ethnic diversity of full-time faculty have been more limited. Between 2005 and 2013 the percentage of Asian American–Pacific Islander faculty members climbed nearly 2% (to 9.13% of faculty) and Hispanic faculty members grew by nearly 1% (to 4.2% of faculty); Black/African American faculty gained an even more modest one-fifth of 1% (to 5.46% of faculty; NCES, 2010, Table 264; NCES, 2015b, Table 315.20). While the growth in women faculty is trending upward, and some racial and ethnic groups are seeing (at best) modest growth, the trends need to be accelerated if the faculty's composition is to keep pace with the changing nature of the student body. Moreover, such continued growth in diversity among faculty has implications for the kind of environment in which faculty will work—a point to consider when you think about what kind of faculty member you want to be. Chapter 3 will help you explore this environment further.

What "Types" of Faculty Are There?

The traditional image of a faculty member is someone who works full-time at a single institution in some combination of teaching, research, and service as her or his three main duties; diligently earns tenure; and likely works at the college or university for 30 years or more. Some have described this person as the *integrated* faculty member (Finkelstein & Schuster, 2011), reflecting the idea that all three traditional areas of faculty work are present in and performed by one faculty member.

However, this image no longer matches the reality. Researchers (Finkelstein & Schuster, 2011; Kezar, Maxey, & Eaton, 2014) have observed that faculty work has become increasingly unbundled in recent years, with faculty being hired to perform only portions of the traditional integrated faculty role. Part-time faculty now account for 43% of the faculty workforce (Finkelstein, Conley, & Schuster, 2016). There also has been a steady decline in the presence of tenured and tenure-track faculty members in the last 40 years, from more than 78% of faculty in 1969 (Schuster & Finkelstein, 2006) to 33% in 2009 (Kezar et al., 2014). Even these figures do not reflect the full nature of the evolution in the faculty, since a growing number of full-time faculty are not eligible for tenure. Some estimates put the numbers of full-time faculty not eligible for tenure as high as 20% of the overall faculty workforce (Kezar & Maxey, 2013), and this group now accounts for the majority of new full-time hires (Finkelstein et al., 2016).

This relatively new category of full-time faculty has a wide range of titles and varied duties, with little of the consistency that we have come to know with the tenure-track ranks. These new faculty members are often hired to carry out a single dimension of traditional faculty work—teaching, research, or service (Finkelstein & Schuster, 2011)—and have titles including lecturer, instructor, or specialist. Titles sometimes reflect the duties for which people are hired (Kezar & Sam, 2010). For example, clinical professors—common in medicine and other professional programs—are hired because of their applied and practical knowledge and are expected to engage in professional work (e.g., treating patients) even as they teach students; research professors, however, are hired specifically to conduct scholarship (Mallon, 2016). Institutions also hire individuals who have been distinguished practitioners (e.g., journalists, politicians, educational leaders) and confer the title of "professor of practice" to reflect their professional accomplishments. The structure of the faculty and its work is far more diverse today than it was even 25 years ago.

These changes in the structure of faculty positions have important implications for you as you shape your faculty career. You may have already experienced this in your job search; as more doctoral graduates seek fewer tenure-eligible faculty positions, the competition for these jobs becomes more intense. And now, if you are in a tenure-eligible position, the growing rarity of those positions also has several impacts. First, fewer tenure-track positions may mean fewer colleagues are eligible to serve on some or all committees, which might mean you will be asked to engage in more service than if you had entered the faculty 20 or 30 years ago. Second, fewer new tenure-track hires each year may mean that institutions provide fewer resources and are less intentional about support for early career faculty success. Third, you may have fewer tenure-track peers and thus be more likely to experience feelings of isolation. If this is the case, it becomes all the more important for you to have clear career goals, identify your needs, be proactive in seeking out sources of support, and create networks—including outside of your department and even your institution.

Where Do the Faculty Work?

Faculty work in a wide variety of college and university settings, and the requirements of faculty work in each of these settings vary just as widely. Each category of institution has significant or subtle distinctions in mission; has different expectations about the desired mix among teaching, research, and service; and serves different types of students.

The Carnegie Foundation for the Advancement of Teaching offers one commonly used way to categorize colleges and universities (see Carnegie Classification of Institutes of Higher Education, 2016). This categorization identifies research/doctoral and master's-granting universities, baccalaureate colleges, baccalaureate/associate degree colleges, associate degree colleges, specialized (e.g., art, medicine) colleges, and tribal colleges.

Research universities most often come to mind when we imagine a faculty career, perhaps because that is where most of us receive our advanced degrees. As Table 1.1 shows, there are literally thousands of institutions in the United States alone, and research universities, where those who become faculty are typically prepared, represent just a small percentage of the total number.

Therefore, as you might expect, most faculty do not go on to careers in research universities. Data from the National Center for Education Statistics (Table 1.2) indicate that in fall 2013, only 38% of full-time faculty worked at research universities. As a result, most of us as faculty members go on to work in institutions that are different from those that prepared us with our graduate degrees. Indeed, the data in Table 1.2 suggest that around 50% of full-time faculty on the tenure track go on to work at master's, baccalaureate, or community college (associate degree) institutions.

These facts are important for several reasons. As a graduate student, you should know the higher education landscape so that you can make an informed choice about your career trajectory. What type of institutional setting might be appealing to you? What would a good workday look like? As a new or experienced faculty member, you should have this typology in mind as way to understand the institutional context and what our institutions expect of us as faculty members. In either case, knowing your professional context is important in considering what your options are in shaping your faculty career.

TABLE 1.1

Number of Institutions by Carnegie Classification in 2016

Type of Institution	Number of Institutions	Percentage of Institutions (%)
Research/doctoral universities	335	7
Master's colleges and universities	759	16
Baccalaureate colleges	574	12
Baccalaureate–associate colleges	403	9
Associate colleges	1,113	24
Special focus, four-year	1,002	21
Special focus, two-year	444	10
Tribal colleges	35	1

Source. The Carnegie Classification of Institutions of Higher Education, 2016, Basic Classification.

TABLE 1.2

Percentage of Full-Time Faculty in the United States by Carnegie Classification 2000, Fall 2013

Type of Institution	Percentage Tenure Track—Any Rank (%)	Percentage All Full-Time (%)
Research universities	44	38
Master's colleges and universities	28	23
Baccalaureate colleges	11	9
Baccalaureate–associate colleges	1	1
Associate colleges	11	21
Other	6	8

Source. Compiled by authors from data at NCES, 2013a.
Note. Number of full-time instructional staff employed by degree-granting postsecondary institutions by Carnegie Classification 2000 academic rank.

The Nature of Faculty Work

There are multiple images of the professor. One visual portrays the professor wearing a tweed jacket, strolling across a residential campus engaged in stimulating conversations with a small group of students. Another portrays a professor toiling away at her lab bench in the late hours of the night or furiously making calculations on a whiteboard. Yet another image might be of a professor on stage, giving a lecture to a room of hundreds of students (some deeply engaged and others not) or perhaps addressing a room full of colleagues at an international conference. All of these are, to some degree, accurate. In this section, we examine how faculty spend their time and how that time is generally allocated.

How Much Do Faculty Work?

Any faculty member will likely tell you that he or she works *a lot*. One of the freedoms of faculty life is the ability to work anytime and anywhere. Yet that same freedom, together with the demanding nature of faculty work, can pose challenges and lead to long hours. As early as 1942, one researcher found that full professors worked 58 hours per week, associate professors worked 52 hours per week, and assistant professors worked more than 60 hours per week (Charters, 1942). Data compiled by Finkelstein and colleagues (2016) suggest that full-time faculty in the early 2000s were working between 47 and 51 hours per week, with a mean of 49.2 hours per week, depending on the emphasis of their work (teaching or research). More recently, a study at Boise State University (a doctoral degree–granting public institution) found that the faculty workweek averaged 61 hours, with full professors reporting the most hours, followed closely by assistant, and then associate professors (Ziker, 2014), suggesting that Charters's figure was not out of line and perhaps has gone up a bit over the decades. The same study found that professors worked about 10 hours per day during the workweek and then another 10 hours spread across the weekend (Ziker, 2014). As Duffy (2015) has noted in challenging the myth of the 80-hour workweek, faculty can often overstate how much they work. However, a faculty job can easily extend beyond the 40-hour workweek; one of our goals in Chapter 10 is to help you find strategies to manage your time.

How Do Faculty Allocate Their Time?

If faculty work a great deal, how is that time allocated among the range of roles and duties? Perhaps surprisingly, most time for most faculty is related to teaching or working with students. A triennial survey by researchers at UCLA (Egan et al., 2014) provided a breakdown of how faculty at baccalaureate degree–granting institutions spent their time in a given semester or quarter. Some highlights are as follows:

- A significant amount of time was spent teaching or preparing to teach. Most faculty (61.1%) spent 5 to 12 hours per week in the actual act of teaching, while 46.6% spent an additional 5 to 12 hours in preparing for teaching or grading.

- Most faculty taught at the undergraduate level. Less than half of the respondents (46.1%) had taught even one graduate course in the prior two years.
- Research and scholarly activity were relatively limited compared to many people's expectations of faculty work. More than two-thirds of the faculty (68%) spent 0 to 8 hours per week on research and scholarly writing, 20% or less of a 40-hour workweek; 60% had two or fewer professional writings published or accepted in the preceding two years.

These findings roughly mirror those from the study at Boise State (Ziker, 2014). In that study, the researcher found that professors spent about 35% of their time during the week on teaching and related activities, with additional time spent on those tasks over the weekend. Assuming a 40-hour workweek (not the reported norm for these Boise State faculty), then 60% of professors' time was spent on teaching and related activities. Much less time (about 5% of time during the workweek) was spent on scholarship.

Early career faculty are often surprised by the amount of administrative work required of them (Gravett & Petersen, 2007; O'Meara et al., 2008). The Boise State study (Ziker, 2014) found that participants spent 30% of their time in meetings (with colleagues or students) or responding to e-mails. A fair portion of faculty time can be spent advising students; drafting letters of recommendation; serving on boards or lending expertise in other ways; and serving on departmental, college, or university committees (O'Meara et al., 2008). Finkelstein and colleagues (2016) note that the percentage of time faculty at 4-year institutions spend on campus service (e.g., committees, meetings) climbed in the last 25 years.

What Shapes Faculty Time Allocations?

The ratio in which these activities take place varies widely for individual faculty members. Nearly three decades ago, in his book *The Academic Life*, Burton Clark (1987) observed that the academic profession had become a series of tribes (subcultures), with relative uniformity (e.g., the professor at a small liberal arts college during colonial days) replaced by a sense of fragmentation. The singular concept of what it meant to be a professor was gone. Since that time, others have similarly noted the decline of the integrated professor (Kezar, Maxey, & Eaton, 2014; Finkelstein & Schuster, 2011) and the growing differentiation of faculty work. Faculty time allocations are influenced by, among other things, institutional type (and bureaucratic structure), disciplinary differences, and social characteristics.

First, different institutional types have different missions and different expectations of how faculty time is calculated, as well as how it is allocated as a result. Faculty in high-status institutions, the research and doctoral universities, might teach one or two classes a semester, often as small graduate seminars rather than large undergraduate courses; have graduate student support for teaching and grading; and be expected to consistently publish and seek (and earn) grants and contracts. At the other extreme, community college faculty likely teach only lower-division undergraduate courses, as many as five or more a semester, with large class sizes and no expectation of (or reward for) scholarly activities. Somewhere between these extremes, faculty members at master's or comprehensive universities and liberal arts colleges might teach three or four courses a semester (spread across the undergraduate and graduate levels); they likely are expected to engage in research, but with more flexible expectations and more focused on practice than their research university colleagues. In short, each type of institution has a different mission; attracts a different type of student; and provides different options for, and expectations of, faculty work.

Table 1.3 provides a percentage breakdown of how faculty nearly 20 years ago allocated their time between teaching and research across different college and university types. As the table shows, teaching filled a substantial portion of most faculty members' time (even more than suggested in our earlier discussion), although the percentage increases steadily from research universities through liberal arts institutions, while the percentage of time spent on research declines correspondingly.

Today, although teaching continues to take the majority of faculty members' time, trends indicate that faculty at some institutional types are spending more time on research. Milem, Berger, and Dey (2000) noted a 20-year trend (between 1972 and 1992) where faculty at all institutional types reported increasing amounts of time spent doing research over that period.

TABLE 1.3
Full-Time Faculty Percentage Time Allocation by Institutional Type, 1998

	Teaching (%)	Research (%)
Research	49.2	27.4
Doctoral	52.6	21.3
Comprehensive	64.6	10.6
Liberal arts/baccalaureate	68.1	8.1
All faculty	60.8	15.1

Source. Adapted from Schuster and Finkelstein, 2006, Table A-4.5.

This additional time spent on research does not necessarily come at the cost of time spent on teaching; instead it might be added to existing work based on expanded scholarly expectations (Schuster & Finkelstein, 2006). Milem and colleagues (2000) make this point also, finding that faculty at four-year institutions spent more time on teaching even as time on research increased. More recent work (Finkelstein et al., 2016) has found that faculty in universities are spending increasing amounts of time on teaching-related work while faculty at other institutional types (e.g., comprehensive, liberal arts) are spending more time per week on research. While the specific expectations regarding scholarship might vary by institutional type (an issue we take up in Chapter 6), these findings suggest that even at institutions where scholarship might have less emphasis, faculty were more engaged in that work than in the past.

Institutional type and context also affect how faculty think about and spend their time because of the nature of the institution's bureaucratic structure. Institutions such as public comprehensive universities typically have more bureaucratic cultures—with a greater emphasis on accountability, policies, and rules and regulations—while research universities and liberal arts colleges typically have fewer of these constraints. To some degree this context may vary by whether the institution is public or private (e.g., public research universities might have more rules and accountability mechanisms than private research universities) or unionized (e.g., unionized institutions have collective bargaining agreements by which they must abide).

First, the degree of bureaucracy can greatly impact how faculty think about time. A professor at a research university might teach one to three courses per year and be expected to fill the remaining time as she chooses—with a balance among individual projects, supervision of doctoral students, and service to the institution. In contrast, a professor at a large, public, unionized, comprehensive institution might have to account for 24 or 30 units of her time per year by receiving workload credit for supervising thesis students or taking on leadership roles as part of service. This latter type of environment can be a surprise to faculty just arriving out of graduate school in a research university environment.

Second, the nature of the academic discipline also makes a difference in how faculty spend or think about their time. For instance, if you are in the sciences, you might well be expected to build a lab when you arrive, as well as prepare grant proposals to support your scholarship, and thus have a reduced teaching load as a result. In contrast, if you are a social scientist, you might be able to begin a research project immediately on arrival (or even continue one already in progress) and face limited expectations to bring in grant dollars. Or perhaps you are in a discipline or at an institution that has large sections of introductory courses and you teach a large section and receive extra workload credit as a result, thus reducing the number of courses you teach compared to colleagues.

Third and finally, social characteristics play a role in shaping how faculty spend their time. For instance, in a study of science and engineering faculty at top research universities, Link, Swann, and Bozeman (2008) found that females in engineering spent more time engaged in service and teaching, and slightly less time on research, than their male colleagues. This same fact was found across higher education by Schuster and Finkelstein (2006), who noted that, in 1998, female faculty spent approximately 66% of their time on teaching compared to 59% for males. This trend has continued in recent years, and data also confirm that women continue to spend more time than men engaged in campus service (Finkelstein et al., 2016).

We share this information for several reasons. First, faculty work, including how we think about and allocate our time, varies depending on the institutional context, just as Burton Clark (1987, 1997) argued. Thus, you should understand your institutional context when you think about your career. Second, even within a single institutional type (e.g., a comprehensive public institution), there can be great variability in how faculty spend their time as driven by a variety of factors, including discipline, bureaucratic structures, and social characteristics. Third, early career faculty often believe that they should be conducting research and writing all of the time. While your institution's expectations have a role to play, these figures show that most faculty spend most of their time teaching (although there is such a thing as too much time spent on teaching). Finally, one of our goals is to help you find balance as a faculty member. As these data suggest, finding such a balance can be challenging; it is easy for faculty work to spill over into personal time and life. Indeed, just because faculty are working many hours does not necessarily mean they are happy with the situation or that it is time well spent. Our hope is that if you are able to assume agency and author your career, you will also be satisfied with the balance that you find.

The Broader Context of Faculty Work

The larger context of our work as faculty members has a great impact on our experiences. In this case, when we speak of context, we do not mean the type of institution; rather, we mean the larger trends and forces shaping higher education more generally. Being aware of these trends and forces is important, since they can present opportunities for sculpting your career as well as potential challenges to or limitations of your professional choices.

In their book *Rethinking Faculty Work: Higher Education's Strategic Imperative*, Gappa and colleagues (2007) offer a succinct analysis of significant trends shaping higher education at the time. We use these trends here as framework to understand the higher education context because those trends are at least as relevant today, if not more so, than when their book was written:

- *Constrained resources and growing competition.* A college education is costly to provide. College and university campuses take considerable resources to maintain, and cutting-edge technology is expensive. In addition, the labor-intensive nature of education means that most campus budgets are composed of faculty/staff salaries, which translates to limited fiscal flexibility when times get tough. While state support for higher education has been declining for some time, the drop was exacerbated during the Great Recession. As a result of these trends, administrators and faculty are under increasing pressures for entrepreneurship to underwrite the cost of college, privatize operations, and rein in education's cost. Add to this the expanded presence of for-profit institutions (although recently these institutional types have been in decline), as well as the growth in competency-based education, certificates, and badges, and it is clear that competition for funding and students is growing.

- *Declining confidence in higher education and calls for greater accountability.* In recent years, colleges and universities have come under increasing scrutiny (even as resources declined) for the cost of education, their use of resources, and student outcomes. Today, the media carry stories about student loan burden and the return on investment for a college education, the un- or underemployment of college graduates, and questions about how faculty spend their time. In this context, calls are ongoing for greater accountability for how institutions spend resources, the outcomes students attain, and faculty productivity. The accountability language often leads to a more managerial culture, with less direct faculty control over the institution and more checks and balances on faculty work.

- *Growing student diversity.* The undergraduate student body is increasingly diverse, and that diversity will continue to grow. Furthermore, diversity is not restricted to race or ethnicity. Colleges and universities are serving more students who are older than traditional-aged college students (ages 18–24), who are working while attending college, and who come from a wide range of socioeconomic and educational backgrounds. This increased diversity has translated into growing enrollments in public community colleges and comprehensive institutions along with declining enrollment at more selective liberal arts colleges. While increased access to higher education is positive, such access also poses challenges to faculty and their institutions in terms of meeting student needs and facilitating learning and success, since most colleges have been set up for the more traditional student who took classes during regular working hours.

- *Growing role of technology.* The impact of technology and the Information Age is woven throughout higher education. The ability to digitize nearly everything and the use of electronic course management platforms have affected how we teach, raised questions of intellectual property, and shaped students' expectations of instructors and instruction. Indeed, the Boise State study described earlier found that faculty spend 13% of their time on e-mail (including e-mails with students [Ziker, 2014]). While the initial fanfare about massive open online courses (MOOCs) appears to have dissipated, faculty are still asked to teach more courses online, and a recent UCLA survey showed a climb from 14% of respondents teaching at least one course online in 2010–2011 to 17.4% doing so in 2013–2014 (Egan et al., 2014). As with the other trends already discussed, the growth of technology in higher education can open up opportunities for faculty growth and learning, yet also pose challenges.

These trends have important implications for faculty and the work we do. The trends point to a more market-driven focus in higher education, where institutions are competing for students and resources. With higher education seen more as a personal investment than a public good, students and their parents are often more concerned about what they get for their money (e.g., skills, employability) than about learning more broadly. This market focus also contributes to a greater emphasis on outcomes and on accountability for those stated outcomes. Institutions are seeking ways to contain costs, convey that college is affordable, expand access, and provide customer service as a way to attract and retain students.

As a result, early career faculty quickly realize that faculty life is not quite like their graduate school experiences. For instance, budget constraints and pressures for accountability have contributed to a rise in new types of faculty appointments (e.g., full-time non-tenure-track faculty) as well as reduced faculty autonomy and control. There is a greater focus on timely graduation and being responsive to students (not necessarily bad changes), as well as the growing expectation that faculty collaborate more to achieve institutional goals. Institutions are increasingly offering courses at night or on weekends and in various configurations (six weeks, eight weeks, hybrid or online, etc.).

As a result, faculty often feel entrepreneurial pressures and a sense of "ratcheting" (Gappa et al., 2007, p. 17)—that they are pulled in many directions and face varied demands, all with seemingly equal importance and all needing to be done right away. Few are the days, if they ever really existed, of the professor sitting at a coffeehouse having a leisurely conversation with students or colleagues about ideas. Today's professors are often moving from a meeting to a class session to office hours before fitting in some grading and working on a grant application.

Faculty Satisfaction

Given this context, one might think that faculty life would be less appealing to those who are already in the role. However, the available data suggest that faculty members are, by and large, happy in their roles. The Higher Education Research Institute (HERI) at UCLA regularly surveys faculty at undergraduate institutions across the nation. In 2013–2014, HERI surveyed more than 16,000 faculty (Egan et al., 2014). Looking globally at satisfaction, the responses were relatively positive:

- About 74% of the faculty said they were very satisfied or satisfied with their jobs overall.
- Asked whether they would come to the same institution again, 69% said definitely yes or probably yes.
- They were even more positive about their role as professor. More than 75% said they definitely or probably would elect to be a college professor again. Only 4% said they would likely not choose the same career.
- In the same survey, however, 35% of respondents said they had considered leaving academe for another job in the last two years, and 49% had considered leaving their institution. Just 48% of respondents were very satisfied or satisfied with their salaries.

Similarly, the Collaborative on Academic Careers in Higher Education (COACHE) surveyed more than 9,000 pretenure faculty at doctorate-granting institutions about their experiences and satisfaction (COACHE, 2010). This study, which had a narrower population, looked at, among other issues, indicators of global satisfaction (with the department and the institution) and compared faculty responses across 12 academic areas. Broadly, faculty satisfaction with the department or institution varied by discipline, with faculty in the professions (e.g., business and education) more likely than others to feel that the chief academic officer cared about their quality of life.

Notably, the COACHE survey results (COACHE, 2010) also shed light on how satisfaction might vary by gender. While the results did not suggest broad differences in satisfaction by gender within the 12 fields of study identified, the findings indicate that men in the social sciences are significantly more likely than women in the field to

- be more satisfied with department as a place to work,
- say they would choose to work at the institution again, and
- give a positive overall rating of the institution.

In Chapter 3, on climate and culture, we take a more detailed look at how institutional and disciplinary culture can shape the experiences of women faculty and faculty of color.

The 2013–2014 HERI survey (Eagan et al., 2014) also asked faculty members to identify sources of stress in the prior two years. Perhaps not surprisingly given the high achievement levels of faculty members, the faculty identified themselves as their greatest source of stress: 35% said that self-imposed high expectations were an extensive source of stress in the preceding two years. Conversely, just 8% of faculty respondents identified students as extensive sources of stress, the lowest-rated item on the list. Beyond these items, Table 1.4 identifies sources of stress in the preceding two years that faculty members identified as extensive or somewhat stressful. High on the list are organizational issues (red tape, changes in responsibilities) and personal or family issues, such as managing household duties and lack of personal time. These data indicate that faculty, like the rest of adults in the United States, confront professional and personal challenges that add to their stress. However, as you likely already know, and as we discuss in Chapter 10 on finding balance, the ability of faculty to work anytime and anywhere most surely adds to the already substantial levels of stress that come from today's modern world.

O'Meara and colleagues (2008) note evidence suggesting that faculty job satisfaction has been on the decline over the last several decades due to growing workloads, increased expectations to earn tenure, work-life balance challenges (particularly for women), and less collegiality. That said, both O'Meara and colleagues and Gappa and colleagues (2007) stress that, when looking across professions, data for the last two decades consistently show faculty to be more satisfied than those who work in most other professions. Despite its challenges, we still believe that a faculty career is a wonderful opportunity.

TABLE 1.4
Faculty Respondents Identifying Sources of Stress,
All Baccalaureate Institutions

%	Source of Stress: *Extensive* or *Somewhat*
85.2	Self-imposed high expectations
78.2	Institutional procedures and red tape
75.2	Change in work responsibilities
74.2	Managing household responsibilities
74.2	Research or publishing demands
73.9	Lack of personal time
73.0	Institutional budget cuts
65.1	Working with underprepared students
63.4	Teaching load
63.0	Committee work
62.6	Review/promotion process
61.7	Personal finances
61.5	Students
60.8	Child care
57.5	Colleagues
55.8	My physical health
54.7	Faculty meetings
36.6	Job security
34.0	Subtle discrimination (racism, sexism, prejudice)

Source. Compiled from Eagan et al., 2014, pp. 37–38 (weighted national norms—all respondents).

Concluding Thoughts

The context for faculty work and the nature of the job have changed markedly over time, and both will likely continue to do so for the foreseeable future. Today's faculty members are increasingly diverse and work at a wide range of institutional types. They are more often called on to work in more entrepreneurial and high-accountability environments, where there may be less autonomy, and to work collaboratively with colleagues who reflect a growing array of faculty employment categories. Despite challenges, faculty are, on balance, satisfied with their jobs. We hope you are—or soon will be— counted among them.

2

YOUR FACULTY CAREER

I n the introduction, we provided an overview of the professional growth perspective that O'Meara and colleagues (2008) offer, which serves as the framework guiding our thinking for this book. O'Meara and colleagues (2008) analyzed and critiqued the literature on faculty work and faculty careers and identified a narrative of constraint, describing faculty as victims rather than agents, receivers rather than creators, isolated rather than in relationships, and cognitively focused rather than engaged with their work and the world at an emotional level. In response, O'Meara and colleagues (2008) offered their counternarrative.

In this counternarrative, which the literature also supports but seldom names, O'Meara and colleagues (2008) argue that learning and growth are at the center of faculty work. Faculty have agency and develop additional agency over time. They learn and grow through "professional relationships embedded in communities" (O'Meara et al., 2008, p. 171) with a broad network of colleagues on and off campus. Moreover, identity, whether implicit or explicit, matters in the teaching, scholarship, and service that faculty do, for these acts are not merely external, objective experiences but part of a personal endeavor arising from commitments to ideas, fields, questions, students, and others. These ideas underpin this book.

O'Meara and colleagues (2008) present another key idea that also underpins this book: the concept of narrative. As O'Meara and colleagues (2008) note in their rationale for challenging the narrative of constraint, narrative focuses our attention on and frames an issue in a particular way (e.g., faculty as either constrained and acted on or growing and acting on). But the idea of narrative also provides a sense of a story that is unfolding before us, something that is "living and unfinished" (O'Meara et al., 2008, p. 154), with chapters yet to be written and stories yet to be told.

Imagine your individual faculty career as a narrative. Faculty members might have careers lasting 30 to 40 years, and while it may seem difficult to imagine when you are just starting out, each career has an arc, a story line that one can follow. Often that story line is visible only in hindsight as we look back at the choices that we have made (sometimes unconsciously); only then might we see the career as something more than just a series of discrete research projects, articles, and books; exhibits curated; classes taught; and roles played. However, starting now to imagine what you want your career to look like later can give you an advantage.

We also like the idea of narrative because it reminds us that a faculty career is one with chapters. For example, it is tempting as an early career faculty member to focus almost solely on retention and tenure and then to feel reactive, powerless, and stressed as a result. This outcome is entirely understandable at a certain level, given the importance of tenure. But Alexander (2008) reminds us that the pretenure years are, at most, just one-quarter of a career; Alexander challenges us to think much bigger than tenure. Therefore, if we can identify these pretenure years as the early chapters in a much longer story, we are more likely to feel that we still have some control to make choices, even at this stage. Then the pretenure years become more than a time when we are trying to decode expectations and please our senior colleagues; they become a time when we are beginning our professional commitments, building relationships, and laying foundations for a long and fulfilling career.

Our goal in this chapter is to help you start thinking about that story line now and give you strategies for authoring your professional narrative. While forces around us—the type of institution at which we work, our students, trends in society—surely shape our careers and work, we can be active in defining our narrative. Kerry Ann Rockquemore (2013), a mentor and coach for faculty, has stressed the importance of early career faculty owning their careers and setting their own standards based on an internal compass rather than external validation. Similarly, O'Meara and colleagues (2008) have argued that faculty are actors "in the design of their own developmental trajectory" (p. 165).

In this chapter we give you some strategies for thinking about the kind of career you want to have and the kind of faculty member you want to be. We begin by sharing what the trajectory of a faculty career might look like based on existing literature. Next, we introduce the idea of a *sweet spot*—an aspirational place where you integrate the three areas of faculty work with your personal and professional identities. Then we offer advice for finding your passions to guide your faculty career, and finally we discuss developing a sense of belonging and handling fear of failure.

The Faculty Career Trajectory

As you think about shaping your faculty career, understand that how you spend your time as a faculty member will likely change. For instance, early career faculty members are often initially protected from service roles and find that service commitments increase with time. You will have choices to make not only early in your career but also on the path to becoming a senior faculty member. In Chapter 1 we looked at how faculty in general allocate their time. In this section we expand on that discussion in Chapter 1 to examine specifically how the amount of time faculty members spend on various tasks evolves over the course of a faculty career.

As you might expect, assistant professors spend more time on teaching and instruction than their more senior colleagues. Eagan and colleagues (2014) reported that across 4-year institutions nationally, 18.1% of assistant professors reported spending 13 or more hours per week on teaching-related work, compared to 13.6% of associate professors and 9.9% of full professors. Similarly, 38% of assistant professors spent 13 or more hours per week grading or preparing for teaching, compared to 33.3% of associate professors and 30.5% of full professors. This distribution of time may reflect the fact that, as others (Baldwin & Blackburn, 1981; Olsen & Sorcinelli, 1992) have observed, teaching becomes easier over time as faculty master the content, preparation, and grading. Moreover, Boice (2000) has noted that early career faculty often overprepare for teaching. Thus, as you progress in your career, you might well find that you save time on teaching by preparing less. However, depending on your institution and your goals, you may also elect to teach different courses or even develop new ones of your own, which may negate some or all of the time savings from less preparation.

When it comes to research and scholarship, associate professors appear more constrained than their colleagues. The study by Eagan and colleagues (2014) found that more full and assistant professors (25.6% and 24.3%, respectively) than associate professors (17.9%) reported spending 13 or more hours per week on research and scholarly writing. In their study of science and engineering professors at research universities, Link and colleagues (2008) found that assistant professors devoted a greater percentage of their time (40%) to research than associate and full professors, with a notable drop after receiving tenure. Associate professors reported that 33% of their time was spent on research, and full professors reported a slight climb to 35%. This distribution of time could reflect the fact that assistant professors are generally expected to engage in some level of research to earn tenure (starting research projects also can take considerable time). Once having earned tenure, however, some associate professors may elect to spend less or no time on research, while those who earn full professor status are likely to have been engaged in scholarship to reach that rank—reflecting another choice you may make in your career.

As your faculty career advances, you will likely spend more time engaged in service to both the institution and the profession. In the study by Eagan and colleagues (2014), senior faculty reported spending more time serving on committees, attending meetings, and engaging in other service. For example, 5.7% of full professors and 5% of associate professors said they spent 13 or more hours per week in committee work and meetings, compared to 1.6% of assistant professors, who were far more likely to report 1 to 4 hours per week of committee work and meetings. Similarly, 13.8% of full professors and 8.5% of associate professors, compared to 4% of assistant professors, indicated 13 or more hours per week in other administrative activities. Echoing these national findings, the study by Link and colleagues (2008) of science and engineering faculty indicated that time spent on service increased with rank. More broadly, senior faculty in the Eagan and colleagues' study (2014) also reported more engagement outside of their institutions. More than half of associate and full professors indicated they were engaged in 1 to 8 hours of community service each week, compared to less than half of assistant professors. In addition, while just 15.7% of assistant professors were engaged in 1 to 8 hours per week of consultant or freelance work, 26.4% of full professors and 22.1% of associate professors were engaged at this level.

Most likely, these findings reflect the tendency for faculty to become more engaged in their communities and the profession over time, as well as the limited time that early career faculty have for such endeavors. Indeed, Bogler and Kremer-Hayon (1999) pointed out that faculty concerns over time moved from their own professional survival as early career faculty to greater concern for the institution and profession. Ultimately, these claims suggest that you can expect to take on more of a leadership role as your career progresses, with more time spent in meetings, in the community, and in other leadership capacities. These roles might include department chair, associate dean, or perhaps even journal editor or officer in a professional association.

Another critical element in how you might spend your time as your career progresses is the evolving nature of your personal life. Responsibilities to parents, partners or spouses, and children are an important part of life, albeit one not often discussed in academe. Eagan and colleagues (2014) found that childcare and household work are a central part of life for many faculty, although less so for full professors. In this case, nearly 40% of assistant and associate professors spent 13 hours or more per week on childcare and household duties, while just 26% of full professors did so. It is also likely that the most senior faculty have older children who require less of their time and energy or are men who traditionally shoulder less household responsibility. This pattern may mean it will be easier for you to be on campus more frequently or take on more outside leadership roles as you advance in your career and the need for a flexible schedule to accommodate children diminishes.

To help you think about the trajectory of your career, we borrow the family metaphor that VanOosting (2015) has offered to frame the relationship between students and professors. While we apply VanOosting's comments more specifically to students in Chapter 4, here we explore the metaphor to think more broadly about the faculty career. As early career faculty members, particularly in our first three years, we often feel like a *child*. New to our role and our campus, we typically feel a bit lost, unsure of where to go and how to proceed, and eager to please others (who, it seems to us, control our fate). Surprised by the complexity of the role, we look to others for guidance, although who in this scenario can be trusted as the parent may not always be clear. Over time, we learn to navigate these waters, albeit carefully. As we mature in our careers, usually the latter stages of the pretenure years, we may assume the role of *older sibling*. By now, we have probably figured out some routines and are attuned to the culture of our departmental family. As newer faculty come in behind us, we are in a position to share our experiences and give guidance to help these people join the family.

Once we earn tenure, we begin to move into the *parent* and then *grandparent* roles. As parents, we set the rules for the family, give input into hiring and tenure decisions, take leadership roles on key committees, and perhaps even serve as department chairs. We also interact more with the outside world as we become more visible in our fields and take on leadership roles in professional associations. Finally, in the later stage of our careers, we assume the role of grandparent, with the pleasure of taking on a more nurturing and supportive role. Having the benefit of years of experience, we can mentor new faculty and share our wisdom with the profession, encouraging and supporting the next generation of scholars.

We share these data and ideas for several reasons. First, they help us illustrate a point that O'Meara and colleagues (2008) have made and that we echo throughout the book: a faculty career is a developmental one. As you move through your career, your role, interests, and opportunities will continue to evolve. While these new opportunities can create stress, they are also opportunities for learning and growth (Baldwin & Blackburn, 1981; Ernst, 2012). Second, knowing this context is important for shaping your career. Although you cannot predict all of your interests or options early in your career, considering what kind of faculty member you want to be now, early in your career, can and should be informed by as much knowledge as possible of how your career will look in the future. Having this understanding now helps you make choices as they arise along the way. Third, having a sense of how you expect your time allocation to evolve can be useful in thinking about how you want to spend your time now to put a firm foundation in place for your ongoing success.

Introducing the Sweet Spot

When we think about the nature of faculty work and when we have felt most successful, we think of something we are calling the *sweet spot*. In sports like tennis and baseball, that term is used to describe the location where the ball hits the racquet or bat in the most efficient way. In those contexts, hitting the sweet spot means that the athlete hits the ball with maximum force and accuracy while experiencing the least amount of negative feedback (e.g., vibrations or sting). It just feels natural, and if you have ever experienced it, you know what a rush it can be.

A faculty career can be a lot like this analogy. Like an athlete who must pay attention to many things (e.g., her own mechanics, the flight and speed of the ball, the placement of opponents), a professor is engaged in teaching, scholarship, and service all while juggling personal and professional relationships and individual identity and goals. When we think of the sweet spot as it applies to faculty, we see it including an integration of teaching, research, and service. However, this integration takes place within a larger context. Specifically, you are integrating these components of work not only with each other but also with your sense of self and who you want to be as a professional and for the rest of your life.

While we take up strategies for creating your sweet spot in Chapter 13, and we touch on the idea throughout the book, we want to introduce you here to its main components.

One of the main goals as a faculty member is finding ways to *integrate* your teaching, research, and/or service work. For example, perhaps you are able to teach a course that contains substantial overlap with your scholarly interests, or perhaps you lend your professional expertise to the community (service), which leads to a scholarly or creative product. In these hypotheticals, you are able to gain efficiency in your efforts as a result of overlap across the areas of faculty work.

Creating our sweet spot also includes tapping into our sense of *self*. The idea for how we want to spend our time and energy as faculty is influenced by who we are and what we value. We discuss this idea a bit more later, but we come to our commitments (O'Meara et al., 2008) and our goals at least in part through our background, experiences, and core values. Our family and friends, formative experiences, and current contexts have shaped who we are and who we hope to become, which in turn shape the choices we make as professors. Acknowledging and considering these elements is important in helping us shape our careers.

Finally, creating our sweet spot also includes drawing on our *professional identity*. Of course, this identity is not unrelated to self, but it is shaped by a variety of other factors. As Bess (1992) noted, our professional expectations and sense of professional self are shaped by our profession or discipline (e.g., how we were socialized in graduate school and rewarded by the profession), our institutional context (e.g., research versus comprehensive university), and the stated and unstated expectations from our department, school or college, and university. Giving thought to this professional identity can assist us in making choices and crafting our sweet spot. Figure 2.1 provides a visual for how we think about this sweet spot.

The sweet spot is not solely about efficiency or effectiveness; our potential for happiness and success is at its height when we can create our sweet spot. Not everything we do, particularly early in our careers, feels like a

Figure 2.1. The sweet spot within professional identity and self.

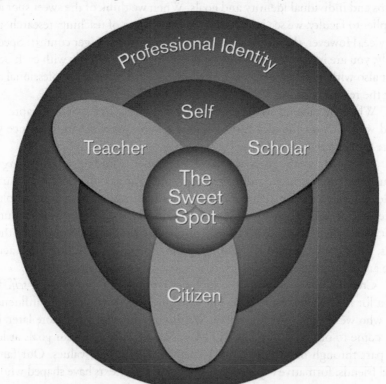

natural fit, nor does it all come together nicely. We might be teaching in one area of our field, doing research in another, and serving in a different area. Perhaps this work feels only loosely connected to who we imagine ourselves to be as a professor or a person. Moreover, it may take time to uncover our professional and personal identities and determine how these influence our careers. As with athletes, however, with time, practice, and self-discovery, it is possible to create your sweet spot as a faculty member.

Creating Your Sweet Spot: Identifying Your Passions and Your Place

Because our personal and professional identities are so important in working toward our sweet spots, understanding them can be a very individualized process; no two sweet spots are likely the same. In this section, we introduce the idea of self-authorship, which is closely related to agency, as a lens for thinking about how to create your sweet spot; discuss the importance of passion in our work; and provide questions to help you think about your own personal and professional identities.

Self-Authoring Your Career

Self-authorship (Baxter Magolda, 2001; Kegan, 1994) is the process by which we come to take control of elements of our lives, most of which involve relationships of some kind or another, and see them objectively, rather than allowing them to control our behavior, emotions, and how we value ourselves and our work. Self-authorship is like intrinsic motivation; it comes from within, but it is a cognitive function. It requires recognizing that we are allowing other people, processes, or things to own us, control us, and determine our value. Once recognized, we can then engage in a cognitive process that involves reframing in such a way that we objectively look at these external forces, evaluate them for their importance and truth value relative to our own identities, and decide their meaning and importance.

The work of being a professor is intimately connected to who we are as humans; most faculty members do not simply go to work, do some things, and come home to be a different person with family and friends. But the reality of faculty life is one of constant critique and evaluation of deeply personal issues, such as your thinking, your writing, your values, your performance in the classroom, and your relationships with colleagues. Being evaluated can feel like the individual self is being assessed rather than the work product. No wonder faculty experience so much stress!

In many ways, this entire book is about authoring your experience and life as a professor and taking an active role in shaping the narrative for your career. For example, perhaps the "revise and resubmit" you received was devastating on first read, but on the second read you were able to depersonalize the feedback. You assessed what was valuable and understood that this one perspective did not define you as a scholar, let alone a person. Or perhaps you choose to engage in more community service than your senior colleagues might recommend because it is a core part of why you became a faculty member and because you are confident that your other work will meet expectations for tenure. Managing the tenure process, becoming a great teacher, and working with your colleagues all require you to put into the palm of your hand those things that threaten your sense of self, cause you doubt, and make you dissatisfied with your job, so that you can examine them as objects distinct from yourself and assess their value.

Of course, to make these judgments and decisions, you must have a clear sense of what is important to you as a person and a professor. Reflecting on your identities, why you chose the career you did, and what you want that career to look like can help you uncover these values and provide the foundation for authoring your career.

The Power of Passion

A related and important part of authoring your faculty career is identifying your passions. O'Meara and colleagues (2008) have pointed out that one of the defining features of faculty growth is our ability to identify and make commitments to ideas, projects, and institutions. Making these commitments comes, at least ideally, from identifying those things that we care most about as people and professionals. While passion and feeling are seldom discussed in academe (perhaps because of the image of the formal, objective scholar), much of what we study and do is driven by things about which we care deeply (Neumann, 2006). Lindholm (2004) studied faculty at various ranks and found common features to be a great passion for their work, a sense of intrinsic motivation, and a desire to contribute. The opportunity to pursue our passions is one of the great privileges of the autonomy we have as faculty, and identifying those passions is an asset to shaping our careers.

Note that we are using the term *passions* as a plural. We think it is possible and likely to identify our passions in multiple areas. For instance, you likely have a passion for your discipline but also for specific projects or subtopics within your field. You might also be able to identify passions for particular approaches to teaching, such as a deep desire to engage students in critical thinking in your field or to use your classrooms as ways to inspire undergraduates to pursue advanced study. With experience you might also discover passions for service, such as working with a professional association or leading your department. Attending to your passions is what sustains you when the going gets tough or when you become overwhelmed with other parts of your job.

In the best of all worlds, we can even connect these subpassions to a larger sense of professional or personal mission. For example, of the authors of this book, Haviland thinks of himself as a problem-solver and sees his career as using research, service, and teaching to help institutions work better to serve all students. Ortiz sees her research, service, and teaching as avenues to provide voice and promote equity for underrepresented students and faculty. Henriques, in contrast, focuses more on supporting individual growth, using a passion for science as a way to understand the world and to mentor and nurture others on their professional journeys to excel and become change agents. These personal missions have informed our choices about projects, teaching philosophies, and time allocation.

Even as an assistant professor, you have choices about how you want to spend your time and the practices in which you engage; that freedom will expand with time. For example, summarizing research, O'Meara and colleagues (2008) noted that women and faculty of color tend to interact more with students, use more active and collaborative learning, and engage students in more diversity-related experiences than do White or male faculty. Quite likely these practices arise from the professional and personal commitments of these scholars. Indeed, O'Meara and colleagues (2008) noted that faculty of color were more likely than White faculty to want to be in academia to create social change. We see this as a good thing, as this kind of professional and personal mission can provide the passion that drives a rich and productive career. At the same time, any choices that we make in terms of the scholarship in which we engage, the advocacy we assert, and the communities with which we align may have consequences as some work is rewarded more than others. (We address expectations related to scholarship in Chapter 6.) Knowing the expectations and values of your colleagues and institutions is important so that you make decisions considering possible outcomes.

Uncovering Your Passions and Identities

If getting to the sweet spot involves uncovering our identities and passions, how do we get there? How can you start to uncover what you want the narrative of your career to be? At the end of Chapters 4, 5, 6, and 8, we offer prompts that you can use to think about your passions, vision, and goals in specific areas (e.g., teaching, research, relationships with colleagues). However, taking a broader view, you might want to work toward drafting a one-paragraph mission statement about your faculty career. There is no one way to do this; you might write it in the past tense (as if someone were reading it at your retirement party) or you might write it as a goal statement given where you are today.

Writing such a mission statement requires reflection. To help you generate some ideas, we pose some big-picture questions in different areas for your consideration. First, think about why you are here as a faculty member or on the faculty path at all. You began this journey for specific reasons: you loved something enough to devote years of study in a graduate program and were committed enough to do what was necessary to obtain your faculty position. With that in mind, consider the following questions:

- What do you love about your subject or what you study?
- Why did you think that becoming a professor was a way to best serve that passion?
- What do you hope to accomplish as a faculty member? What problems are you hoping to address or conditions are you seeking to improve?
- Imagine your retirement party and consider the following questions: What do you hope others (colleagues, students, etc.) will say about your contributions? What three characteristics of your career would you hope to be most proud of?
- What are the practices and behaviors of the faculty members whom you admire most?

Second, give thought to what your background, including your family and early life experiences, contributes to who you are as a professor. Many of us have had a fascination for our subjects since we were children. It can be helpful to connect with those initial aspirations and excitements. Perhaps you are continuing a family tradition in academics or in occupations related to your field. Maybe there was a significant event in childhood that motivated you to become a professor. Consider the following prompts:

- When did you first experience the desire to inquire or create?
- Was there a teacher or family member who sparked your interest in your subject?
- Where did you get early encouragement to pursue your passion?

We address these more foundational parts of your life to acknowledge that motivation to achieve comes early, and connecting to that early motivation is a way to use it in the present. Some of us also think about the role we play in our families. Are your goals and success a reflection of your family? Did your family make sacrifices so that you could pursue your education? These are important motivators; we want to make our loved ones proud, we want to serve as role models for siblings and cousins, and we may excel and achieve so that we can help support our families. Do not discount these motivators, because when the academy becomes a bit insane, these motivators can help ground you.

Third, consider your social identities. Maybe you study how your subject plays out differently depending on gender or ethnicity. Maybe because you are a member of an underrepresented group, you take a different teaching approach to your subject, or maybe you experience your life as a professor differently. Maybe you know that your research changes the health and well-being of specific populations. Ask yourself the following questions:

- How does being a [fill in your relevant social identity] reflect itself in my scholarship, research, or creative activity?
- Does the impact you want to make relate to your identity (your gender, race or ethnicity, sexual orientation, etc.)? How? What would this impact look like in practice?
- How does this social identity affect the way in which you experience your field, your department, and your institution?

The preceding questions are by no means exhaustive. Our goal is to model questions you might ask and to give you permission and encouragement to think beyond the tasks of faculty work to look at how that work can be integrated with your personal and professional self. We caution you: doing this work takes time. As we have progressed in our careers, we have become better at uncovering our values and goals, and creating our sweet spots. Yet for us, with more than 50 cumulative years of faculty experience, it is still a journey—just as it will be for you.

Belonging, Learning, and Taking Risks

We would be remiss if we talked about agency and self-authoring without addressing the fear of failure or rejection. Our main messages in this chapter have been twofold: (a) to start thinking about the long-term trajectory of your career *now*, even as you are at the beginning and (b) to be an *agent* in shaping the career you want even before you have tenure. Shaping your career need not, perhaps cannot, wait until you have earned tenure. We urge you to think and act now to look for new challenges—to find ways to grow, to learn, and to become the professor you want to be.

However, seeking to grow and learn involves taking risks, which is where things can go wrong. We might let a fear of failing stop us from taking the risk in the first place, foreclosing an opportunity, or we might take the risk and not succeed, leaving us to feel rejected or that we have failed. This sense of rejection might come after submitting material for publication, trying something new in the classroom, pitching an idea to our chair or dean, or even running for a service role on a committee.

An added dimension that can make risk-taking even harder for some than others is the *imposter phenomenon*. Coined in the 1970s by Clance and Imes (1978), the term describes an experience, typically among high achievers, in which people believe that their success is due to external factors (e.g., luck, misunderstandings by others) rather than their own skill and knowledge and worry about one day being exposed as an imposter (Clark, Vardeman, & Barba, 2014). This mind-set has been associated with reduced self-esteem, anxiety, depression, overworking, and burnout (Brems, Baldwin, Davis, & Namyniuk, 1994; Clark et al., 2014). While relatively little research has taken place on faculty and the imposter phenomenon, indications are that faculty do experience it (Brems et al., 1994; Hutchins, 2015), it affects all genders (Hutchins, 2015), and younger or less experienced faculty are more likely to feel like imposters than older or more experienced colleagues. Risk-taking is difficult enough, and the imposter phenomenon likely makes it more so.

Nonetheless, failure is a common part of faculty life—albeit one that is barely discussed. One accomplished professor (Looser, 2015) mused that if she created a curriculum vitae (CV) to show her failures, it would reflect more than 1,000 instances of rejections in the form of submitted publications, jobs sought, and grants pursued. We assure you that she is not alone! We offer the following advice:

- Do not let a fear of rejection or failure stop you from trying something new or taking smart, calculated risks.
- Do not let the experience of failure or rejection stop you from learning, recalibrating your plan, and trying once again to achieve your goals.

So when we encourage you to embrace risk-taking, are we suggesting that, as you pursue tenure, you should disregard expectations of your institution and move blissfully ahead? Of course not. We are suggesting, though, that you should think deeply about the kind of career you want to have, be creative about finding ways to fulfill expectations for tenure that are aligned with your own goals and identities, and be willing to take calculated risks that move you toward your goals.

The question is not whether you fail or experience rejection as a professor—because you will—but rather how you handle and explain it.

Your senior colleagues know that early career faculty have a "fragile expertise" (Alexander, 2008, p. 73). Fresh out of graduate school or perhaps a postdoc, you are still mastering your discipline, teaching, scholarly and creative activities, and new roles. Senior faculty expect you to experience failure and rejection just as they have; they do not expect you to be a flawless professor right out of the gate. What they are looking for is that you are growing, learning, and building a foundation for success. They want to know why you chose to pursue certain paths, hear what you learned from the experience, and see what you have done as a result.

Concluding Thoughts

We return to an idea from earlier in the chapter: narrative. Your career narrative is something you not only build for yourself but also share with others to help them understand your trajectory. Your narrative helps explain your goals, choices, passions, commitments, lessons learned, and actions taken. It can be a formal, written narrative (for tenure, as we cover in Chapter 9), but it may also be an oral narrative shared with colleagues over coffee or a meal. We encourage you to start building your narrative today. If you are going to experience failure and rejection with some of your professional efforts anyway, these might as well be related to agentic choices you make rather than to confining tenure-related boxes into which you try to fit. We hope this book helps you with that process.

3

ASSESSING CLIMATE AND CULTURE ON YOUR CAMPUS

*F*it is a word frequently used in faculty searches and emphasized during orientation when a new member joins a faculty and campus community. Campus interviews are largely opportunities to judge if our future colleagues—ones who may well be with us for the life of a career—align with our values, expectations, behavior, vision, and so on. These considerations are important, as the culture and climate of our departments and institutions have a great impact on the satisfaction and success of early career faculty.

On one hand, fit is often critiqued as code for a host of beliefs and attitudes that leads to the exclusion of individuals who do not fit a community's dominant profile. At times this code takes precedence over objective assessments of productivity and other achievements in the evaluation of early career faculty, including the ultimate evaluation of tenure and promotion.

On the other hand, when used fairly, fit is a real phenomenon in higher education, one that is usually a manifestation of culture and climate. In higher education, culture operates on multiple levels. Each discipline, each institutional type, each campus, and each college and department within a campus have their own cultures. Climate is institution- or campus-specific but can also vary depending on college or department. In this chapter we distinguish between *culture* and *climate* and outline how these impact the experiences of early career faculty, make recommendations as to how you can assess the culture before being hired or soon afterward, and give you tips for how to work within one's particular culture and climate.

The Difference Between Climate and Culture

The terms *culture* and *climate* are often used interchangeably, and on a day-to-day basis, such casual usage may be fine. However, as you seek to develop your understanding of your institution's climate and culture, you should have a more refined understanding of each term.

Culture

As with most institutions, each institution of higher education has a *culture* that reflects its norms, values, practices, beliefs, and assumptions (Kuh & Whitt, 1988). This often unspoken culture, which James describes in Inset 3.1, guides nearly all elements of organizational behavior, from the development of mission, policies, and interpersonal interactions to resource allocation.

> **Inset 3.1.**
> **Words From Early Career Faculty: The Unwritten Rules of Culture**
>
> *So, there is the formality of what is supposed to be done. Then there is what people do and what's okay and what you are encouraged to do, and the informal stuff differs so strongly by departments and by the culture of a department. —* James

Culture is, in short, how we do things. For example, are faculty in their offices daily or seldom seen? Do students address professors as "Doctor" or by first name? As with culture in general, campus culture evolves, but it does so quite slowly, typically over decades. On a rare occasion, a tragedy or other calamity prompts a more rapid change of culture, but even then the transformation of culture may take years. Thus, for faculty members, campus culture is something that is experienced as relatively stable.

Kuh and Whitt (1988) outline and define several drivers of institutional culture that can be readily seen and evaluated. The *external environment*—such as where the institution is located (rural, suburban, urban), the dominant attitudes of the general public about higher education, the culture of the region of the country in which the institution is located, and the proclivities of local philanthropic organizations—influences the campus in multiple ways. For example, a rural, small private institution with an emphasis on experiential learning due to the ongoing support of the largest employer in the area will likely have a culture where a faculty member who wants to use practice-based pedagogies and be actively involved in the external community will be well regarded and rewarded. Contrast this with an urban university that is relatively disconnected from the neighborhood and considered to be elite, creating an attitude of distrust in the community. Here this same faculty member might struggle because community engagement and applied research may be practices that university colleagues do not value.

The *internal environment* of the institution itself holds a number of influences on campus culture. Some are quite obvious, such as religious affiliation, single-sex student populations, minority-serving-institution status, and other characteristics of institutional type (public, private, research, comprehensive, etc.). At times the academic program may be quite clear, especially in institutions that are clearly liberal arts colleges or technical institutions, but the quality or philosophical emphasis of the academic program may be harder to detect.

Other internal influences may be more obscure or less easily detected, such as the institutional or organizational *saga* (Clark, 1972), which is essentially the story that the institution tells about its development and evolution through nearly mythical people and events. Sagas define how people feel about the institution and indicate points of pride about it. Personal values and perspectives contrary to or speculative of the saga (e.g., challenging the value of the institutional mission that evolved over the prior 80 years) are suspect and may make fit difficult. The *institutional ethos* operates in a similar way, developing when "deeply held beliefs and guiding principles" result in an "underlying attitude that describes how faculty and students feel about themselves" (Kuh & Whitt, 1988, p. 47).

Bergquist and Pawlak (2008) posit that six cultures are present within colleges and universities. The *collegial* culture is discipline based, with a focus on the dissemination and creation of knowledge in an environment where faculty governance is robust and noncompetitive, rather than adversarial. Here faculty focus on the principles of liberal education, including the holistic education of future leaders. The *managerial* culture focuses on organization, goals, objectives, and institutional capacity. It considers the purpose of higher education to be more functional and skill based, placing a premium on developing citizenship in its students. The *developmental* culture embraces the personal, social, and professional growth of its members. The purpose of the institution and education is to develop mature individuals who also help the institution to mature.

The *advocacy* culture challenges the institution to behave in equitable ways, where distribution of resources is related to the distribution of power. Here, oppressive structures are assumed to exist and to impact faculty and students in different ways, according to their membership in groups that may oppose one another. The *virtual* culture is postmodern in nature and takes a global perspective in creating learning networks. The *tangible* culture "finds meaning in its roots, its community and its spiritual grounding" (Bergquist & Pawlak, 2008, p. xiv). In this culture, education is localized with a commitment to individual interactions based on shared values. No campus has just one culture; in fact, campuses probably have layers of multiple cultures, although one or two may stand out as particularly prominent. The interactions among these cultures can result in not only tensions (e.g., conflict between collegial and managerial cultures) but also opportunities for institutional growth.

Climate

Climate is the result of individuals operationalizing culture through their behavior and attitudes that then become a part of the institutional climate (Peterson & Spencer, 1990). Ultimately, climate relates more to how it feels to be a member of one group or another on campus, as a result of behaviors and attitudes that emerge from the culture. When Nancy talks about ego and self-interest, she offers a good example for a particular climate that she is learning to navigate (see Inset 3.2).

Inset 3.2.
Words From Early Career Faculty: A Climate of Self-Interest

It's about self-interest. You have to be careful of how you present your ideas, because the egos are so big here, and I've realized that even though we're all in academia, [often] students are not the focus. It is not about the students, it is about you being with ego, it is about you trying to demonstrate to other faculty members that [you are] superior in [your] thinking. —Nancy

Climate began to be applied as a way to describe how subgroups experienced universities when research on *chilly climate* documented the ways in which women were disenfranchised (e.g., Hall & Sandler, 1982; Sandler, 1986). This research, for example, found that women students were less likely to be called on in class, more likely to be interrupted, and inadvertently discouraged from participation in more so-called masculine disciplines such as science and math. Sandler (1986) explained that women faculty members also experienced chilly climates in their departments when they were referred to in gender stereotypical terms or given more caretaking or housekeeping roles.

Later, campus climate was analyzed in reference to the experience of non-White students, faculty, and staff. In this research, internal components of the racial climate contain the following dimensions: (a) the institution's historical legacy of inclusion or exclusion, (b) structural diversity or the demographic composition of a campus, (c) psychological factors such as the attitudes and beliefs of community members, and (d) how constituents interact with one another (Hurtado, Milem, Clayton-Pedersen, & Allen, 1998). Milem, Chang, and Antonio (2005) later added an additional dimension, the organizational/structural dimension, to account for structures, practices, and policies such as admissions, tenure, promotion, budgeting, and hiring. While these authors primarily focused on climate in terms of race or ethnicity, we can easily see the connection with the chilly climate women experience and extrapolate those principles to the experiences of faculty who come from other nondominant social identities, such as low socioeconomic class or lesbian, gay, bisexual, or transgender (LGBT). If there is a history of exclusion, low structural diversity, negative psychological factors, or negative interactions, then members of a target group have a difficult time develop-ing a sense of belonging to the institution; thus, through consistent negative experiences, their work and satisfaction are ultimately compromised.

The Impact of Campus Culture and Climate on Early Career Faculty

As suggested previously, climate and culture are complex constructs. In fact, they are so complex that once we are in a university for a while we may take the values, norms, and behaviors in that environment for granted in a way that we did not when we started. Behaviors, experiences, and interac-tions just start to seem normal to us in a way they might not have at first. In this section, we examine how those influences on culture and climate— such as discipline and institutional type, the academic culture, minority-serving-institution status, structural diversity, and other variations within an institution—can affect your faculty career.

Disciplinary Cultures and Institutional Type

Our initial mode of socialization in higher education is our socialization into our disciplines. Faculty reproduce themselves in the doctoral students they mentor and guide into the professoriate; thus, our doctoral-level education experiences shape our expectations for what our own lives will be like as fac-ulty members and what it means to be, for example, a physicist or a historian. We also learn what this academic identity means on a larger scale, beyond our university. Burton Clark's (1987) well-known book *The Academic Life: Small Worlds, Different Worlds* chronicled the impact of discipline on faculty experiences and expectations. These expectations and cultures shape our time allocations (to lab, home, studio, or field), salary structures, teaching loads, grant productivity, and so on. Within an institution, these disciplinary cul-tures make a difference as they influence how early career faculty experience their workplace; being an assistant professor in a college of education may be quite different than in a college of natural science or business, as our dis-ciplinary colleagues have differing expectations for how we behave, what we need, and how we succeed. James, an early career faculty member, is refer-ring to this when he talks about department cultures in Inset 3.1 earlier in the chapter. A very simple example of how cultural expectations may differ is that in more applied disciplines it may be important that early career faculty quickly become involved in the field of practice, where in the sciences it is more important to establish one's lab and quickly seek external funding for a research program.

Thus, as doctoral students, although we come to expect that our first job will be in a place just like the one where we studied, you may find yourself at a different type of institution. In fact, as noted in Chapter 1, most faculty work at places unlike their doctoral institutions. Terosky and Gonzales (2016) recently studied the experiences of faculty who began their careers at institutions different from those to which they aspired when entering the job market. The messaging they received in graduate school and the subsequent disappointment they felt from their advisers caused them to feel "less than" and compelled to justify their choices when working at nonresearch institutions. For those who continued to want to move to research-intensive universities, the inability to do so led to dissatisfaction in their current positions. However, many found that they valued contributing to the deep learning of their students and conducting research that they enjoyed and that had applications in their local communities. Discipline and institutional climate can impact early career faculty in multiple ways.

Cosmopolitan Versus Local Orientations

Merton (1968) offered a distinction between cosmopolitans and locals in regard to community influences that many analysts have adopted to describe faculty; that distinction is instructive here. The term *cosmopolitan* is used to describe a faculty member who prioritizes being part of a larger disciplinary community beyond the institution, forming networks across institutions, and developing a reputation that extends beyond the home university or college. This type of disciplinary identity is often particularly strong at doctoral universities with a high research presence, where being a member of a discipline encompasses national and international communities. In contrast, especially at comprehensive public teaching institutions, faculty members may be expected to be more *local,* in that their identities are situated in the institution rather than in the wider discipline. These cultures become impactful for early career faculty if their expectations for their careers stand in opposition to the expectations of their institution.

Because most of us earn our degrees at doctoral universities, often some of the most selective public and private universities in the country, we are typically socialized to create a career that is more cosmopolitan in nature, with a focus on developing a strong scholarly reputation. At these institutions, research productivity dominates the faculty experience. You likely saw your major professor do very little teaching and contribute relatively low amounts of service to the department or university. Thus, like being socialized into a discipline, you were also socialized into the culture of an institutional type.

Academic Culture

Bergquist and Pawlak's six academic cultures (2008) also provide examples for ways in which culture may impact early career faculty. For example, many of us have been socialized in a collegial culture where disciplines are centered and autonomy and faculty governance are valued, but we then find ourselves as faculty in an organization that emphasizes a managerial culture where processes, controls, and outcomes define the expectations and rewards. In this kind of environment, administrative control of the curriculum and an emphasis on increasing graduation rates may limit the breadth and depth of academic majors and frustrate faculty who are focused on autonomy in their academic programs.

Similarly, faculty members who value an advocacy culture may find it difficult to work in one where the focus is on serving those students and faculty best prepared for college-level work, rather than working to correct past inequities in education. A culture that values developing individuals, collaboration, and interdisciplinary work may be at odds with the control and systems of a managerial culture and the more individualized and political nature of the collegial culture. Given that early career faculty members today are more likely to grow up with technology and lean toward the virtual world, connecting across physical boundaries, there is potential for conflict with a more tangible culture that considers instruction and work as place-based and relies on face-to-face interaction.

Minority-Serving Institution Status

Culture and climate converge more explicitly when the impact of institutional type is considered for women's colleges, historically Black colleges and universities, and tribal colleges and universities. Institutional culture may reflect the cultural values, traditions, and norms of the group represented by high numbers of faculty, staff, and students, thus creating a welcoming, engaging, and supportive climate for those group members. In the relatively new, federally designated Hispanic-serving, Asian and Pacific Islander–serving, and Native-serving institutions, culture and climate may struggle to reflect the presence of these groups. Although the structural diversity may meet a federal designation, this may not be enough to change the climate or culture. Thus, you should not assume that as an early career faculty member you will find an easier path to tenure and job satisfaction at this type of institution.

Structural Diversity, or Lack Thereof

Structural diversity, a part of the racial climate model described by Hurtado and colleagues (1998), is critical to the satisfaction of faculty from underrepresented groups (women, minoritized and LGBT populations, or people from low socioeconomic status groups). Because of historical legacies of exclusion, predominantly White institutions tend to have cultures and climates that reflect the values of traditional academe in terms of what is considered good research, what is appropriate service, and how much teaching is valued. Moreover, the cultures of some fields may be more supportive of individuals from diverse groups than others. For example, Alexander (2008) suggests that women faculty in education may find more support and success than their female counterparts in engineering because the latter field has fewer female scholars.

As a result of limited structural diversity, faculty of color and those from other minoritized groups may experience bias in promotion and tenure decisions. The foci of their research may be questioned, they may be using new methodologies that are suspect, service in their communities could be undervalued, and senior colleagues may fail to understand how teaching evaluations may reflect students' discomfort with minoritized faculty rather than faculty members' actual teaching effectiveness. When there are low numbers of faculty from these groups on campus, these faculty members tend to feel isolated and a sense of otherness, whether they experience targeted bias or not. In fact, in one study, 44% of the faculty of color who perceived a hostile racial climate expressed a desire to leave their institutions (Jayakumar, Howard, Allen, & Han, 2009). This is an example of the complex cycle that a lack of structural diversity creates: isolation, bias, and hostility lead to dissatisfaction and a desire to leave, making retention of faculty of color difficult and furthering the problem with structural diversity. Relatedly, repeated experience with a hostile or chilly climate where one's competency is questioned can leave minoritized faculty members with doubt about their own competence and abilities (the imposter phenomenon is discussed in Chapter 2), much like the long-documented research on how a chilly climate can impact women (Hall & Sandler, 1982).

Being a *token* faculty member—one of only a few members in your minoritized group on your campus or in your department or college—has a major impact on climate as it has many implications for satisfaction and success and even your desire to stay at your institution (Atherton et al., 2016). If you come from one of these groups, you might be expected to represent your group on committees throughout the university; formally advise students from your groups; or, more likely, become a de facto adviser as these students begin to seek you out. Representation is also apparent in the additional pressure that minoritized faculty feel when their personal performance, good or bad, is perceived to represent their entire group (Turner, Gonzalez, & Wood, 2008). Because *token* implies that there are few like faculty on campus, finding communities of support and mentors is also a challenge for new faculty members (Atherton et al., 2016). Mentorship or lack thereof from one's affiliation group—a topic we take up more in Chapter 4—has been shown to be one of the strongest factors in the satisfaction and retention of new faculty (Turner et al., 2008).

Cultural Variations Within Institutions

Climate and culture naturally manifest at different levels in the institution. The environment of greatest impact for early career faculty is the home program, department, or college. Here are the day-to-day interactions and the communities that first welcome and later are the first evaluators in retention, tenure, and promotion processes. (Different campuses each have their own titles and language around the tenure and promotion process: promotion, tenure, and reappointment; retention, tenure, and promotion; tenure/reappointment/promotion; appointment, retention, reappointment; periodic review of faculty; we call this process RTP.) Like our graduate programs, our departments have the tendency to seek to hire people like themselves. The recent calls to diversify faculty may lead to early career faculty finding themselves in departments with more traditional academic values, few women and members of non-White groups, and perhaps an aging faculty—all reflective of decades of hiring White males. While not always the case, these differences may lead to challenges to values or work style. This experience is not limited to minoritized faculty, but it is more likely to be the case with them. Examples of enforcing traditional academic values may be resistance to newer research methodologies (O'Meara, Bennett, & Neihaus, 2016) and marginalization of research that focuses on liberalized or more critical topics.

Cultural differences may also relate to how department or college faculty *work*. Is it customary for faculty to come to the office daily, or do they primarily work from home (Rockquemore & Laszloffy, 2008)? Is it okay to structure office presence or course assignments around child care responsibilities? You may feel quite a bit of isolation if your work style is to come to the office daily while more senior faculty are seldom there (O'Meara et al., 2016). Department and college cultures might also have expectations for socializing with colleagues in other public situations. Are you in a department that socializes together or includes families and partners in events? You can imagine that if you continually avoid these events, fit will be difficult to achieve. Culture and climate are important and complicated, multilayered concepts. Both affect the experiences and careers of faculty in varied ways, and as an early career faculty member you need to be able to assess and work within the culture at your institution.

Assessing Campus Culture and Climate

Assessing campus climate and culture should begin as you consider entering a faculty search pool and should become more focused during the campus interview. However, with the tough academic market

Inset 3.3.
Words From Early Career Faculty: Assessing Campus Culture

You have to figure out what the game is before you know how to—before you figure out how to play it. —Sarah

and other pressing issues (finishing a dissertation, relocating, etc.), many new assistant professors do not begin to consider climate and culture until long after they arrive on campus. However, as Sarah discovered, figuring out climate and culture early allows you to be strategic about your professional choices (see Inset 3.3).

More often, once you are on campus you will be triggered to think about climate and culture when you ask questions like, *Why does this happen in this way? What is it that I'm not getting here?* and *Why is this so difficult here, when it was so easy at my doctoral institution?* Alternatively, maybe you are told, "That is not the way we do it here," or "You need to really understand what it takes to be liked here." These kinds of issues are often referred to as *politics*, and politics and alliances are parts of the culture and the climate at an institution. You may have experienced some politics in your doctoral education (with dissertation chairs, funding, and other opportunities), but for the most part you were insulated from these. When you become an assistant professor, politics are more profound.

Bates (1984; cited in Kuh & Whitt, 1988, p. 104) suggests that the following six "life problems" or orientations of organizations be the basis for assessing campus culture: the *affective* orientation (relationships, social expectations); the orientation to *causality* (attributions for problems); the *change* orientation (willingness to take risks or innovate); the *hierarchical* orientation (risk-taking, innovation); the orientation to *collaboration*; and the orientation to *pluralism* (intergroup relations).

Using this model as a base, we suggest that early career faculty or candidates develop questions that could be used to quickly assess culture and climate (see Table 3.1). Answers to the questions can come from a variety of sources, including individuals, publications, websites, and policies, and ideally should be triangulated with more than one source. Because the campus culture has multiple levels, these questions can also be applied at the program, department, or college level.

Considering the earlier discussion of the impact of Bergquist and Pawlak's six academic cultures (2008) on early career faculty, it may also be

TABLE 3.1
Strategy for Success: Assessing Your Institutional Culture and Climate

Question	Sources of Information
What is the structural diversity of the student body? Of the faculty?	Admissions fact sheets, institutional research dashboard on the website
Are there faculty associations or groups organized around social identities?	Website, ethnic or gender studies colleagues, administrators
What is the story of the institution? Who are the legends? What are sources of pride?	Longtime personnel; slogans on T-shirts, banners, or publications; websites
What are the priorities of the campus leadership?	Presidential messages, stated goals, strategic plan
Who are the influential people on campus?	Colleagues, e-mail messages, public statements
What are the current challenges?	Colleagues, public statements, campus events, posters/flyers, news sources
What is the role of faculty governance?	Faculty senate meetings; membership of the senate; collective bargaining agreement
What are the students like on campus?	Athletics, student organizations, Greek system, commuters
Is the faculty unionized? How predominant is the union?	Retention; tenure and promotion policies; websites; mythology or messages about grievances, administrators, or faculty
What does the purpose of education seem to be?	Messages about preparing citizens, advancing knowledge, providing access and equity, career preparation, and so on
How are merit and excellence talked about?	Focus on national rankings, negative remarks about underprepared students, bulletin boards, websites
Is the focus more local or cosmopolitan?	Competitor institutions, external funding expectations, valued publications
Is there a developmental approach or a sink-or-swim mentality related to students? Faculty? Staff?	Gatekeeping discourse and courses; resistance to support services; website of programs and services; sentiments of students, faculty, and staff

helpful to consult their Academic Cultures Inventory (see Inset 3.4), which helps you assess what cultures are dominant at your own institution. Twelve root statements reveal beliefs, values, meanings, purposes, and fears about the institution. Understanding how these cultures operate within your own institution help you to frame your expectations and deconstruct what you see and experience around you.

Working Within the Culture and Climate You Have

If you are really lucky, you find a perfect fit in your first tenure-track appointment, but most of us still need a little help in transitioning to a new environment. Here we offer some strategies that might be helpful to you in working within the culture and climate of an institution.

> **Inset 3.4.**
> **Resource for Success: Assessing Academic Culture**
>
> Academic Cultures Inventory (2008) by W. H. Bergquist and K. Pawlak
>
> This 72-item survey can determine which of the six cultures are predominant at your college or university. Its focus on your perception of the institution and its members aids you in accessing strategies in their book to help you navigate those cultures successfully.

- *Make your expectations known.* In the on-campus interviews with the department chair and dean be clear, if possible, about what you value and what it will take for you to succeed. Once on campus, meet with these individuals within the first month of arriving and again state your expectations for colleagueship and support. Moderate this, so as not to appear overly needy, by stating only what is absolutely necessary for you to transition well to the new institution.

> **Inset 3.5.**
> **Words From Early Career Faculty: Finding Relationships**
>
> *[A colleague's] got his stuff together pretty well, so he's doing okay. But from what I understand, his first couple of years were tougher than mine. . . . I think part of that was not reaching out to people. I think he sort of thought that people would reach out to him, and in our department it just doesn't happen. —James*

- *Find those who share your professional priorities.* In Terosky and Gonzales's study (2016), those who eventually found satisfaction in teaching and in self-defined research goals cited their ability to find like-minded colleagues at their institutions as an important form of support. Find those people and make them part of your colleague circle, including like-minded senior colleagues, who can help you navigate. As James explains in Inset 3.5, do not leave this important part of socialization to others or expect that they will reach out to you. We discuss this topic more in Chapter 4.

- *Find those who are like you.* If you are in an institution where proportionally few faculty or students are from your affiliation group, find or develop communities of safety on campus. You might join established groups, such as a Latinx Faculty Consortium, engage with student organizations, or start a monthly coffee meeting with colleagues who share your social identities.
- *Build your own social network off campus.* When a cultural mismatch exists, for whatever reason, faculty members often need to develop code-switching behaviors—that is, using behaviors and espousing values of the dominant culture that are contrary to a person's identity. This approach helps an individual to function within the environment, but it also takes a personal toll by calling on him to consistently work beyond his comfort zone. Becoming a part of your own community outside of campus, where your culture is the norm, can be a way of sustaining and reenergizing yourself.
- *Build your professional network off campus.* Likewise, becoming a part of your discipline and developing networks external to your campus—regionally, nationally, and internationally—are ways to counter an isolating experience on campus. Professional organizations often have a variety of early career faculty research and professional development activities where you can develop a network of colleagues and support. These may also be avenues to develop collaborative research projects or funding opportunities. External networks are also places where you can share your experiences in a safer environment, which may help to normalize the experience—as others likely have similar experiences on their campuses—and to learn successful strategies from others.

Concluding Thoughts

Bergquist and Pawlak (2008) recommend that through *appreciative inquiry* we can focus on what is right and working in our environments, in essence redefining the way we are looking at our institutions. This cognitive reframing is important for many reasons. As mentioned earlier, campus cultures are slow to change, meaning that it is in your best interest to learn how to thrive and succeed in your institution, no matter what the current culture. The academic market does not make it easy to shop for positions and find a campus that fulfills all of our needs, which makes our ability to reframe all the more important. We are not suggesting you change who you are to fit, but rather to be strategic so that being your authentic self is not fraught with conflict and misunderstandings. The recommendations noted in this chapter can help you develop tools, networks, allies, and defense mechanisms that make it more likely that you can better assess your climate and culture, avoiding the delay that Karen experienced in her early years (Inset 3.6).

> **Inset 3.6.**
> **Words From Early Career Faculty: Seeing the Big Picture**
>
> *It took me about two to three years to really understand the politics. I was a brand-new faculty member. I never worked in academia before. This whole environment to me was very complex. Very new. So it took me time to learn it because learning it was not my only focus. I was also learning to be a teacher. I was learning to get on my feet, so it was part of this. I feel like if I worked in academia before I probably would have quickly analyzed the situation in front of me, but it took me a longer time to see the entire picture. —Karen*

Exercises

Following are reflective questions that might be useful to you as you consider the campus climate and culture you need to thrive or in which you currently find yourself:

1. What kind of culture do you need to thrive as a faculty member?
2. How satisfied are you with the culture of your department? Why? What aspects of it align with your values and your approach to the work you do as a professor?
3. If the culture of your department is not healthy for you, why? What aspects are not aligned with your values and approach? What can you do about that?
4. How do you experience the climate at your campus? What role do you believe your gender, race, ethnicity, sexual orientation, or other social identities play in your experience? Where might you find support? Which of the recommendations in this chapter are you likely to employ?

4

BUILDING AND MAINTAINING POSITIVE PROFESSIONAL RELATIONSHIPS

Positive professional relationships are central to a fulfilling faculty career. While faculty work may often seem like a solo enterprise, we get ideas, learn, and achieve goals through the relationships we develop. In summarizing literature on faculty professional relationships, O'Meara and colleagues (2008) note that the ability to have strong relationships with both students and colleagues makes a difference in job satisfaction, including bolstering fulfillment with teaching, supporting scholarship, and providing access to allies. Neumann (2006) found that ideas for inquiry often emerged through conversations in the classroom and with colleagues. Moreover, our relationships shape our professional reputation. For example, over time our reputation as a teacher precedes us (to our benefit or detriment) with new groups of students; the same is true with our reputation for follow-through on projects or the respect we show our colleagues. Tending to your professional relationships is a key component of your faculty career and your ultimate success.

In this chapter we provide suggestions and strategies for how to think about and nurture positive professional relationships. Your professional relationships extend beyond your faculty colleagues and students to include campus administrators and staff as well as colleagues at other institutions. We provide comments and tips for working with each of these groups. However, before we do, we want to begin the chapter by discussing what can be a rather ill-defined and amorphous concept: *collegiality*.

Collegiality

You have probably heard the term *collegiality*, a word used in higher education quite frequently and often described as the central feature of faculty life (Bess, 1992). The concept of collegiality is seen by some as so important, in fact, that there have been debates about whether it should be formalized as the fourth criteria for tenure (AAUP, 2016; Connell & Savage, 2001; Flaherty, 2013; Schmidt, 2013; Strippling, 2010).

Collegiality as a term has not necessarily been well-defined. While we often understand it as more or less "being nice" to each other, the term has far richer meaning (Haviland, Alleman, & Cliburn Allen, 2017). Bess (1992) has offered a multilayered definition of *collegiality*, which is beyond our scope here. For our purposes, we note that collegiality confers both rights (to have your voice heard, to influence decisions) as well as responsibilities (to support a common purpose, to act in good faith and trust that others are doing the same, to support others without expectation of immediate reciprocity, to share concerns appropriately; Haviland et al., 2017). Collegiality might be thought of as a sense of professional trust and respect that translates into supportive behaviors that facilitate pursuit of shared goals within a department, a school or college, or a university.

In this sense, collegiality is the cornerstone of a central value in faculty life: working together to advance the academic enterprise. Faculty engagement in making decisions about the academic programs of the department or university is critical, as is faculty participation in larger areas of shared governance (such as budget oversight). When fully realized, collegiality greases these wheels, leading faculty to engage in honest debate based on trust, to act in the collective (rather than self-) interest, and to commit to the greater good. Collegiality is also a value that encourages us to support and look out for the interests of our individual colleagues, and while this sentiment can be valuable for each faculty member, O'Meara and colleagues (2008) have noted that women faculty especially value collegiality.

Collegiality has a central role in faculty life, facilitating academic governance and playing a role in how much of the institutional work gets done. To be perfectly frank, whether collegiality is a formal part of the tenure process or not, being respected and trusted, being seen as someone with integrity, and being liked by your colleagues does in fact make a difference in the decision. We see it happen.

While often applied only to faculty, here we apply the collegiality concept even more broadly to guide our interactions with staff and administrators on a campus. Given the complexity of today's university, through collegiality more

Inset 4.1.
Words From Early Career Faculty: Missing Collegial Relationships

I just don't have anybody here to reflect ideas off of in the same kind of way. If something's turning in my head, I can't just walk down the hallway and talk to whoever I see.
—James

[In grad school] I used to go down the hallway . . . and have tea with one of my colleagues. We would chat for 15 minutes and then go. That is something I really miss, especially coming out of grad school, that kind of connection to other people.
—Sarah

broadly understood we can accomplish our individual and shared goals. A department, a college, and a university are all communal workplaces, and success in those environments means building relationships; acting with respect, trust, and integrity; and recognizing a larger shared purpose.

Relationships With Faculty Colleagues

Relationships with faculty colleagues can be a source of anxiety and frustration for early career faculty members. We often arrive right out of graduate school and expect to find a community like that of which we were a part: a scholarly community with long conversations with colleagues on issues big and small and colloquia on a range of topics. What we often find, however, are faculty members who teach multiple classes, serve on committees, juggle family commitments, and try to squeeze out time for scholarship. Rather than coming in with other doctoral students, we might find we are the only new faculty member in the department or that we have relatively little day-to-day contact with our colleagues. James and Sarah both speak to this isolation in Inset 4.1.

No surprise, then, that early career faculty repeatedly report their surprise and even dismay at the isolation they find as they step into their position (Austin & Rice, 1998; Bogler & Kremer-Hayon, 1999; Gravett & Petersen, 2007; Trower, 2010). (These feelings of loneliness are often compounded by the fact that we have moved to a new area for our job and lack social connections as well. Inset 4.2 offers some tips for connecting in your new community.) Seeking engagement with faculty colleagues, early career faculty frequently report missing a sense of community, being shocked at the individualized and competitive nature of faculty life, and being surprised by the time it took to feel like part of the community (Austin & Rice, 1998; Bogler & Kremer-Hayon, 1999; Gravett & Petersen, 2007). Often, professional interaction with their *tenured* colleagues leaves pretenure faculty least satisfied (Trower, 2010).

We share this information not to discourage you, but rather for two reasons. First, we want to normalize the fact that early career faculty often feel lonely and isolated when they step into their roles. Second, we want to assure you that you can take steps to change the situation.

With that in mind, here are tips and suggestions both for how to be a good colleague and how to build healthy relationships with your faculty colleagues:

> **Inset 4.2.**
> **Strategies for Success:**
> **Becoming Part of a New**
> **Community**
>
> Use the following strategies to get connected socially when you move to a new area:
>
> - Volunteer.
> - Find a gym, yoga studio, or other space for physical health.
> - Seek out a church, synagogue, mosque or other spiritual center.
> - Use meetup.com to find interest groups you might want to join.

- *Reach out to your colleagues.* Early career faculty often look to senior faculty and administrators to reach out to them (Cawyer & Friedrich, 1998). While this hope is not unreasonable, the reality is that reaching out does not always happen as we might like. This does not mean those administrators and senior faculty are not open to building relationships with you; they might just need you to take the lead. So, drop by someone's office for a chat or take that person out to coffee to learn about his work and to share yours.
- *Be present at department and college events, including meetings, colloquia, and the like* (Alexander, 2008). It may not always feel like these events are the best use of your time when you have teaching and scholarship to worry about. However, being visible, accessible, and present at the majority of events shows your colleagues you care and puts you in a position to meet and interact with people. You might even decide to be in your office with the door open at strategic times when most faculty are around.
- *Take the time to talk with others when the opportunity presents itself.* Your days will quickly fill up, and there will be moments when it feels like the last thing you have time to do is chat with colleagues. Resist that urge. Get to the department meeting early so that you can make small talk, enjoy the quick hallway conversation about movies, and prop yourself in a colleague's doorway to ask how her weekend was (Kirk, 2013). These moments take little time, but they build the trust and familiarity that provide the foundation of relationships.

- *Be involved in things outside your department.* Your campus likely has a center for teaching and learning (it may go by another name) that offers workshops and events. It may even have programs specifically for new faculty. Participate. Doing so may connect you not only to more senior faculty but also to early career faculty like yourself who can provide support.
- *Be kind, patient, and considerate of the interests of others* (Bess, 1992). One of the foundations of collegiality is the idea that our colleagues consider and look out for our interests even if we are not around at the time to do so. Develop a reputation of acting with integrity and trying to understand your colleagues' perspectives.
- *Avoid taking sides in department factions.* This suggestion can be difficult, to be sure, but it is an important skill. Particularly in larger departments, faculty may have organized into smaller groups, perhaps based on disciplinary differences or even past political fights. Try not to get caught in this dynamic. First, interact with as many different faculty colleagues as you can so that it is clear you are not aligning with any particular cluster or clique. Second, remember that you do not need to be engaged in their battles. Remain noncommittal should they try to engage you in their debates, and do not repeat what one group might say about the other. That only causes trouble.
- *Follow through.* One of your most precious resources is your professional reputation, and you build that reputation slowly, over time, as your colleagues come to know you as reliable and dependable. We encourage you to take great care in completing the work you take on (e.g., on department committees, in associations) to ensure that it is always timely, thorough, and professionally done. You do not want to develop a reputation as a colleague whom others cannot trust. In general, it is better to say no to something (a topic we discuss in Chapter 10) than to take on work and not deliver.

Finding Mentors, Allies, and Sources of Support

Most of us have heard how important it is to have a mentor. Companies have mentoring programs, universities set up mentoring programs for first-year students, and early career faculty are encouraged to find a mentor or develop a mentor network. But what *is* a mentor and why is that person so important?

Bode (1999) defines a *mentor* as "a guide or a sponsor—one who looks after, advises, protects, and takes a special interest in another's development" (p. 119). Rockquemore and Laszloffy (2008) draw a distinction between a mentor and a sponsor: a mentor provides you with tips and support, while a sponsor uses her power or position to advocate for you with others and help advance your career.

There are multiple potential benefits for early career faculty in a mentoring relationship. A mentor can serve as a friend who gives social and emotional support, a career guide to help with professional development, a source of information about an organization, an intellectual guide with whom to collaborate on scholarship, or any combination of these (Sands, Parsons, & Duane, 1991). Kiewra (2008) notes that, aside from opening doors and providing opportunities for you, being involved in a scholarly partnership with a mentor can allow you to watch a senior expert work, which can reveal an accomplished expert's thought processes and work patterns. Mentors can also provide a sense of connection to the campus community and reduce isolation, something that can be particularly important for women and faculty of color who often describe a more isolating work environment (Boice, 1993; O'Meara et al., 2008).

Finding mentors can certainly be challenging, particularly when we are new to a campus. Following are some tips and strategies for building mentoring relationships:

- *Think of a support network, rather than trying to identify a single mentor.* Too often we are in search of the elusive holy grail of mentoring: a single person who can meet all of our professional needs. This tall order is likely to fail. Like Michael and Karen in Inset 4.3, we encourage you to build and access a network of experienced colleagues whom you can tap for advice on varied topics (e.g., research, teaching, relationship with your chair; O'Meara et al., 2008; Rockquemore & Laszloffy, 2008; Terosky & Gonzales, 2016). Build a team that can help meet your varied professional needs.
- *Use both formal and informal means to find mentors.* Many faculty development centers offer mentoring programs for early career faculty. However, research also suggests that the informal relationships that develop through other means are the most meaningful for faculty (Terosky & Gonzales, 2016; Trower, 2010). We encourage

Inset 4.3.
Words From Early Career Faculty: Searching for Mentoring

It's just continuous reaching and looking for mentorship. It can be exhausting. —Karen

Listen, I need some help on this area. I'm going to go to this person and I'm going to ask the question. —Michael

Inset 4.4.
Words From Early Career Faculty:
Look Beyond Your Department

Get out of the department now and then. And I mean this in the best way possible, but it was actually one of the most helpful things that I've learned, that there's much more on campus outside of these [office] walls.
—Michael

Try to build the strongest relationships you can in your department, but also . . . be working with people across colleges, across universities.
— James

you to take advantage of formal mentoring programs as well as build your own support network.

• *Build your network from both inside and outside your institution.* You can collect mentoring and advice from your graduate school advisers and professors, senior colleagues within and outside of your department, and even more experienced junior colleagues who are not too far removed from your current experiences. Your department chair may also be an important resource for advice and for identifying others to whom you can reach out. Early in your career, your graduate school professors may be the ones who know your work best and can give you advice and feedback on publishing. Senior colleagues from outside your college or discipline may be of limited help in advising on tenure standards in your department but might provide valuable and objective advice on how to handle relationships with department colleagues. Both Michael and James share their advice in Inset 4.4.

• *Be proactive in building and nurturing your network.* Tell colleagues that you are looking for someone who could mentor you in a particular area (e.g., teaching or a particular area of research) and ask them if they have any suggestions (Rockquemore & Laszloffy, 2008). Be intentional about building genuine relationships with members of your network (Bode, 1999) by taking them to coffee, getting to know them, and sharing ideas and resources with them.

Ultimately, your relationships with your faculty colleagues on and off campus can be some of the most rewarding and valuable components of your professional life and serve as a resource throughout your career.

Contrary to the image of the professor toiling alone at her desk, the wheels of faculty life are greased by our colleagues. As Alexander (2008) and others (e.g., O'Meara et al, 2008) have said, it is almost impossible to succeed in faculty work without support and guidance from others. Relationships with faculty colleagues can help us learn about the institution and its culture, give us tips on teaching, refine ideas for scholarship, and even just help us pass some time during the workday. We encourage you to think about a professional support network that is broad and diverse, one that is built to meet your varied, individual needs as a faculty member. At the same time, be both patient and persistent as you build these relationships. Be thoughtful about whom you identify to collaborate with on projects, to ensure that the work will be productive, and be sure that you can trust others' discretion before sharing too much personal information or something that might come back to hurt you later. While the relationships may

> **Inset 4.5.**
> **Words From Early Career Faculty: Reaching Out to Colleagues**
>
> *I'm having to work harder . . . building in a lot more collaboration— [i.e., with a colleague in another state] whose interests are very similar to me. And I just wrote to him and said, "Hey, I've got this data. Do you have anything that might compare with it? We can submit a bigger study together; if not, maybe you're still interested in just writing this with me." I've been really active about that, and that's not nearly as easy as walking down the hall and chatting.*
> —James

not develop as quickly as you would like, if you put in the effort (as James describes in Inset 4.5), it will be worth the time.

Working With Disciplinary Colleagues

As faculty, we have colleagues who are part of our broader discipline. These faculty colleagues can play a central role in professional success and growth, and tending to these relationships is an important part of building our reputation. For instance, as the quote in Inset 4.5 shows, James addressed his lack of engagement with departmental colleagues in his specialization by reaching out to others off campus for collaboration and intellectual growth.

Building strong relationships with disciplinary colleagues can be particularly important for minoritized faculty, given their small numbers in many fields and on many campuses. For these scholars, off-campus colleagues may be among the few options for finding others who share the same research interests. These off-campus colleagues can also be key sources of emotional and professional support.

There is no one way to build your network of disciplinary colleagues, so we offer several ideas:

- Participate in preconference workshops offered by your professional association for early career faculty.

- Attend the less formal conference presentations, such as roundtables and poster sessions, where you can engage in one-on-one and small group conversation.
- Identify colleagues you would like to meet at a conference and then reach out to them before a conference to see if they would like to grab coffee or a meal to discuss their work.
- Look for mentoring programs within your scholarly associations. Many associations have programs to connect more junior scholars with senior scholars.

In Chapter 10 of their book, Rockquemore and Laszloffy (2008) also offer helpful ideas for connecting with others beyond your campus, including looking for gender, racial, or ethnic organizations in your field (e.g., Latinx sociologists) and posting questions to electronic mailing lists and discussion boards. For this final suggestion, we offer a caveat: Be sure that whatever you post is professional and appropriate, because your own campus colleagues might see it.

Relationships With Staff Colleagues

As a faculty member, you come into regular contact with the administrative staff in your department office almost from the moment you accept the job offer. These individuals, who have titles such as department assistant or department coordinator, are typically involved in managing the hiring paperwork and ensuring that you have what you need to get started on your teaching and scholarship. You will continue to interact with these individuals on an almost daily basis for the rest of your career. As your career progresses, you will also encounter staff in a variety of other roles. For instance, if you secure grants, you will work with staff who manage grants and contracts at your institution.

We have one overarching piece of advice: Treat these individuals with the respect and kindness they deserve, and they will make your professional life immensely easier. Your relationships with these professionals should be nurtured with as much care and respect as your relationships with faculty colleagues. In many ways, administrative staff hold the keys to the academic kingdom. While department chairs come and go and deans change, a staff member may remain in the position or at the institution for years. When you wonder about deadlines, where a form goes, or how to purchase something, they are the ones most likely to know the answer. And when you need to help a student solve a problem, it is likely a staff member can call her friend of 20 years, who just happens to work in the registrar's office, to sort out the issue.

With this in mind, here are tips for building effective working relationships with staff members. We focus on staff in your department, but the same principles apply to staff across campus:

- *Identify staff roles and duties almost as soon as you get to campus.* While duties vary, office staff often help you obtain desk copies of books, place book orders for your courses, and handle paperwork for things such as travel and equipment purchases. However, there may also be school- or college-level staff who you will need to work with for some of these items. Talk with your chair and with the staff themselves to learn who does what and how the staff would like you to access them for help. For instance, is there a single point person to approach who then directs with whom you'll work? Do people prefer e-mail or in-person requests?

- *Plan ahead and be patient.* Just like you, administrative staff have multiple demands on their time. Remember that they do not work for you per se; they work for the department or the institution. While part of their job is to help you do yours, their overall duty is to make sure the department runs well. On any given day, they are likely supporting the chair, handling multiple requests from other faculty like you, processing student paperwork, and even responding to a request from the dean. Even in a small department, the work can be overwhelming, and staff are having to continually reprioritize. Unless it is a simple question, plan your requests ahead and give the staff plenty of lead time to complete them.

- *Be active in getting to know them.* Just as with your faculty colleagues, your staff colleagues have full lives outside of work. Take the time to get to know them and show interest in their lives. Depending on when you come to the office, they may be the only ones around. Take a few moments to ask about their day, recent movies, or the weather. Nurture a healthy, professional relationship with these colleagues.

- *Show your appreciation for the work that they do.* Staff help faculty and students in big and little ways, seen and unseen. It might be something as little as expediting paperwork or as big as calling in a favor to get a policy exception. Just like everyone else, staff want to make a difference in what they do and want to be appreciated for it. Appreciation does not have to be a grand gesture. Sometimes, just noticing and saying, "Thank you," is sufficient. If you are going to grab a cup of coffee, see if they want one, or perhaps give each staff member a small gift card and thank-you note around the holidays or at the end of the academic year.

Relationships With Administrator Colleagues

Any college or university has multiple levels of administrators, although their roles and titles vary depending on the complexity of the institution. For example, at a smaller institution, department chairs may report directly to a single academic dean, who reports to the president. At a larger comprehensive or research university, the department chair may report to a dean or associate dean of the school or college, who then reports to a provost. Larger campuses have numerous administrators with titles like director, associate vice president, and vice president. The modern university is a complex place, with divisions such as academic affairs, student affairs, finance, alumni relations, and research—and all of these have administrators. Fundamentally, an administrator's role is to manage the work of the institution and his unit. This can mean setting policy (as with a dean or provost); interpreting and implementing policy (as with a chair); or developing programs and services for students, faculty, or staff (as with the faculty development center).

While your main contact early in your career will likely be with your department chair and maybe your dean, your contact with other administrators will grow over time. What's more, administrators can also be important mentors and allies for all faculty, including early career faculty. In academic affairs, many administrators were once faculty themselves and likely moved through the ranks to professor. They know what it is like to be starting a career and can be a source of support. Moreover, they likely have a good understanding of the campus as a whole and provide a wise voice from outside your department. Other administrators, even if they were not once faculty, can be valued colleagues and may even open up opportunities for you down the road (e.g., you may develop an interest in helping to build the research infrastructure, support faculty development, or support a campus-wide effort like general education).

With these roles in mind, following are tips for working with administrator colleagues:

- *Identify key administrators and their roles as soon as you arrive on campus.* Campuses often hold a new faculty orientation during which more senior administrators visit to introduce themselves. Remember their names and faces so that you can greet them on campus and introduce yourself to them. Find out their responsibilities. You might even locate an organizational chart for the campus or its divisions to find out who does what and who reports to whom.
- *Feel free to reach out and get to know them.* As you talk with other faculty, you will learn a bit more about administrators, their interests,

and their backgrounds. You might find, for instance, that the vice president for faculty affairs has the same research interests that you do, or that you went to the same graduate school. Feel free to contact that person's office and ask for a short appointment so that you can introduce yourself, learn about her or him, and seek her or his advice on your own career. Treat every campus administrator as a potential part of your support network.

- *Respect the organizational chart when making a request.* Over time, you will develop relationships, even friendships, with administrators and will become comfortable with these colleagues. Remember, however, that you still work in an organization and that your actions have implications for (and reflect on) your chair and dean. Therefore, be mindful when you need to work through your chair or dean rather than through a campus administrator. Seeking advice from an administrator about a professional challenge or your career goals is one thing. However, if you are about to pitch an idea for some big project that would take time from your teaching or otherwise affect your work in the department, first talk to your chair and your dean so that they do not hear the idea from someone else.

Relationships With Students

Finally, we discuss students. Almost regardless of the type of institution in which you work, most of your professional relationships include contact with students. Of course, the nature of the contact may vary. You may teach large lectures of 60 to 100 students or more. Perhaps you have small graduate seminars with fewer than 10 students, or maybe much of your contact with students is through a team that works in your lab or in mentoring (graduate) students in research. Whatever the case, think carefully about the kinds of professional relationships you have with your students and about the kind of professor you wish to be.

VanOosting (2015) speculates that the relationship that faculty members have with students goes through four stages over the course of a faculty career. In the first stage, he says, faculty are like *older siblings.* As an early career faculty member, it is likely that you will be close in age to your students; this fact has both pros and cons. In VanOosting's second stage, the professor is more of a *friend.* While the age gap may be a bit larger, it is still not terribly significant. These faculty members and their students might have more extended interactions and conversations on academic matters that then flow into grabbing coffee or a beer together to continue the conversation, perhaps discussing personal matters along with academic topics. Both of these stages provide opportunities to connect with individual students. As someone who might be able to speak the students' language, you can help them advance into adulthood, learn professional norms, and discover how to succeed in academe.

VanOosting's (2015) later stages involve more "adult" faculty roles. In the third stage he suggests that around the time faculty earn tenure, they become more like *parents* to their students. Once tenured and progressing to full professor, we are more engaged in setting and enforcing the rules through policies and decisions that affect students' education. At this point, our outlook might change a bit, as we take on a less individual and more institutional perspective related to students and our department. In the fourth stage, as we wind down our career, we become like *grandparents*—benevolent, patient, and indulgent of students' foibles. With the longer perspective of a career and life, we seek to share our wisdom in a relaxed and supportive way.

Relationships with faculty can make a significant difference in students' lives. At the same time, the line is very fine; familiarity can quickly become overfamiliarity and lead to blurred professional boundaries. In some cases, faculty and students work together on projects (e.g., in a lab or on a research project) where contact is less structured and where conversation may even turn to everyday, less academic topics. Such relationships can be rewarding and benefit both the student and faculty member. However, students may latch on to a professor (particularly one close to their age), or a faculty member may take advantage of being in an authority position. Such relationships can easily morph into behavior that can be perceived as sexual harassment.

We cannot stress enough the importance of maintaining a professional relationship with your students. Meet with students with your door open, avoid oversharing personal information or discussing topics not appropriate for the workplace, and set clear professional boundaries. For instance, some faculty choose not to connect with students on social media, or they set up nonpersonal accounts for teaching and instruction. Most campuses today have policies designed to limit romantic relationships between students and faculty. You should be familiar with your campus policy. In Chapter 5 we consider more specific suggestions related to teaching. Here we offer tips to consider for your professional relationships with students.

- *Expect different relationships with undergraduate versus graduate students.* As you interact with undergraduate students, particularly freshmen and sophomores, you will likely find that they need more concrete coaching and guidance on things like study skills and time management. Moreover, much of your interaction will likely be fairly structured (e.g., classroom time, office hours). Graduate students, in contrast, may be closer to your own age. You may also find yourself working with them in less structured ways and for longer periods of time (e.g., lab projects, theses, or dissertations). Be ready to perhaps learn things about their lives that you might not want to know and also to have much more casual conversations while maintaining appropriate boundaries.

- *Be professional, fair, and consistent with all of your students.* Getting a reputation for being anything other than these qualities will be hard to undo. Your role with each student with whom you interact is that of teacher. Each student should have the same opportunity to learn from and receive support from you. Will you connect more with some students than others? Of course. But be careful not to play favorites, such as by sharing some information (e.g., about assignments) with some students and not others.

- *Be human and be yourself.* Students generally want to like you and to learn from you, and they will work harder for you and give you more latitude if they feel that they know a little bit about you as a person. When you see them on campus, ask them how they are doing; share appropriate details about what you did over the weekend or use relevant personal vignettes about your life (as a student, as a professor, as a parent) in class. These conversations help build positive relationships.

- *At the same time, be careful about oversharing.* Think before you share a personal vignette in class or in a one-on-one conversation with a student. Any story shared in class should help to illustrate a point but not cast you in an unprofessional light. For instance, you might share a story about being in a fraternity to illustrate social stratification and privilege; talking about your participation in fraternity parties, however, seems less wise. The risk for oversharing is even greater during chats with one or a handful of students, where the conversation is often more casual and wide-ranging. Our advice is not to share anything that you would be embarrassed for others to know. Assume that what you say will be shared with others.

- *Carefully consider how you want to be addressed.* Some new professors are eager to use their title as a doctor with students while others eschew the idea as hierarchical. We do not have a recommendation but do suggest you consider a couple of things. First, for women and other minoritized faculty, asking students to use your title may be a way to show you expect respect and to augment your credibility; this strategy may also be useful if you are close in age to your students. Second, consider the department's culture. While you might want to use your academic title, the norm in your department may be otherwise. In this case, using your title might make you stand out and run counter to your colleagues' habits. You might still choose to do so, but mindfully consider the pros and cons before you make your choice.

Concluding Thoughts

The professional relationships you build with your faculty colleagues, staff, administrators, and students are central to your success as a faculty member. These relationships connect us to our campus and our disciplines, provide inspiration (and partners) for scholarly endeavors, help us accomplish our work, shape our reputations, and offer fulfillment. Building and nurturing these relationships takes time, care, and intention. We encourage you to think carefully about the kind of professional relationships you want to have, as well as strategies for developing those relationships, as part of your career. Doing so is worth the investment of your time and energy.

Exercises

Following are exercises that might be useful to you in developing your professional relationships.

1. Ask senior colleagues both on and off campus (e.g., your chair, graduate school teachers) whom they identify as a model of a good colleague and why. Try to get them to be concrete about their models' behaviors and actions. Use this information to create a portrait of the kind of colleague you want to be.
2. Think about your professional goals for the next several years. Then, think about the knowledge and skills you need, but may not yet have, to accomplish those goals. Based on your goals and your needs consider the following:
   - What are your top two to three needs for mentoring right now?
   - Who are people (faculty, staff, administrators) on campus who can help you learn and grow professionally?
   - Create a plan for reaching out to each of those people.
3. Reflect on the following questions:
   - What are your core values for professional relations?
   - What is one personal characteristic of yours that is related to professional relationships and of which you are proudest? Why?

- What is one personal characteristic of yours that is related to professional relationships and of which you are least proud? Why? What can you do about it?

Goal-Setting Activity:
Building Your Professional Relationships

We provide here a step-by-step process for you to start to think about the kinds of things you might want to accomplish as a colleague during the next several years of your career.

1. Brainstorm several goals or things you would like to learn or accomplish as a colleague in the next three to five years. How do you want to be perceived by your students and colleagues on and off campus? With whom do you want to build professional relationships?
2. Try to arrange those goals in some kind of order. For instance, does one lead to another? Or could one be accomplished in a year or so while another goal might take two to three years to accomplish?
3. Now for each goal, ask the following:
    - What are some challenges I might encounter in reaching that goal?
    - What resources (e.g., people, information, skills) do I have to help me reach that goal?
    - What specific steps will I take, and by when, to reach that goal?

You might consider using a table like Table 4.1 to help you think about these questions. We have filled in the first row to give you an example.

TABLE 4.1
Shaping Your Professional Relationships

Goal	Challenges I Might Encounter	Resources I Have	Steps I Will Take and by When	Accomplished? When?
1. Connect with a research partner from a different campus	• Difficult to identify someone with similar interests • Colleagues already too busy	• Network of existing colleagues • Google, Research Gate, and other tools to identify shared interests • Ability to network	• Online search for other researchers at my same career stage • Attend poster sessions/ roundtables at conferences to meet those with similar interests • Share draft of my work for feedback to initiate/ explore a relationship	
2.				
3.				
4.				
5.				

Some other goals you might consider for your professional relationships include

- building positive relationships with department or college staff members,
- developing a clear philosophy for professional relationships (with clear boundaries) with students, and
- connecting with one senior faculty member from another department or college on the campus as possible mentor or coach.

PART TWO

THRIVING IN YOUR FACULTY WORK

SHAPING YOUR CAREER AS A TEACHER

As we have discussed, faculty members spend a good portion of their time teaching. Almost 46% of assistant professors spend between 9 and 16 hours per week in classroom instruction; more than 18% spend 13 or more hours per week (Eagan et al., 2014). Then, of course, there is time spent preparing for teaching and grading, with 30% of assistant professors reporting more than 13 hours per week on these tasks (Eagan et al., 2014). These figures likely do not capture the random e-mail exchanges and brief hallway conversations faculty have with their students on a daily basis. For most faculty, much of their time and energy goes to teaching and interacting with students. However, our doctoral programs generally do little if anything to prepare us well for this component of faculty work (Golde & Dore, 2001; Rice et al., 2000).

Our goal in this chapter is to help you think about teaching as a part of your faculty career. This is not a how-to chapter on teaching in the classroom; many wonderful resources are available on that topic, and we do not presume to say something they have not—or to do it nearly as well. Throughout this chapter, we identify resources that we have found especially helpful. While we touch on some teaching tips and related strategies in these pages, our main goal here is to help you think about the context in which you teach (the goals, the students), your role as an educator relative to other components of your faculty work, and what part teaching plays in your faculty identity. We begin by looking at the way teaching and learning have evolved in higher education before turning to specific teaching-related topics. Then we discuss course evaluations. We next consider how our social identities may impact how we approach teaching and our classroom experiences. We close with exercises and activities you can use for growing and developing as an educator.

The Changing Landscape of Teaching and Learning

In the last 40-plus years, the landscape for the educational work that faculty do has changed greatly. On one level, the shift has been from a focus on *teaching* (or what faculty do as the center of attention) to one on *learning* (or what happens to students who are in our classrooms). On another, related level, the student population coming to college is increasingly diverse, which brings important implications for how faculty should consider their educational role.

From Teaching to Learning

In the mid-1990s, Barr and Tagg (1995) made the case that higher education needed to move from a faculty-centric focus on teaching to a focus on student learning. This article is widely cited when people talk about shifting the mind-set in higher education from a concern about processes (teaching) to a concern about outcomes (learning). Along with this shift have come pithy sayings, such as that we are moving from the idea of the faculty member as the sage on the stage to one where he or she is the guide by the side.

This shift has influenced how faculty work around teaching and learning in multiple ways. First, one change in our faculty work has been in how we think about our teaching. Many of the common images of a professor even today include a gray-bearded White male holding forth with an engaging lecture to a hall full of students sitting in rapt attention with a mixture of admiration, respect, and perhaps a small dose of fear. Apart from the problematic gender and racial assumptions of this image, it fails to capture what actually happens pedagogically in today's college classroom. While 50.6% of faculty reported "extensive lecturing" as a teaching method in 2013–2014, classroom practices are far more diverse. For example, 83% described using class discussions, 70% used real-life problems, 61% used small-group learning, and 56% graded with rubrics (Eagan et al., 2014). Moreover, 22% used multimedia to flip the classroom (Eagan et al., 2014), which pushes learning of new material outside of the classroom (e.g., reading, recorded lectures) and then uses class time to engage students in more active learning strategies with which they apply the material. (We should note that flipping does not require the use of technology or multimedia, although the two have become more associated with flipping in recent years.) Berrett (2014) has noted that college classrooms are moving to the place where students rather than faculty members are at the center of the action (through presentations, group work, and problem-based learning).

Second, and as might be expected with a move from teaching toward learning, focus has been growing on student learning outcomes (SLOs) over the last several decades. While the shift to SLOs in higher education dates to the 1990s, it has gained substantial momentum in the last 15 or so years as higher education accrediting bodies (including disciplinary accrediting associations) have stepped up expectations for colleges and universities to articulate and assess student learning. Depending on your discipline, you may now quite likely find that your program must have learning outcomes at multiple levels, including at the level of the individual course (e.g., what course completers should know or be able to do) and the academic program (e.g., five or six things all graduates of a program should know or be able to do), with course activities or the courses of the academic program—or both—mapped to those outcomes to show how the outcomes are to be achieved. Moreover, regional (e.g., WASC, Middle States, Higher Learning Commission) and disciplinary accreditors often expect institutions to have institutional or

> **Inset 5.1.**
> **Resources for Success: Assessment**
>
> The following are practical, easy-to-read guides to learn more about assessing student learning both in an academic program and in your own classroom.
>
> Allen, M. J. (2004). *Assessing academic programs in higher education*. Bolton, MA: Anker.
>
> Angelo, T., & Cross, K. P. (1993). *Classroom assessment techniques: A handbook for college teachers* (2nd ed.). San Francisco, CA: Jossey-Bass.
>
> Suskie, L., & Banta, T. W. (2009). *Assessing student learning: A common sense guide* (2nd ed.). San Francisco, CA: Jossey-Bass.
>
> Walvoord, B. E., & Banta, T. W. (2010). *Assessment clear and simple: A practical guide for institutions, departments, and general education* (2nd ed.). San Francisco, CA: Jossey-Bass.

unit-wide learning outcomes that cut across all academic programs. Inset 5.1 provides references to four books that we have found to be very helpful how-to sources when it comes to assessment.

Third, the focus on student learning outcomes adds a new layer to faculty work and can most definitely pose challenges. For example, if graduate school does a poor job of preparing us to teach, it does an even worse job of preparing us to assess student learning. Thus, for most of us, the language and expectations around assessment are foreign. Couple this fact with little if any institutional support (e.g., What is a rubric, and how do I develop one?) and the need to coordinate program-level assessment with other colleagues, and the difficulty is clear. Moreover, if you are stepping into a department that already has a culture of assessment, this may well shape the expectations students have of you, from clearly stated outcomes and specific directions for assignments to well-developed rubrics.

Still, when done well, assessment can be useful for students and faculty. For instance, collaborating with our colleagues to articulate and then assess learning outcomes across our program can spark conversations that can be extremely productive for program coherence and quality as well as intellectually enjoyable. In addition, articulating course and program outcomes can benefit individual faculty and students. For faculty, learning outcomes for a course can help us decide where to allocate our energy and precious class time; for students, having clearly articulated outcomes can be a road map of what they should be gaining from courses and the program.

Both the move to more student-centered pedagogies and the focus on assessment of student learning have implications for what students expect of us as faculty in the classroom. They may arrive in our courses expecting to be engaged in ways beyond lecture or even discussion. They may expect clearly defined assignments and grades based on rubrics that provide feedback and clarity. As a faculty member you need to talk with your colleagues to get a sense of the culture in the department around both pedagogy and assessment, so that you know what students may be expecting and can adapt your practice accordingly. In the Exercises section at the end of this chapter, we give you some ideas for how to learn about the culture around teaching and assessment in your department.

The Changing Student Body

In addition to changing expectations about teaching and learning, higher education is also serving an increasingly diverse student population, one with characteristics that are decidedly different from students of 40 or 50 years ago. As Table 5.1 shows, the undergraduate student body has changed dramatically in the nearly 40 years between 1976 and 2012, with a 25% decline in the number of White students, a 29% gain in the number of Black or African American students enrolled, an 11% gain among Latinx students, and a 12% gain among Asian Americans and Pacific Islanders. These changes are almost certain to continue as the US population becomes more diverse. In addition to the racial and ethnic changes, the number of women enrolled in college has changed dramatically, with women now making up 57% of the undergraduate population.

Colleges are not just more diverse; more of the U.S. population is going to college. According to data from the National Center for Education Statistics (NCES; 2013b, Table 302.60), in 1976, of the overall 18- to 24-year-old population, 6.4% were enrolled in community colleges and 20.2% were

TABLE 5.1
Changes in Undergraduate Fall Enrollment, 1976 to 2012 (in thousands)

	1976		2012		Change in %
	Number	%	Number	%	
White	9,076.1	83	11,981.1	58	−25
Black	1,033.0	9	7,878.8	38	29
Hispanic	383.8	3	2,962.1	14	11
Asian American/ Pacific Islander	197.9	2	2,979.4	14	13
American Indian/ Alaska native	76.1	1	172.9	1	0
Two or more races	—	—	505.1	2	2
Nonresident alien	218.7	2	782.9	4	2
Male	5,794.4	53	8,919.1	43	−10
Female	5,191.2	47	11,723.7	57	10

Source. Compiled from NCES, 2013c, Table 306.10.

enrolled in four-year institutions, for a total of 26.6% enrolled in college at some level. By 2012, those figures had climbed; 12.7% of traditional-age students were enrolled in community colleges and 28.3% were enrolled in four-year colleges, for a total of 41% of the traditional college-age population enrolled in college. NCES (2014, Table 303.40) is forecasting a slight gain in the percentage of adult students (age 25 and above) enrolled in colleges and universities, with a 2% gain between 2012 and 2023, further adding to the diversity of the college population.

The growing access to higher education means that the students we work with are more likely to reflect our broader society, with characteristics or experiences that do not always match up cleanly with how higher education is structured or how we as faculty have been prepared for our roles. Consider some of the following characteristics and experiences that many of today's college students may have:

- *College readiness.* As more students attend college, there is the chance that more of them are underprepared for the rigors of college work. Most institutions, not just community colleges, run multiple sections of developmental education courses in math and English to support undergraduate students who need additional instruction in these areas. This trend even continues to graduate study. One small study (Ortiz, Filimon, & Cole-Jackson, 2015) of faculty teaching master's students in the field of student affairs for 18 years or more found that these instructors felt that their graduate students today were less prepared than in the past, academically as well as interpersonally and intrapersonally.

- *Multiple roles.* Students, whether adult students or those in the traditional (18- to 24-year-old) age range, are increasingly juggling multiple priorities while going to college. They may have obligations to their parents and siblings, have children of their own, work one or more jobs while going to school, or manage a combination of the three. Rather than being able to spend a full day on campus, their day may be broken up, as they have to leave campus to work, take a parent to an appointment, or take care of a child before returning for class in the afternoon or evening.

- *A (mostly) wired generation.* Many of today's students have a relationship with technology different from that of their predecessors. They rely on their cell phones and other mobile devices to interact socially and to produce work, are used to instant communication (e.g., text or Snapchat), and may have great facility with shooting and editing videos. However, they may not have the habit of checking their e-mail or be familiar with how to communicate professionally using that tool. These characteristics shape both what they expect from and how they interact with their professors.

- *Enrollment of veterans.* Universities are seeing a growing population of military veterans in recent years and will continue to do so. These veterans bring a wonderful set of skills and perspectives to college campuses. At the same time, many may have trouble adjusting to the traditional undergraduate culture, and some may be struggling with physical or psychological injuries brought on by combat, making the college experience all the more difficult for them.

- *Other challenges.* Finally, we are increasingly aware of the kinds of hidden challenges college students may face. For instance, students may arrive with or discover learning disabilities that make studying and succeeding in college without appropriate accommodation difficult. Some students may struggle with mental health issues that can shape their experience and may also affect their behavior in the classroom as well as their interactions with faculty and peers. They may be anxious about violence on campus (Ortiz et al., 2015).

Further, there is a growing awareness of a fairly sizeable population of students on college campuses who may be homeless or food-insecure (Crutchfield, 2012) and therefore lacking even basic needs as they seek to get an education.

The changing nature of American society, as well as the changing nature of the student body, means that students today are juggling multiple demands on their time and multiple challenges in their lives. While they may arguably be more committed to their college education than students of 50 or more years ago, the contexts in which they pursue that education are decidedly different. Knowing the characteristics and needs of the students we serve are critical for faculty, as this knowledge can inform choices we make about assignments, policies regarding late work, and a host of other matters. Inset 5.2 provides some ideas and strategies for you to get to know more about your students, who they are, and how you can support them.

Even the most student-focused faculty member might find it challenging to identify and respond to the varied needs of today's student body, and doing so may be all the more complicated because graduate programs do not prepare us well to teach. As a result, we must continually learn, grow, and evolve as teachers. This is true for how we teach (our pedagogy) as well as how we think about and interact with our students. Indeed, these two issues often go together, for as we get to know more about our students (who they are, their needs, their

> **Inset 5.2.**
> **Strategies for Success:**
> **Learning About Your Students**
>
> Knowing what your students' lives are like outside of the classroom can inform your practice as a faculty member. Here are some ideas for learning about the students in your classroom:
>
> - Do an anonymous survey or poll (e.g., using clickers) to find out things like how many students are the first in their family to attend college, work full- or part-time off campus, or are a caretaker for a child or other family member.
> - Talk with your more experienced colleagues in the department about characteristics of students in your courses, challenges the faculty have encountered, and ways they have addressed those challenges.
> - Visit the campus institutional research office website and look for reports on student characteristics, graduation rates, and so on.

goals and skills), how we teach often evolves in tandem. It is a career-long journey.

Thoughts on the Craft of Teaching

Although we have said this chapter is not a how-to on teaching, we would be remiss if we did not share advice based on our own experiences and the good work of many others. As we noted at the start of the chapter, many good books and resources on how to teach are out there, and we do not wish to duplicate them. Here we want to highlight some strategies and topics—such as preparation and grading—that might be of interest.

Through the work of many thoughtful scholars, we have a fairly good sense of how good teachers in higher education approach their work. For instance, Arthur Chickering and Zelda Gamson (1987) outlined what they referred to as seven principles for good practice in undergraduate education. Ken Bain (2004) has studied numerous "excellent" professors from across the nation. Much of what these scholars identified may seem like common sense, yet the principles can be very difficult to enact. For the sake of space, we blend and merge their ideas in the following list. Good instruction involves the following:

- *Knowing and communicating your stuff.* Good teachers, whether they are well-published or not, are up-to-date and well-versed in the major ideas and developments in their fields and are able to communicate this information clearly and simply so that others can learn. Moreover, they at least intuitively grasp how people learn and apply that understanding in their teaching.
- *Planning with students in mind.* Rather than starting to plan a course with the teacher at the center, excellent teachers start by asking themselves what students need to know and learn. (Remember our earlier discussion about learning outcomes?) As they plan, teachers return to these questions with a rigor equal to their scholarship.
- *Making learning relevant.* The best teachers focus on course objectives that students can take with them and apply as they move through life.
- *Creating a dynamic learning environment.* Good faculty members create a learning space that challenges students to solve problems and engage in authentic work, is safe for risk-taking, and gives students some control over the experience. Students work collaboratively,

perhaps fail, and learn from their peers and instructors along the way.

- *Respecting students.* Excellent teachers regard students as individuals who want to learn and are capable of learning; they do not blame students for the students' struggles. They develop appropriate professional relationships with the students, letting the learners see a bit about their professors as humans. They treat students, as Bain (2004) writes, with "simple decency" (p. 18). This means communicating high expectations, respecting diverse ways of learning, and providing varied ways to demonstrate that learning. It also means regular and ongoing feedback so that students can chart their own growth.
- *Reflecting on your work.* Good teachers regularly reflect on their own effectiveness, based on how students seem to be learning and on their own instructional goals.

These principles provide a succinct framework within which faculty can think about teaching, student interactions, expectations of students, and shaping the learning environment. We recommend Bain's work (2004) in particular as a very accessible, succinct, and valuable way to learn from some of our most effective colleagues. As he and others (e.g., Jones, 2008) note, teaching is about more than content and the act of instruction; it is about respecting and developing positive professional relationships with students.

Your Teaching Philosophy

Whether we know it or not, we all have a philosophy of teaching: our set of assumptions about our role as a teacher, students' roles as learners, and how we might best go about facilitating learning. This philosophy, tacit or explicit, guides our choices and decision-making about assignments, pedagogy (lecturing, active learning, etc.), and even grading. Moreover, your teaching philosophy is not static; rather, it changes and evolves as you learn about your students and yourself.

We encourage you to take some time to articulate your teaching philosophy and to reflect on it periodically. While you do not need to have an extensive philosophy statement, the exercise of crafting one is helpful, and it is good to have a statement of philosophy available for use in your syllabi as well as in your tenure and promotion materials (see Chapter 9). Inset 5.3 provides some ideas for questions you might ask yourself as you think about your instructional philosophy as well as some websites that might be useful.

Inset 5.3.
Strategies for Success:
Your Teaching Philosophy

Consider questions such as the following as you sketch out your teaching philosophy:

- If someone told you that you could have just one goal as an instructor, what would it be?
- Why should a student take a course with you as the instructor?
- What is the relative importance of theory versus practice in your courses? Why?
- What do you hope a student who took one of your courses would remember from that course or do 10 years later?

Following are websites with ideas and support for thinking about your teaching philosophy:

- This link to a University of Minnesota tutorial on teaching philosophies (goo.gl/ymRxHz; University of Minnesota, Center for Educational Innovation, 2015b) includes steps for drafting and finalizing your philosophy as well as samples from multiple fields (goo.gl/A3Ibhp; University of Minnesota, Center for Educational Innovation, 2015a).
- The University of Michigan has published an occasional paper, including a rubric and references, on drafting a teaching philosophy (goo.gl/Pnzvvt; O'Neal, Meizlish, & Kaplan (2007).

Preparing for Teaching

Boice (2000), who studied new faculty effectiveness and strategies for support, argued that new faculty in particular were likely to overprepare for teaching and that such preparation actually was *not* rewarded with better student ratings or more effective instruction. As Inset 5.4 shows, the early career faculty in Haviland's study were no different. Boice argued for preparation for teaching in brief regular sessions, where you start planning for a given class meeting by jotting down some brief notes for just five minutes or so before moving on to another task. Done daily, these sessions can produce class outlines and activities that support student learning but avoid overpreparation by the instructor.

While preparing to teach can take an enormous amount of time, early career faculty should put limits on that preparation. The desire to prepare to perfection is natural, because teaching is perhaps the most public act we do regularly as faculty. This desire can be even more intense for women and faculty of color, who are more likely to have their intellectual authority challenged by students in their classrooms and feel pressure to be perfect in each class session (Harlow, 2003; Pittman, 2010).

However, as one new scholar interviewed by Royles (2014b) quickly realized, not every class can be awesome. And as another new scholar interviewed by Royles (2014a) noted, sometimes it is when we feel least prepared that our classes turn out the best. But for this to happen, we have to be able to trust ourselves (what we know, our ability to communicate, etc.) as well as our students.

Faculty have varied approaches to preparation for teaching. In Inset 5.5, for example, the stories of Sarah and James describe different strategies. As a new mom, Sarah realized that she had to find ways to prepare within the time frame that she had available. James, in contrast, prepared for undergraduate class meetings by generating a list of topics and questions for discussion that day. (We recommend just a touch more preparation.)

You will likely find your own level of preparation somewhere between that of these two scholars. Following are some strategies you can use to prepare for a full course and/or an individual class meeting:

- *Visit your classroom ahead of time.* Once you know your assigned room, visit the space. How is it arranged? Are chairs fixed or movable? How much whiteboard space is there? Will you need to bring your own markers and an eraser, or are they provided? Is a computer there or do you need to bring your laptop? If you find a situation that poses a real obstacle for your teaching style, consult with your chair immediately.
- *Consider Table 5.2 as a tool for helping to plan a class session.* Haviland used this format at the top of each class outline in the early years of his

---

Inset 5.4.
Words From Early Career Faculty: Reflections on the First Year of Teaching

I guess I didn't realize . . . how much time I spent on teaching. —Carl

I was totally overprepared for my first lectures. I would approach it almost like a dissertation. —Karen

---

Inset 5.5.
Words From Early Career Faculty: Streamlining Teaching Preparation

I had an outline of what I wanted to cover. . . . I would simply mark it off the list and say, "Hey, we have talked about that," and a lot of times students would ask something and another would jump in and would add something more to it. It happened in a free-flowing kind of way. —James

[Having a baby, I realized,] well, I've got two hours to do this lecture. It's not going to be the best lecture in the world, but it's going to be fine. —Sarah

TABLE 5.2
Sample Planning Table for Class Meeting

Class Meeting Lesson Plan		
Week 3	Topics	Readings Due
Outcomes	Activities	Handouts

career. The content for the second row of the table (topics and readings due) was taken directly from the course calendar in the syllabus, while the third row allowed him to map out desired outcomes, main activities, and associated handouts for the day to form an agenda. While the content of these lesson plans will evolve as you learn, they make course planning in future years far easier, as you know what you need ahead of time and are just making minor adjustments.

- *Take notes about what worked well and what did not work well after each class session.* You will invariably have ideas (both in the middle of the class and right after) about what you might do differently in the future; capture those insights immediately. Did you ask a brilliant question that sparked discussion? Did something come up that you wished you had prepared as part of the course? Do you have ideas for changes to readings? You can record the insights on the class notes or on the syllabus itself, but however you do it, you will thank yourself later.

Your Syllabus

The syllabus plays many important roles in teaching. It is a road map for your course, telling you and your students where you are headed and when you are expecting to get there. It is also a tone-setter: the syllabus can help motivate, engage, and inspire students about course content. Finally, the syllabus is also a contract, laying out not only what you expect of students in terms of performance but also what you will do for students as their instructor. Inset 5.6 provides some useful resources on crafting a syllabus. We also offer some suggestions and resources for thinking about your syllabi:

- *Be sure your syllabus reflects campus guidelines.* Many campuses have policies and required syllabus statements about incompletes, withdrawals, and accommodations for students with special needs. Your department or college may even have a required syllabus template.

Consult with your department chair and be sure your syllabus is tightly aligned with campus, school, or college expectations.

- *Use the syllabus to shape expectations.* Hargittai (2015) provides specific tips on how to use the syllabus to provide clear expectations for the course. Her tips on structuring the syllabus, as well as referring back to it at the end of each of class so that students can see what is coming next, provide insight into how to have a syllabus that students are likely to use. Dmochowski (2015) provides a nice strategy for using a syllabus to create a positive learning environment, using it to tell students 10 things she loved them doing, including coming to her for help, making eye contact during a lecture, and asking questions. In winter 2015 James Lang (2015a; 2015b) published a two-part article

> **Inset 5.6.**
> **Resources for Success: Writing a Syllabus**
>
> - The Center for Teaching Excellence at Cornell University provides a useful overview of how to create a syllabus, including a "rubric" to judge your work (goo.gl/3Tk7PA; Cornell University Center for Teaching Excellence, 2017).
> - The Center for Teaching and Learning at the University of Washington also provides a nice overview, including course design and assessment of learning (goo.gl/9M9Bmx; University of Washington, Center for Teaching and Learning, 2017).
> - The Center for Teaching at Vanderbilt University offers resources on syllabus construction, as well as useful references and links to other sites (goo.gl/Nz8gVk; Vanderbilt University, Center for Teaching, 2017).

on the functions of a syllabus; we highly recommend this resource to you. He describes how a syllabus can be used to build excitement about the class, give students a sense of control, and even have them reflect on their own learning.

Pedagogy

As with the other topics in this chapter, the question of pedagogy is far too vast to cover in depth here. However, thinking about your approach to teaching is important, as is understanding that how you think about and practice

Inset 5.7.
Words From Early Career Faculty:
Using Pedagogy to Save Time
and Energy

The whole idea of doing more active
learning, small group—it was easier
for me. I didn't have to prepare so
much. And I just taught them how
to think, and I really feel like I pre-
pared them for what's ahead.
—Catherine

teaching will likely change over the course of your career. In discussing the literature on faculty and instruction, Jones (2008) notes that faculty often begin their teaching practice focused on themselves (their own priorities and comfort areas), then over time shift to a focus on subject (conveying content), and only later begin to really consider students' needs and how best to facilitate learning. Perhaps for these reasons, newer faculty often rely heavily on lecture, which almost surely contributes to the common problem of overpreparation (Boice, 2000).

You can draw comfort from knowing that early career faculty become more confident in the classroom over time (Olsen & Sorcinelli, 1992), and as they do, their approach shifts to discussion-based and active learning strategies that recognize students as agents in their own learning (Jones, 2008). In Inset 5.7, Catherine illustrates this point nicely, saying she discovered active learning helped students learn better even as the approach saved her time and energy.

You will want to consider multiple questions as you plan and practice your pedagogy, and many of these questions and their answers tie back to your teaching philosophy. For example, how much will you seek to spark discussion and use active learning versus how much do you plan to lecture? Lang (2016) has written that, as appealing as discussion can be, instructors often have to address cultural norms that may impede robust discussion before discussion can flourish. What will your approach be, for example, to attendance, late work, food in class, or cell phone and laptop use? Commentaries by Mason (2015), as well as LaFrance and Corbett (2014), lay out a range of strategies that faculty might adopt, from developmental to more punitive.

As we noted earlier, many books, periodicals, and other resources provide useful options and ideas for thinking about pedagogy. We recommend that you add some of the items in Inset 5.8 to your list of resources to consult on an ongoing basis.

Grading

One of the most challenging aspects of teaching is grading. Even experienced faculty members struggle with how much time to allot for grading, and how much and what kind of feedback to give. Grading can easily expand to fill the time available, so managing the task is important. Here are some thoughts to help you do so:

- *Have clear expectations.* At the start, clearly lay out your expectations and the assignment parameters. In your syllabus or a separate document, be very specific about what you want your students to do and provide in the assignment. Try to imagine an excellent assignment: What parts would it have? What would the final product look like? This strategy may increase the chance that you will get higher-quality work and should also allow you to expedite grading since each product will have a similar format.
- *Plan your grading time.* Jenkins (2015) offers concrete suggestions to manage grading. Among these, he estimates how long it will take to grade each paper. If it is 20 minutes per paper and he has 20 papers, then he knows he is looking at about 6.5 hours of grading; he then divides that time into smaller blocks to stay fresh while doing the task. You can

Inset 5.8.
Resources for Success:
Books and Resources on Teaching

Books

The following have been useful to us in our own growth as teachers. The second and third books both provide specific and concrete strategies for thinking about, planning for, implementing, and wrapping up a course.

Bain, K. (2004). *What the best college teachers do*. Cambridge, MA: Harvard University Press.

Davis, B. G. (2009). *Tools for teaching* (2nd ed.). San Francisco, CA: Jossey-Bass.

Svinicki, M. D., & McKeachie, W. J. (2014). *McKeachie's teaching tips: Strategies, research, and theory for college and university teachers.* Belmont, CA: Wadsworth, Cengage Learning.

Periodicals and Websites

- Pedagogy Unbound: *The Chronicle of Higher Education* has a section in which faculty can share ideas and resources on teaching and learning. This "Pedagogy Unbound" section provides commentary and summaries of current resources for thinking about instruction.
- Commentary by James Lang: Also in *The Chronicle of Higher Education*, James Lang, director for the Center for Teaching Excellence at Assumption College, has a regular column on teaching.
- Tomorrow's Professor (tomprof.stanford.edu/welcome): Moderated by Stanford professor Richard Reis, this website/Listserv allows you to sign up for a feed with insights and advice on teaching, faculty careers, and more.

even put grading times on your calendar to be sure you have scheduled this commitment.

- *Be strategic with your comments.* If you are making comments on papers, consider the purpose and nature of the comments. If you are providing formative feedback designed to help students get better (perhaps it is early in the term or a first draft of an assignment), then more comments may be appropriate. If, however, you are providing summative feedback to explain a grade, a few well-placed comments and an overall summary may be sufficient.

- *Use technology to your advantage.* You will almost certainly find yourself making the same comments on paper after paper. You can save time here in a variety of ways. First, if you use abbreviations or shorthand, give your students a list of your abbreviations at the start of the semester so that they can decipher your feedback and you can grade more quickly. Second, if you grade electronically, keep a file of your most common feedback (perhaps you will need one file per assignment). Then simply copy and paste from that main document into the student's paper as needed. Alternatively, we had a tech-savvy colleague who used the macros function in Microsoft Word to generate comments about lack of clarity, the need to develop an idea, and the like.

- *Consider using a rubric.* Rubrics describe the strengths and flaws of the student work at different levels of performance. They can be a great way to streamline your comments, since a well-done rubric describes the basic reasons for a grade. Moreover, rubrics can help students see what you expect in the assignment; designing them can help you think through an assignment more clearly. Inset 5.9 provides resources on grading and rubrics.

Inset 5.9.
Resources for Success:
Grading and Rubrics

We have found the following to be very useful in streamlining our own grading practice, as well as in learning about various types of rubrics and how to create useful ones.

Stevens, D. D., & Levi, A. J. (2005). *Introduction to rubrics: An assessment tool to save grading time, convey effective feedback, and promote student learning.* Sterling, VA: Stylus.

Walvoord, B. E., & Johnson Anderson, V. (2010). *Effective grading: A tool for learning and assessment* (2nd ed.). San Francisco, CA: Jossey-Bass.

Advising and Supporting Your Students

Most of us who become professors were good students; knowing how to learn and succeed in school is almost intuitive for us by the time we start to teach in a college classroom. However, many of our students are still developing these skills, and many also face multiple academic and social challenges to their educational journey. Part of our role as professors is to support that journey. Here are some ways you can do that:

- *Be sensitive to the kinds of things that students will need to have made explicit for them.* Students may arrive in class unclear about how to read your syllabus or use it to manage their assignments. They may be unfamiliar with how to use a rubric, navigate through a learning management system, or send a professional e-mail to their professor. While this may be particularly true for first-year students, sophomores, and transfers, it may be the case for juniors and seniors as well. Observe your students and provide coaching and guidance when you think they need it.

- *Know your campus resources.* Where can students get support for and feedback on their writing? Where can a student with a disability go to get support? Are tutoring services available? Where is the counseling center, and how should you refer a student in distress? These questions should be covered in faculty orientation, but you can also reach out to your department chair or your faculty development center for information.

- *Learn about the requirements for the programs in which you advise students.* What are the required courses? The prerequisites? Know when key courses are offered (only in spring? only in alternating years?) and know the sequence so that you can advise students when to enroll and guide them on prerequisites. If your program uses professional advisers, get to know them so that you can refer students appropriately and also learn about the program(s) yourself. Talk to your chair and senior colleagues to learn about the program(s) as well.

- *Make note of when registration begins each semester as well as the course enrollment timeline.* You should expect to be busy seeing students in the weeks leading up to registration, so plan accordingly. You may want to offer expanded office hours and reach out to your advisees to invite them to come see you before registration begins. Also, once the semester has begun, be aware of the date by when students in your course must be registered so you can be sure students who are sitting in your classroom actually belong there!

We conclude this section on the craft of teaching by summarizing some of our most important suggestions to make your work as a teacher easier:

- Visit your classroom ahead of time to be familiar with the layout and any equipment you might need to use.
- Take notes after *each* class meeting (and after the course ends overall) about what worked and what you would change.
- Be clear and specific about your expectations for an assignment.
- Consider using a rubric to grade each assignment and share it with students in advance.
- Use technology to expedite grading, including perhaps copying and pasting your most frequent feedback.
- Be familiar with your program's requirements, campus resources for students, and timelines for registration.

Course Evaluations

Receiving the results of your course evaluations can be one of the most challenging and even emotional aspects of the teaching part of faculty life. Just because you put a great deal of thought, care, planning, and energy into a course does not mean that every student will recognize your hard work, and seeing their assessments on course evaluations can be difficult. This kind of disappointment is felt by faculty at all levels, from the newest professor to the most senior scholar.

Moreover, there is evidence that a professor's gender, race, or ethnicity can influence students' perceptions of their instructors. In summarizing literature from the 1980s and 1990s, Anderson and Smith (2005) note that the studies have found men receive more positive course evaluations than women. Pittman (2010) found the same in her summary of the literature on course evaluations. Bavishi, Madera, and Hebl (2010) studied how high school students in college preparatory courses evaluated the competence, interpersonal skills, and legitimacy of college faculty (African American, Asian American, and White) based on their CVs. They found that African Americans were rated lower than Asian Americans and Whites on perceived competence and legitimacy, and African Americans and Asian Americas were rated lower than Whites on perceived interpersonal skills. Moreover, African American women were the lowest-rated group across each dimension.

One of the key points we want to make here is that students' ratings of instruction are influenced by many things, including the students' own characteristics, their expectations of who a professor is or should be (Bavishi et al., 2010); the discipline and the subject matter of the course; and, yes, perhaps even students' mood that day. At least hypothetically, students in a field where there are more women professors might be more used to seeing women in this role and respond with less bias on evaluations. Alternatively, students in a course where the content is more controversial or political might come with more suspicion of a professor based on the student's own identity or the professor's, or both. Many factors in the course evaluation are outside of your direct control.

So what is there to do when the course evaluations come in and are not quite what you had hoped? First, you might take some comfort in knowing you are not alone; thousands of professors in the country share the same experience. Second, scan the evaluations and then try not to think about them for 24 hours. Sitting with the evaluations and brooding over the results is not a recipe for joy; give yourself some space before going

> **Inset 5.10.**
> **Strategies for Success:**
> **Putting Course Evaluations in Context**
>
> 1. Skim the evaluations, then put them aside for at least 24 hours.
> 2. Take the course evaluations and put them in two piles. One pile is for those you regard as positive, and one pile is for those you regard as negative. This is a great, tactile way to see that the negative evaluations are usually much fewer than the positive ones.
> 3. Ask yourself: Does any of the negative feedback ring true? Is any of it actionable—something you are willing and able to address?

back to them and really reading the comments. At some point, ask yourself what feedback was on target (even if it hurts!) and what feedback you can act on or address. Then be ready to let the other feedback go. Third, reflect on what about the evaluations is upsetting to you. Did you receive a low score in one area? How many students *really* rated you low in that area—one or two? Or, as is often the case, did one or two written comments really get under your skin? Fourth, consider seeking out a more senior, trusted colleague (e.g., your chair) to share the evaluations and your concerns. That person can help you implement some of the strategies we have outlined here. Inset 5.10 summarizes some of our tips for putting your course evaluations in the proper context.

Finally, a brief word about online instructor evaluation websites such as RateMyProfessor. Our advice is simply this: Handle with care. We encourage you to think carefully about what you hope to learn by visiting your online ratings before going to such a site. While the value of university course evaluations is a subject of debate in the field, they are designed to provide professors with information to be used to improve their practice, and they are more likely than online commercial sites (which may attract those at the ends of the very positive and very negative spectrum) to get a broader sample of your students. So, before visiting an online site, consider what you hope to gain and also what you might lose (e.g., confidence). If you do choose to visit the site, take what you see with a grain of salt.

Learning and Growing as a Teacher

We close this chapter by noting that learning to teach is a process that continues for an entire career. While the learning often feels most intense in the early part of our careers, professors continue to evolve and grow as teachers over time. Like so much learning, this process of learning to teach is a social act. While we have recommended books and online resources that we have found useful, we know of no substitute for the trial-and-error act of teaching and for using the people around us to get better at what we do. Thus, we share the following resources and tips for growing as a teacher:

- *Faculty development center.* Almost every campus has an office devoted to supporting effective teaching and learning. The offices go by various names (Center for Teaching, Teaching Excellence Center, etc.), but they are likely to offer resources such as workshops, individual consultations, and even peer observations. Familiarize yourself with the center on your campus as soon as you arrive and make use of its resources.
- *Department chair.* Most department chairs are senior colleagues who have faced the same teaching challenges as you. They also want to support and mentor junior faculty. We encourage you to meet with them periodically to learn from them. For instance, perhaps you can meet once per semester to discuss course evaluations from the prior semester, how current courses are going, and strategies for preparing for and teaching courses the next semester.
- *Other colleagues.* Beyond your chair, other colleagues are also useful resources. Some may have taught the same courses that you are now teaching; at the very least, they probably have the same students. Your colleagues can give you invaluable guidance on how and how much to prepare for a course, how to manage the students, and teaching strategies that might work. Depending on the colleague, you might even ask for a peer observation of your teaching. You could choose to have it be just a casual observation with informal feedback at the end, or if you want, you might ask your colleague to write a more formal letter for your tenure file. Rockquemore and Laszloffy (2008) recommend going to coffee or lunch with colleagues and talking teaching on a regular basis. Inset 5.11 has some tips and resources for making peer observation useful. You could also ask if you might be able to observe colleagues teaching, to see how they interact with

students and structure their classes.

- *Videorecord yourself.* While most of us might not like to see ourselves on video, watching yourself teach as someone else might can help you get better at teaching. Record a class session and then watch and evaluate your teaching. Do you stand in one place or move about the room? Is the cadence of your speech too fast, too slow, or just right? Are you making eye contact and engaging with your students as individuals? Getting a sense of how others might be experiencing your instruction can help you make changes *and* build your confidence.
- *Mid-semester feedback.* As a new instructor, or even when teaching a course for the first time, gathering mid-semester feedback from students can be very useful. We recommend putting just two or three questions (see Inset 5.12) on paper and having students fill out the paper anonymously. We want to offer a couple of cautions or caveats. First, talk with your department chair before doing this so that you are clear on any guidelines for collecting the feedback; you want to be sure not to interfere with the formal

---

Inset 5.11.
Strategies for Success:
Making Peer Observation Useful

- Invite a colleague whom you trust and respect as a teacher to observe you.
- Agree in advance if this will be an informal observation for your growth or if the colleague will prepare a letter to put in your file.
- Meet before class to tell your colleague what your goals are for the class and what you would like them to focus on for feedback.
- Meet after class to reflect on your efforts and receive feedback from your observer.

Inset 5.12.
Strategies for Success:
Mid-Semester Feedback

Consider asking two or three questions such as the following at the midpoint of a course:

- What practices or elements of the course thus far have best supported your learning?
- What is happening in the course that you would like more of to support your learning?
- What else might I do in the course to better support your learning?
- What practices or elements of the course thus far have interfered with or not supported your learning?

course evaluation process and to have your chair's support. Second, be sure to allow time in the next class session to review and discuss the feedback. Report back to students on what the main themes were, thank them for all of their feedback, and be specific about what you plan to change or explain why you will not make certain changes.

- *Your students.* You can and should learn about teaching from your students. Office hours conversations can be an opportunity to probe for perspectives about how group work is going or whether the reading seems relevant. Haviland has been known to leave 30 minutes on the last day of class (after course evaluations are done) to debrief with the students about what worked and did not work for their learning. He treats it as a conversation, soliciting their feedback, explaining why he did certain things, and noting their replies. This conversation can be very enlightening; just be sure you go in with specific prompts (e.g., relevance of readings, feasibility of an assignment) to guide the discussion.

Concluding Thoughts

The nature of teaching and the students we serve have changed considerably over the years. Today's students are far more diverse, and many come to college with more commitments and experience than students in the past. It can be very easy for teaching to cause anxiety and take more time than perhaps it should—particularly for early career faculty. However, teaching can also be an immensely rewarding part of the faculty career. One of the most invigorating parts of teaching is finding ways to grow as an instructor, learn from your students, and develop new ways to support their learning. We hope this chapter has provided some tools and strategies to help reduce some of the stress that may come with teaching and make it a more manageable and enjoyable task—and something that you can make one of your professional commitments (O'Meara et al., 2008).

Exercises

Following are some ideas for exercises that might be useful to you in building your knowledge and skills regarding the teaching-related topics we discussed in this chapter.

1. Take a colleague to lunch or coffee and ask some or all of the following:
   - What are the norms in the department regarding lecturing versus other pedagogies?

- What are the norms in the department for giving in-class exams versus papers? Multiple-choice versus written exams? For assessing student learning in general?
- What are the biggest personal and academic challenges students in your program face?

2. Visit your university's or college's website and find out where they post the schedule for registration, add/drop, and withdrawals. Then put the dates for this year on your calendar and bookmark the site!

3. Develop a list of the location and contact information for the following offices and services:
- All ally programs (LGBT, autism, veterans, etc.)
- Career services/planning
- Counseling
- Disabled students' services
- Ombudsperson
- Tutoring, learning, and writing support
- Veterans' support

4. Draft your teaching philosophy. Share it with your chair and a couple more experienced colleagues you trust to get their feedback.

5. Ask yourself: What do I hope my students will say to others (family, peers, etc.) to describe me as a teacher?

Goal-Setting Activity: Shaping Your Career as a Teacher

The following is a step-by-step process for you to start thinking about the kinds of things you might want to accomplish as a teacher during the next several years of your career.

1. Brainstorm several goals or things you would like to learn or accomplish as a teacher in the next three to five years.

2. Try to arrange those goals in some kind of order. For instance, does one lead to another? Or could one be accomplished in a year or so while another goal might take two to three years to accomplish?

3. Now, for each goal, ask the following:
- What are some challenges I might encounter in reaching that goal?
- What resources (e.g., people, information, skills) do I have that will help me reach that goal?
- What specific steps will I take, and by when, to reach that goal?

You might consider using a chart like Table 5.3 to help you think about these questions. We've used the first row to give you an example.

TABLE 5.3
Shaping Your Career as a Teacher

Goal	Challenges I Might Encounter	Resources I Have	Steps I Will Take and by When	Accomplished? When?
1. *Learn how to hybridize a course*	• *Department doesn't support it* • *Lack of tools/ technology to do the work* • *Not familiar with video-recording and editing*	• *Department chair* • *Faculty development center* • *Colleague at State University has done this*	• *Talk with chair to confirm it is okay to do* • *Look for professional development (PD) on campus or via professional association* • *Attend PD* • *Identify course to pilot hybridizing*	
2.				
3.				
4.				
5.				

Some other goals you might consider for your teaching include

- using more active learning,
- learning how to ask good questions to construct classroom dialogue,
- creating a safe environment for classroom discussion, and
- reducing use of PowerPoints.

6

SHAPING YOUR CAREER AS A SCHOLAR

cholarship is often at the forefront of our minds and the top of the to-do list. But with so many things confronting early career faculty members, it is likely the easiest thing about which to procrastinate. Syllabi must be prepared, lectures and class sessions must be planned, and papers must be graded. These are all on timelines and are pretty much solely your responsibility. Even if you are fortunate enough to have limited service responsibilities in your first term, you may have program, department, and/or college meetings, and you may have advising responsibilities or other programmatic duties. Chapters 5 and 8 give you advice and strategies for meeting these expectations effectively and efficiently.

For the most part, establishing your research program is left to your own initiative, without timelines and often without guidance. (We use the terms *research* and *scholarship* interchangeably here. However we recognize they encompass a range of activities, from empirical studies to creating art to performing music.) The expectation that you carry out a scholarly program comes at a time when you may have, just months before, completed your dissertation, and you are ready to have a rest from doing scholarship and writing. If you had a postdoc, then maybe you find yourself facing something of a blank screen, having published from your dissertation and maybe a postdoc research project and are now sitting at the precipice of identifying new initiatives.

In that first semester or even the first year, you may very much want scholarship and publication to be your top priority, but teaching and other professorial responsibilities typically take precedence; the rest of your energy may go toward the transition you are experiencing to a new role, a new university, and likely a new city or part of the country. Often these transitions leave early career faculty members worrying about their scholarly productivity more than actually making progress on their research. In this chapter we offer ways to learn about the scholarly expectations at your university and strategies to establish your research agenda and produce quality products that have the highest impact, without having a negative impact on your overall sense of well-being. Like other areas we cover in this book, we take the position that when research is connected to who you are as a professor, it strengthens the other dimensions of instruction, service, and self.

Developing a Scholarly Identity

You became a member of a discipline before you were hired at your university and before you began identifying as a teacher or university citizen. Thus your scholarly identity may be well on its way to maturation early in your career. We would like to offer a broader view of scholarly identity beyond your discipline. This identity encompasses not just your disciplinary expertise but how your scholarship reflects who you are as a person (*Which of my personal values are connected to the purpose of my research?*), the mark you want to make on your subject (*Do I want to be the authority on my subject? Do I want to be a lead applied researcher on my subject? Do I want my work to be commercially viable?*), and the life goals you want to accomplish (*Can I involve my family in this work? Will this work take me around the world? Will my work allow me to also lay a foundation for the administrative career I am planning?*). Considering these and other questions can help you develop an integrated scholarly identity.

Understanding the Scholarly Expectations of Your Institution

The first step in developing a research or scholarly program as a faculty member is identifying the research expectations of your institution and considering how these expectations intersect with the traditions and norms in your discipline. We suggest asking two main questions:

1. What *type* of scholarship is expected of me?
2. What *level* of productivity is expected of that scholarship?

In Chapter 3 we said that early career faculty likely know the expectations of their discipline best. Starting your research may mean building a lab, complete with equipment to order and students to hire or recruit, to produce research at your new institution. Or perhaps your discipline highly values turning your dissertation into a book. If you are in the arts, then what matters is likely even more diverse. Whatever the convention of your discipline, if you did not learn these norms in your doctoral program, you need to get a grasp on them now.

But disciplinary expectations can coincide with or contradict those of your institution. For example, the convention in your discipline might be to produce a book before tenure, but at your institution the norm in the department is to have at least three articles published. In most cases, institutional expectations take precedence over disciplinary ones. During your campus interview, you should have been given a copy of all relevant RTP policies that will govern your reviews. These documents should outline what counts in terms of research productivity. They might also suggest how much research productivity is expected. These documents are like anthropological artifacts in that they convey much about the culture as it is and what it wants to become. They often require that you learn to read between the lines and interpret what is valued and how much is expected. If you are in a unionized environmesnt, your expectations may be specifically spelled out. We know of institutions where the policy is that you must have a specific number of publications for tenure, and the department, college, or university specifically says what kinds of publications count. But even in many unionized environments, there is likely ambiguity in what is expected. In nonunionized environments, the language may even be more ambiguous, using qualifiers such as *of the highest quality* or *the top journals in your discipline* or *significant contributions to the field.* An unfortunate adage holds that the more highly ranked an institution is, the less likely it is to be unionized and the less likely that the RTP policies will be specific in nature. Your job becomes figuring out what the policies mean and what you need to do, just as Michael explains in trying to figure out what kind of and how many publications he needs (see Inset 6.1).

The second step is to consider the expectations for productivity, which includes criteria such as number and type of publications, the quality of the publication venues, and your role as author (sole, lead, etc.). The factor that usually best predicts the expectations of your institution for your productivity is institutional type. Table 6.1 portrays a synopsis of what might be the research expectations of different types of institutions for new faculty members. Of course, there are

> **Inset 6.1.**
> **Words From Early Career Faculty: Clarifying Publishing Expectations**
> *You want to publish in the top journals in the specific field that you are working in. But at the same time, it is one of those things that—if I actually managed to get one paper published in the top journal, will it count as much as if I worked on three crappier ones? —Michael*

TABLE 6.1
Research Expectations by Institutional Type

Institutional Type	Scholarly Expectations
Research	• Empirical work in top-tier refereed journals • Externally funded research • Single-authored works • High-impact dissemination • Quantity and quality matter
Comprehensive	• Empirical work in refereed journals • Collaborative work with lead authorship • Research and publications with students • Applied research • Modest expectations for quantity
Liberal arts	• Multidisciplinary collaborations • Theoretical or summative works • Research and publications with students • Quality matters more than quantity

variations to this summary, but in general the table offers a good place to begin to familiarize yourself with expectations of different kinds of institutions.

Knowing where your institution falls on the national reputational rankings and the connection to institutional type is also important. However, be aware that many institutions are striving to move up in those rankings (O'Meara, 2007, 2011). Comprehensive universities may be striving to become doctoral universities. Modestly ranked research institutions want to move into the top 50 national universities (or top 25 or 10, depending on where they start). Liberal arts colleges are also in this game; regionally known liberal arts colleges want to become nationally prominent, those on the national stage want to be in the top 10, and so on. In a national study of faculty, 84% of faculty at public institutions and 89% of faculty at private institutions believed that enhancing the institution's national image was a highest or high priority (Eagan et al., 2014), and doing so is often linked to scholarly productivity and prestige. Inset 6.2 suggests ways you might begin to uncover the expectations for scholarly productivity at your institution.

Rankings and reputations, like it or not, matter to campus administrators. Unfortunately, rankings and reputations are like self-fulfilling prophecies. The higher the ranking, the "better" the student; the "better" the faculty, the more grant money awarded. The best students and the best faculty contribute to the ratings formula, bringing even more into the fold (Astin, 1985). The work of faculty is an important part of these formulas, as the number of publications, the significance of awards, and the amount of grant money generated all contribute to national rankings. Thus, campuses apply pressure, formally through institutional policies or informally through unwritten expectations, for faculty to increase productivity and visibility.

Throughout your time as an assistant professor it is normal to continually ask yourself, "Am I doing enough?" and "Am I doing the right things?" In a national survey of pretenure faculty, getting inconsistent messages from senior faculty about expectations, and a lack of transparency and reasonableness in the tenure process, were perceived as barriers to success (COACHE, 2008). Managing this uncertainty is important (see Chapter 9 on RTP) because the time and emotional energy needed to worry continually about this productivity is better spent actually doing the work.

Scholarly Products and Publication Outlets

> **Inset 6.2.**
> **Strategy for Success:**
> **Ways to Uncover Productivity Expectations**
>
> 1. Ask your senior colleagues how much scholarly productivity they think it takes to get tenure. Only ask each individual once, and do it in the first year.
> 2. Look across your department and college and note who recently earned tenure. Then, using the many online databases, research the number, variety, and quality of publications they produced before they went up for tenure.
> 3. Listen for messages about grant productivity. Do colleagues say that you do not need to worry about external funding before tenure? Are other assistant professors loudly praised when they secure a grant? Is your department chair or dean recommending grant writing workshops or sending you requests for proposals?

Remember that unless you disseminate your research, it rarely counts in RTP processes. We have seen many ways that faculty of all ranks procrastinate in moving a project to dissemination. Collecting data is a great way to procrastinate in the writing process; unfortunately, the more data you collect, the more monumental the task seems of moving it to publication. Reading more and more literature is also an effective way of pretending to be productive while really just delaying dissemination. Part of the way to beat the tendency to procrastinate on publishing is to have a clear plan and target in mind. It seems somewhat nonsensical, but the first step in the process is deciding what type of product you wish or need to publish.

Inset 6.3.
Strategy for Success:
Be Selective in the Scholarly Products You Choose

Articles. In many fields, peer-reviewed articles are essential when it comes to earning tenure and promotion. They have the advantage of being shorter and more focused than some of the other publishing options. However, review and eventual publication can take some time, so plan accordingly.

Books. Books take a long time to complete, so think about their value in your RTP policies and the time you have to produce them. A book in progress at retention, in most disciplines, may not count at all.

Edited books. Editing a book has advantages (you are not really writing the whole book) and disadvantages (chapter editors may miss deadlines or submit sloppy work). In addition, some RTP policies may consider edited books to have limited value. However, these are good ways to build external networks and familiarize a broader range of colleagues with your work. This may be quite advantageous if your institution requires external reviews for tenure.

Textbooks. Given the substantial time textbook production involves, these are better left for later stages of your career.

Book chapters. Being invited to write a book chapter shows that you are becoming recognized in your field. That is a good thing.

(continues)

Depending on the discipline there are multiple options. If the primary scholarly product in your discipline is the conference paper or journal article, then as an assistant professor, do not consider other invitations or options, such as book chapters, textbooks, or newsletter contributions. These should be considered secondary at this stage of your career. If your discipline is in the social sciences, however, you may have a wider range of scholarly products to consider in addition to conference papers or journal articles, such as books, edited volumes, book chapters, technical reports, and so on. The humanities may value the publication of books over other types of publications.

Inset 6.3 presents an overview of common publication types and some of the factors to consider regarding each of the options. With more options for scholarly products, you need to consider factors such as RTP timelines; balance in the kinds of products you choose; and making sure that you have products that are highly valued by your institution, college, or department. Choosing an outlet is a critical decision. Use your senior colleagues, department chair, or mentors to help you strike the balance you need to be most successful in the tenure process. Your career will be long, and there will be other times to take more risk in what you produce.

Once you make the decision about what you intend to publish, then identify the outlet for your work. In most cases, this will be a journal, university press, or academic or commercial publisher.

If you know that top-tier journals are the expectation for productivity, then start there. If a university press is more valued than an academic publisher, start there. Thomas (see Inset 6.4) offers an extensive process he used to determine where he might publish. Regardless of how you determine quality, when selecting an outlet, start at the highest-quality one with the best fit. But also identify at least two backup outlets; if the piece is rejected, then you already have the second outlet selected.

How do you know the best fit? Ask the following questions:

- Does the journal, press, or conference publish work like yours (think of topic, methodology, where those you have cited have published, etc.)?
- Does the journal have the audience you hope to impact?
- Does the maximum page length allow for the scope of the product you are writing?

Inset 6.3. (*continued*)

Book chapters also may be relatively easy to write, taking less time than other products. There are two cautions here. First, book chapters are often the least valued kind of scholarship. Second, you may have very little control over the book's timeline. If editors drop the ball, then it may be years before the chapter is published.

Conference presentations/papers/posters/proceedings. Depending on your campus or discipline, a conference paper may even count toward tenure; at the very least, however, papers are a good way to move a project toward publication by gathering and incorporating preliminary feedback from other scholars.

Newsletter articles. Publishing in professional newsletters or magazines offers another way for your work to reach an extended audience. These are often short, focused pieces that likely show how your work translates to a professional, practical audience. If your discipline values theory-to-practice work, this can be a good choice. But know that in RTP policies, these formats may be considered one of the lowest valued scholarly products.

Each journal has manuscript instructions on its website or in each issue. Journals note maximum manuscript length, publication style or format, restrictions on tables and figures, and so on. Follow those instructions to the letter. You will also benefit from knowing how long it may take for a journal to review and publish an article, since time can be of the essence in your pretenure years. Inset 6.5 highlights Karen's frustration with a journal's review process, as well as her ability to successfully navigate that process.

Inset 6.4.
Words From Early Career Faculty: Being Strategic About Choosing a Journal

A recent grad agreed to be my research assistant, and I had her go through all my target journals, give me abstracts—download the abstract for every article for the past two years for all my target journals. I review all that, confirm that this will be good for this paper, that paper—I have to be strategic because there's a time frame. It's a system. I have all these target journals listed [with] acceptance rate, rejection rate, number of publications per year per journal, how many issues per year, [and] the website.
—Thomas

Inset 6.5.
Words From Early Career Faculty: Working With Journal Editors

I turned in one of my articles, and it went into a black hole. I never heard back. I wrote and I phoned and I sent registered mail. After nine months they told me they accepted it. But then I needed to know when it was going to be published. Again, I wrote and I faxed and I e-mailed and I called. What do I do? Nobody had an answer to it. Then I was sharing that with a colleague of mine who was also faculty and she said, "You know what? I don't know but I know someone who might know." It was a

(continues)

For books, each publisher has a website with its call for proposals. They also indicate what types of books they publish. It may also be a good idea to network with editors at conferences, as they can help you develop your ideas so that what you propose is better customized for that publisher. This step is most easily accomplished at academic conferences, as editors often staff the publishers' booths in the exhibit hall.

The other important component to consider when deciding where to publish, particularly in journals, is how to determine quality. Organizations, including journals, are increasingly turning to impact factors as public metrics of journal prestige and quality. There are a couple of important ideas to keep in mind:

- *Impact factor.* This is a journal's total number of citations over a two- or three-year period divided by the number of articles published. This metric gives the average number of citations per article (goo.gl/rHtcHq; Thomson Reuters, 2017).
- *Tier.* The Scimago Journal Rankings ranks journals throughout the disciplines based on their impact factors. They are ranked numerically and categorized in quartiles, which are colloquially referred to as *tiers* (goo.gl/nrbnac; Scimago Journal & Country Rank, 2016).

Impact factors and tier rankings are based on the number of citations. Generally, the smaller or more specialized your discipline or subdiscipline is, the more likely that the journal has a low ranking because fewer people are available to cite articles therein. If impact factors and rankings are important to your institution, then be prepared to explain lower factors or rankings in your RTP dossier to nondisciplinary peers.

We also want to address a few other options and discuss their advantages and disadvantages. In

> **Inset 6.5.** (*continued*)
>
> *total stranger. Well, [I wrote] to her. She was unbelievably generous. She gave me steps to follow. I did what she told me and within four days, the editor responded. It was insider knowledge on who to talk to. The answer was not what I wanted: it's not going to come out soon, which is really ridiculous. What do I do? Do I withdraw it? It is in press, so she told me, "You are on a tenure track so you don't want to pull it now."* —Karen

vanity presses (subsidy publishing or self-publishing), the author pays to have the book published. There can be some advantages to the author in terms of earning profits from the book if there is an audience. Although some self-publishing houses have high editorial standards, there is seldom peer review and little quality control in terms of subject-matter content. You should beware of these facts if quality of the outlet is a consideration in your RTP process, as vanity presses are considered the lowest quality and your institution may not count them. Open-source publication outlets are online presses, usually journals, where the publication is generally paid for by the author or an organization, rather than the end user. Some of these may offer peer review, especially if the organization pays for publication. Other outlets where authors pay to be published seldom have peer review or other editorial standards and are often considered to be of low quality. Again, we encourage you to be clear on expectations in your department and on campus before choosing your publication outlets. At the very least, you should be prepared to explain your choices as well as make arguments about the quality of publication venue.

Publishing Your Dissertation

If you have recently finished graduate school, then you have just conducted a major research project and have a manuscript that you have spent years developing. For most early career faculty, the first thing you should work on moving to publication is your dissertation. We understand that you may well be very tired of working on the project and wish to never see it again; however, the research is done, it is already written, and this is the easiest way

Inset 6.6.
Words From Early Career Faculty: Publishing From Your Dissertation

I just think that I've always been able to sell this project. It's just like I lucked out. I found archives that no one knew had been there and like knowing what to do with that. Do you know what I mean? I just sort of learned over time how to sell it to more and more and more general audiences. Just because it's my dissertation I've been selling it to grant funders for eight years, and so I sold it even in a preliminary fashion and that's publication. —Catherine

to get moving on your publications. Like Catherine (see Inset 6.6), sticking with it and finding different ways to "sell it" pays off.

Finding your desired outlet is a first step that will make your work most efficient. You need to follow the conventions of your field. If that means your dissertation needs to become a book, then your outlets are focused on commercial or university publishing houses. If the convention is to produce journal articles, then work to determine two or three distinct articles from your dissertation and then search for the right journal.

In many doctoral programs now, not just those in the sciences, dissertations are composed of three separate articles with the expectation that they will be repurposed for later publication. If you are fortunate to be in possession of one of these dissertations, your task is relatively easy. If you are facing a dissertation that needs quite a bit of work to move it or parts of it to publication, you must determine what you need to do. As we have worked with early career faculty, we have seen the following pitfalls in publishing from the dissertation, as well as some useful strategies in addressing these challenges:

- *Problem:* Turning a 200-plus-page document into 30 pages or less seems like an impossible task, so you become immobilized.

  Strategy: As soon as possible, identify the articles that you plan to write and your preliminary publication outlets. Give these articles titles and write an abstract for each of them based on what you know about your findings. Ask your dissertation committee members for advice and recommendations; perhaps you can get an article from your literature review, one on methods, and one or more on your findings.

- *Problem:* The more you think about your dissertation, the more you question its quality and you cannot see how you can possibly get anything accepted for publication.

  Strategy: This is the worst possible mind-set to adopt. It is natural to doubt yourself as you take this work forward, and perhaps you are a victim of imposter syndrome, which makes believing in the quality of the work even harder. But remember that a reputable university granted your doctorate and that your work was guided by a reputable scholar, maybe even the top in your field. Also, do not forget that given the very tight job market for tenure-track faculty, your institution selected you. A lot of evidence is available that your work is, in fact, not worthless. Listen to it and consider finding outlets, even if they are not the top ones.

- *Problem:* You cannot think of a way to break up that literature review. In fact, you think that maybe you need a completely new one.

  Strategy: Worry about the literature review after you have written the rest of the article. At that point, you will have the focus to decide what needs to be in that article and you will know if you need a new, very specific literature review. This strategy allows you to get a sense of how much space you can afford to give it.

- *Problem:* You think you need to completely reanalyze your data.

  Strategy: If feedback from your committee suggested further or different analysis and this fits within the foci of the two or three articles you are working on, then work on this focused reanalysis. If one or two of those pieces call for new analysis, then be sure your analysis is specific to each piece. Refrain from looking at your dataset as one entity.

- *Problem:* It has been a year or more into your position, and you still have not published from your dissertation. You believe your data are too old to get it published.

  Strategy: Although we hope that you will not find yourself in this predicament, it is not uncommon. If you are in this situation, all is not lost. Look at your target journals and note the age of data reported in them. Ask a senior faculty member in your field for advice. If you abandon this work, be sure you have exhausted all possible options, because this research is already done and a new research project will take at least a year before you submit for publication. You may not be able to afford that kind of time.

Designing a Research Program

Even if you are able to publish from your dissertation, you will still want and need to start a new research program once you arrive on campus. If you are in the sciences, this imperative may be even more urgent, since you will need to establish a lab and demonstrate that you can manage a productive research lab early on. Carl makes this point in Inset 6.7. If your field calls

Inset 6.7.
Words From Early Career Faculty:
Needing to Start a New Research Program

Stuff you do as part of your postdoc from prior institutions is enhancing criteria [for tenure] but doesn't count toward that minimum. So there is this weird incentive where as soon as you get here, any time you spend working on papers from data at your previous institution is almost counterproductive. —Carl

Inset 6.8
Strategies for Success:
Getting Your Lab Functioning

Setting up your lab requires you to order equipment (usually from start-up funds) and get the lab functioning. You may be tempted to get students involved in your research during your first semester or year on campus. Be careful not to recruit students to work with you in the lab until you have something for them to do. Having the responsibility of training students and keeping them meaningfully engaged before your lab is ready can cause problems (Gaugler, 2004).

for getting that lab established right away, then be self-controlled in how you do that, remembering that your priority may be publishing from your dissertation. Inset 6.8 offers strategies for getting your lab off to a good start.

In general, we recommend that you avoid collecting any new data until your dissertation work is submitted for publication, if that is appropriate for your discipline. In either case, we hope that you can continue the line of research that you started in your graduate work. This is the easiest approach, as you already have a strong understanding of the research that has been done and that needs to be done. However, if you have truly come to dislike your topic or area, the time to find a new direction is now. Forcing yourself to stay on a trajectory for which you lack passion makes the necessary work more arduous, and you will likely have difficulty staying focused and maintaining the productivity you need to be successful. Treat this like any other project: set a goal for the time needed to reach the decision and map out specific steps and activities to help you make the decision.

We began this chapter with ways to learn about and understand the research productivity expectations of your institution. Knowing these expectations early assists in deciding what kind of time you have to enact your research agenda. High expectations for quantity might mean that longitudinal projects are not the best option for this career stage, unless there are very discrete points in the project where publishing results is desirable and feasible.

Consider having your research and writing projects in different stages at different times. You might think about your projects as moving through the following stages: (a) conceptualization (literature review, design); (b) data collection; (c) data analysis; and (d) writing, revision, and submission. Table 6.2 provides an example of a graphic you might use to guide and manage your work with more specific steps. Be flexible in using the steps as they may not be appropriate for all projects.

As Table 6.2 demonstrates, some projects can and should continue to move forward when others are in process and where some events are outside your control, such as waiting for Institutional Review Board (IRB) or Institutional Animal Care and Use Committee (IACUC) approval or for the review process for conference proposals or journal articles. A chart like this offers a good way to keep track of progress on multiple projects and serves as a motivational tool when each goal is met. Another strategy that may be

TABLE 6.2
Sample Project Management Tool

	Project #1	Project #2	Project #3	Project #4
Literature review	October/November			
Securing resources	October			
IRB/IACU process	December			
Data collection	January–June			
Data analysis	June–July			
Identify presentation outlet(s)	July			
Write conference proposal				
Draft intro and lit review for manuscript	August/September			
Draft remaining sections of manuscript	October/November			
Presentations				
Integrate feedback				
Submit manuscript for publication				
Revise and resubmit				
Final revisions				
PUBLISHED!				

helpful, since there is a bit more public accountability, is to organize your CV as a way to communicate work in multiple stages:

- *Research in progress.* Give each project a title and treat the project like a manuscript from the beginning; note in parentheses the stage of the research.
- *Works in progress.* Identify actual manuscripts that you are preparing for conferences or publication. If these are drafts that have yet to be presented or submitted for publication, indicate the target conference or outlet. If the manuscript has been submitted, is under review, or is being revised, note this status using the style of your discipline.
- *Published.* This section is for manuscripts that have been accepted for publication or published. If these are accepted or in press, note this.

Developing Good Scholarship Habits

Inquiry, discovery, and creation are the hallmarks of scholarship we produce at the university. Key to maintaining momentum with our production is how well we stay curious and motivated. Good scholarship habits begin with finding activities that inspire you to become a part of the dialogue, a part of the field, and a part of the scene. Academics who do empirical research keep up with developments in the field, and those of us whose scholarship is more creative engage in activities that nurture our creativity. Experiencing helps us to ask better questions. Reading helps us to be better writers. If you are in the social sciences, maybe being involved in organizations or communities helps you find inspiration and motivation. Remember, scholarship need not be an isolating process. In fact, collaborating with peers can help us be more creative and productive.

Strategies for Productive Scholarship

For many of us, inspiration and motivation come from our own experiences. Minoritized faculty in particular sometimes face the conundrum of feeling that their work is somehow less valuable because it is focused on their own communities. These faculty members may fear that this work will be less valued in the tenure and promotion processes. While this concern is natural, it should not prevent you from doing work that is meaningful to you and others and has the potential to benefit diverse communities. Manage this tension in some of the same ways we recommend later when discussing collaboration and networking, so that you find colleagues who can support your work and mentor you on how to navigate political issues you encounter on your own campus.

Good time management is perhaps the most valuable writing habit to develop; add willpower and the power to say no, and you are in a great starting place. Jenkins (2015) emphasizes that recognizing writing as a matter of sacrifice and trade-offs is helpful for any early career faculty because you are managing a variety of pressures and tasks simultaneously. Jenkins (2015) stresses that you first must consciously decide that writing is worthwhile and something you really want to do. This connects to motive; identifying and acknowledging your motivation is absolutely necessary to moving forward. Your motive may be that you just want to keep your job. When we work with early career faculty, one of the mantras is, what other profession guarantees a job for life as long as you work hard for six years? This position is a privileged one to have in today's economy and job market. Maybe the motive is ego, which is perfectly okay; seeing your name on a byline or book cover is pretty cool. Hopefully, though, you also have more noble motives. You want to get your

> **Inset 6.9.**
> **Resources for Success:**
> **Reading on Writing**
>
> The resources in this inset provide practical tips on writing effectively as well as strategies for staying motivated and productive. We and others have found them very useful in our own writing and scholarship.
>
> Boice, R. (2000). *Advice for new faculty members:* Nihil nimus. Boston, MA: Allyn and Bacon.
> Lamott, A. (1994). *Bird by bird: Some instructions on writing and life.* New York, NY: Pantheon Books.
> Lasch, C. (2002). *Plain style: A guide to written English.* Philadelphia, PA: University of Pennsylvania Press.
> Lupton (2012) has also provided some useful advice on her blog (goo.gl/5ZDxqB).
> Silvia, P. J. (1976). *How to write a lot: A practical guide to productive academic writing.* Washington, DC: American Psychological Association.

ideas into the world; you want to make things better for students, people, the planet, and so on. Keeping in touch with those motives gives you the willpower you need to sit at the computer or to say no to competing demands; writing cannot get done without these two things. Inset 6.9 provides some suggested resources that we have found useful in our own growth.

Lupton (2012) recommends that you keep writing any way you can. For example, she suggests that once you have an idea, you create a file and write everything you can about it, no matter how rough it is or how (in)complete your ideas are. As noted previously, the kind of formats you choose can also build on each other. For example, a conference presentation, talk, or training session

**Inset 6.10.
Strategies for Success:
Time Management Tips**

1. Write every day at your most productive time. Boice (2000) notes
   that the most successful faculty
   members work at writing daily but
   with moderation and efficiency.
2. Keep your manuscript open for
   quick writes when you have as
   little as 15 minutes free or to jot
   down ideas. Boice (2000) argues
   that writing as little as 15 to 30
   minutes daily can be sufficient.
3. Schedule your writing strategically. For most, blocking off
   whole days is hard. Using a few
   two- to three-hour blocks (or
   less) throughout the week is more
   efficient. Start and stop on time
   (Boice, 2000).
4. On your calendar, write "Off-
   campus meeting," instead of
   "writing." And never disclose that
   you cannot make or schedule
   another meeting because it is your
   writing time. You simply have a
   meeting or are off campus.
5. Always have a backup project so
   that if you hit a block in one, you
   can jump to the other.

can be developed into a chapter or
column. You can begin to develop
an argument in a blog post and use
the feedback to make a publication
better. A series of articles from one
research project can be turned into
a book. In addition to strengthen-
ing writing habits, using various
forums to disseminate your research
and ideas allows you to develop your
expertise further and reach different
audiences. Inset 6.10 provides some
strategies to stay on track as you
write.

Peer Writing Support

Scholarship can be a lonely activity, especially for those who work
independently. Writing groups and
other forms of peer support are
ways to connect with others, solicit
feedback early in the research and
writing process, and create accountability. These groups can take different formats. A traditional writing
group might meet monthly with
members taking turns on sharing
their work to get feedback from
the group. Maybe good peer support for you would be to make a
weekly date with a writing partner
at a local coffee shop and write side
by side, without sharing feedback.
If you are looking for a group close
to your subject or content area, perhaps a virtual or online writing group is
the right choice. Royles (2015) suggests that when forming a writing group,
you consider how long the group will last, what you will ask of participants,
how often you will meet, and what you will do if folks do not follow through
on their deadlines or refuse to take peer review seriously. Taking advantage
of offers from colleagues to read your work is another way to get external
support.

Collaboration and Networks

Networking with colleagues beyond your department or university around scholarship and creative activities has multiple benefits. Karen, an early career faculty member quoted in Inset 6.5, received significant assistance in working with a journal editor from a "stranger" with whom she was connected through a mutual colleague. Senior colleagues in your network likely know folks in many contexts who can support you in various stages of the scholarly process. If your area of research is highly specialized, building a regional or national network can be critical in gaining support for your scholarship. Sharing ideas, resources, and inspiration are all worthwhile functions of these external networks. These networks can also facilitate collaboration in research, with the side benefit of developing important mentoring relationships with senior colleagues in your field. Research has shown that external mentors are key for success for many, especially for women or faculty of color (Turner & Gonzalez, 2015). Stanley (2006) found that true mentoring came from external networks that the new faculty member strategically created.

You will likely be involved with collaborative projects, whether with external or internal colleagues, at different points in your pretenure years. All the benefits of networks can also hold true with collaborative projects. When we work with others, the synergy has the potential to make our projects better, make our thinking more critical, and expand our access to talent and resources. However, as Lupton (2012) cautions, do careful research on your collaborators before making any commitments. Great partnerships are the stuff of legend; poor ones can drain your time and energy, leaving you with little to show for the effort. Some of the same parameters we suggest that you set for writing groups should be considered for scholarly collaborations. Inset 6.11 outlines some strategies to make the collaboration successful. Setting clear expectations regarding amount of work, timing of work, distribution of tasks, and ownership of work—especially if you are managing grant funds across institutions—is vital.

> **Inset 6.11.**
> **Strategies for Success:**
> **Tips for Collaborating on Scholarship**
>
> 1. Start small to test the collaboration. Ask for feedback on a document. Give collaborators a deadline and see if they meet it.
> 2. Consider coauthoring a poster presentation or conference paper.
> 3. Invest time in discussing and agreeing on your shared goals for the work, as well as your roles, expectations, and work styles.
> 4. Agree up front on order of authorship and expectations for what that means.

We recommend that you discuss authorship order and roles early in any partnership. When moving your work to publication, order of authorship has conventions depending on one's discipline. In the social sciences and humanities, single authorship is highly valued, though collaboration is becoming the norm. In the sciences, authorship usually includes all who worked on the project, moving down in order of contribution or lab ownership. Hopefully your doctoral program coached or socialized you in the conventions of your discipline. Merton's (1968) classic work on the prominence of scientists over their careers discusses the order of authorship and what it means in developing notoriety and prominence. First authorship or corresponding author status is important to develop name recognition. Publishing with well-known people, perhaps your dissertation chair, has its pros—access to networks, drawing people to your work—and its cons—the perception of riding coattails or an assumption that the first authorship was a gift rather than being reflective of the larger contribution.

Managing Publication Feedback

One of us had the surprising fortune of receiving "accept" as the first decision in the review process on her first two article submissions, but this turned out to have unfortunate consequences. When subsequent submissions were rejected or required revision and resubmission, she was devastated and developed quite a case of writer's block and submission avoidance. Almost nothing is accepted on first review. Thus, how you manage the review decision and the feedback is significant in moving the piece to publication. Whether the piece is rejected or you are asked to revise and resubmit, read through the editor's summary and then the reviewer comments, trying to focus on the positive feedback. Highlight those comments if you are feeling particularly discouraged. Then read through the entire response, noting the negative comments as to-dos rather than definitive judgments. Harris (2015) recommends that these become a master to-do list that serves as your guidepost for writing the revision. Table 6.3, a table with actual reviewer feedback and author response, is helpful in keeping track of specific comments and how you are making revisions to address them.

In the revise and resubmit, once revisions are complete, construct a letter to the editor noting the major changes you have made and how they align with the editor and reviewer comments. Table 6.3 can also be used in your letter to the editor when you submit your revision. Harris (2015) also recommends, "If you had contradictory comments from reviewers or did not address a major area raised by the reviewers, you should clearly explain your logic and rationale" (p. 2). Editors are not always looking for you to do

TABLE 6.3
Sample Author Response Table

Reviewers' Comments	Authors' Response
Create a graphic of the conceptual framework, perhaps showing peripheral status of the NTTF [non-tenure-track faculty].	We have created Figure 1 (p. 11) to help readers visualize the interplay between Bess's circles of influence and symbolic interaction. We note that a reviewer suggested we use the visual to indicate where NTTF might fall on the periphery of the profession. However, our goal here was not so much to indicate this peripheral status as to depict the meaning-making that might take place as individuals negotiate professional, institutional, and personal values and identities.
Provide richer information on symbolic interactionism for readers.	We have provided a more specific and extended discussion of symbolic interactionism in the Conceptual Framework section (pp. 8–9), highlighting the work of Snow (2001), who extended Blumer's (1980) formulation. In addition, we have revised the Methods section (pp. 11–12) to be more explicit about the connection between symbolic interactionism and the interpretivist lens we adopted given the tight coupling between these concepts.
Identify how participants were identified and why institutions where chosen.	In the Methods section (p. 12), we have explained that the institutions were chosen because they represent a significant portion of institutions in higher education and because full-time NTTF numbers at these institutional types are sizeable (as we note in the Introduction). We have also have addressed our use of purposeful, typical case sampling for participants (p. 12).

everything they and the reviewers ask, but they *are* looking for you to respect their guidance and provide a sound rationale for your choices. Michael's comments in Inset 6.12 reflect this process of reconciling divergent reviewer feedback in a future revision.

If the piece has been rejected, we recommend you do the following:

- Review all of the comments.
  - What do you see as constructive and useful to making the product better? Put these on your to-do list.
  - What seems to be idiosyncratic or not related to your goals for the product? Decide to ignore these.
- Consider the focus and requirements of the next journal (which you have already selected) and work this into the list of to-dos.

Inset 6.12.
Words From Early Career Faculty: Navigating the Revise and Resubmit

My first experience submitting something for a scholarly journal was interesting because they have two reviewers. One of them loved my article, said it was perfect. The other one hated my article, said it was a piece of crap and we will never publish this. What am I supposed to do here? I went back and I looked at the comments from the reviewer who pretty much trashed me. And I do give the guy credit, now that I'm looking back at it. So, that's part of the goal, at some point during the next six months, going back and pretty much reworking the whole paper with the same analysis, still the same research, but just a different approach to it, which I think can work better.
—Michael

- Think of this manuscript as a revise and resubmit, even if it is to a different outlet, rather than a rejection, since that approach helps you stay in a positive state of mind.

Give yourself a very strict deadline to complete the revision and make this the top priority in your research and scholarly activities.

Be Your Best Advocate

We began this chapter by emphasizing that developing your record of scholarship in a successful and timely manner is largely up to you. Your agency is essential to achieving your goals in this area. Your scholarly agenda and productivity are not places to be modest and to defer to others. They are opportunities to set a course, make things happen, and be sure folks know what you are doing. Impressions matter. Seltzer (2015) reminds us that women are the least likely to promote themselves, to cite their own work, or to assign their own books. Minoritized faculty often fall into this same trap but also deal with the complexity that too much self-promotion is seen as disingenuous or overly boastful. Networks, mentorship, and self-care help us to counter these thoughts and behaviors. Our own good work is the best defense against microaggressive colleagues and environments.

Lupton (2012) recommends keeping your online presence active and up-to-date. Consider buying a domain name and setting up a personal website using many of the free or low-cost platforms available. You might also consider a commercial profile (e.g., researchgate.net) if that better meets your needs. At the least, make sure your university webpage is current with your latest publications. Use Facebook and Twitter (or whatever is the latest, favored mode of social media) to share your ideas and announce new publications or grants. Use your campus outlets (newsletters, weekly news, magazines) to announce these as well. Do not be shy about sending a story idea of your work to the campus alumni or research magazine. Like Karen, you may find that sharing your work with others has multiple benefits (see Inset 6.13).

Concluding Thoughts

Research, scholarly, and creative work can be among the least structured of all faculty work and therefore the easiest to let slide in the face of more pressing demands. Thus, it is critical that as an early career faculty member you take the initiative and be proactive in building a productive scholarly agenda. Being savvy about the expectations of your institution is also key, as you want to align your own productivity expectations with those of your department and campus.

Even as you do so, we encourage you to remember concepts from O'Meara and colleagues (2008). First, find ways to pursue work that is important to you personally and professionally as a way to build and honor your commitments. Second, develop and access strong professional relationships as strategies for accountability, writing productivity, and feedback on your work—as well as just basic emotional support.

Remember also that your scholarly career is just getting started, so take the long view and celebrate your achievements as they come. If you publish a book, be sure to have a launch or book signing. Mark each journal article or composition with a special dinner. Celebrating those special moments helps you maintain your momentum and is good for the soul!

> **Inset 6.13.**
> **Words From Early Career Faculty: Share the Joy**
>
> *I never really brag about what I publish. I don't see myself doing that at all. But when [my article] first came out I actually distributed it to our faculty and pointed out where it fits in our curriculum and who might be using it. Because we do need to change a lot of things.* —Karen

Exercises

Here are some ideas for exercises that might be useful to you in building your knowledge and skills regarding the teaching-related topics we discussed in this chapter.

1. Define your desired scholarly niche in your field. Who are your peer scholars? How will you judge your contributions to this niche?
2. Imagine what kind of scholar you really want to be. What are the benefits? What will be the challenges to becoming that scholar? Does that correspond to the kind of scholar your institutional

colleagues would like you to become? How will you mange if it is not?

3. What level of productivity is reasonable for you? Are you being honest in this assessment? Is it enough for tenure at your institution?
4. What kind of help will you need with your scholarship? Do you know the steps to get that help? Are you ready to seek out that help?
5. What kind of help will you need for scholarship? Do you know the steps to get that help? Are you ready to seek out that help?

Goal-Setting Activity: Shaping Your Career as a Scholar

Here we provide a step-by-step process to help you start thinking about the kinds of things you might want to accomplish as a scholar during the next several years of your career.

1. Brainstorm several goals or things you would like to learn or accomplish as a scholar in the next three to five years.
2. Try to arrange those goals in some kind of order. For instance, does one lead to another? Or could one be accomplished in a year or so while another goal might take two to three years to accomplish?
3. For each goal ask the following:
   - What are some challenges I might encounter in reaching that goal?
   - What resources (e.g., people, information, skills) do I have to help me reach that goal?
   - What specific steps will I take, and by when, to reach that goal?

You might consider using a chart like Table 6.4 to help you think about these questions. We've completed the first row just to give you an example.

TABLE 6.4
Shaping Your Career as a Scholar

Goal	Challenges I Might Encounter	Resources I Have	Steps I Will Take and by When	Accomplished? When?
1. *Translate dissertation methodology chapter into an article*	• *Current chapter is too long for journal* • *Not sure of an appropriate journal* • *Need to sharpen philosophical background on the method*	• *New colleague is expert on the methodology* • *Dissertation committee* • *No teaching or meetings on Thursday*	• *Identify two to three possible journals; scan articles* • *Contact editor of one journal* • *Protect two hours each Thursday for writing article* • *Seek guidance from committee and colleague*	
2.				
3.				
4.				
5.				

Some other goals you might consider for your scholarship include

- identifying sources of funding on campus to support research,
- sketching initial designs for a new study,
- identifying potential research collaborators on or off campus, and
- identifying field sites and locations for your research.

7

NAVIGATING THE WORLD
OF GRANTS AND FUNDING

E xternal funding of scholarly work has become increasingly critical to our success as faculty members while also becoming increasingly competitive to garner. This chapter provides you with information about the types of grants and funding you can seek, as well as guidance about how to write proposals. We begin by talking about the why of writing grants before giving a broad overview of types of grants. From there, we look at how to prepare for and write a strong proposal (narrative, budget, etc.) and responding to proposal reviews, before we offer a few words on managing a grant once you have received it.

We are not overly specific about funding agencies or information about where to find funding, as those lists quickly become dated and the possibilities are too broad to cover. Grants.gov, however, is one source that we can mention as it links to grants from multiple governmental funding agencies— everything from the Department of the Interior to NASA to the National Science Foundation to the National Endowment for the Arts and more. On that site you can find current requests for proposals (RFPs), as well as links to the different federal funding agencies. You also want to check out your state's websites to see about state-level funding sources. In addition to pointers about writing proposals, we also provide general information about managing funded programs. Different fields have varying levels of available funding, and research in some fields rarely is supported by grants.

Why Write Grants?

Writing grant proposals is a fair amount of work, so why go to all of that trouble? Perhaps you need an expensive piece of equipment to conduct your research. You may have had some money allocated to equipment or supplies as part of the start-up package when you were hired, but that money gets spent quickly and usually has an expiration date, so you need to figure out how to find funding elsewhere. Even if you are seeking money at the department or college level, you need to make a case for the purchases. Perhaps you need time to redesign a course or develop innovative curriculum to support student success. Sometimes your campus may offer reassigned time or summer salary for these activities. (Reassigned time is when you are released from teaching a course to perform other duties. This is sometimes called *buy-out* or *course buy-out*. Your time is reassigned from typical duties for a specific task.) Occasionally there will be external funding for curriculum innovation and revision.

Of course, you are not alone in trying to secure funding. Grants are more competitive than ever, and even strong proposals often have to go through several submissions before being funded. University and college budgets are stretched like never before. State funding as a percentage of the overall budget for public colleges and universities has dropped dramatically (Mortensen, 2012), so the number of faculty looking outside department budgets to get the supplies, equipment, student researchers, or time to conduct scholarly work continues to grow.

Regardless of the type of funding you are seeking, you need to have a project that is innovative; seeks to answer a question; has definable deliverables or outcomes; and includes all the appropriate equipment, participants, and leadership. The specifics of what you propose to do are not part of this chapter; that is your area of expertise. Your goal is to convince the funding agency that you have the capabilities and capacity to complete the project successfully.

Types of Grants or Funding

The two broad classes of funding for faculty are internal funding from the campus budget and external funding from an off-campus entity. Making a compelling argument is essential for either type, but the level of detail needed for each varies.

Internal Funding

If you are an early career faculty member, you probably do not yet have a track record to demonstrate your ability to get and successfully manage grants. How do you build one? Most campuses have relatively small amounts of money to support faculty who are doing research or scholarly work. These awards may support release time from a class or summer salary, small grants

Inset 7.1.
Words From Early Career Faculty:
Building a Scholarly Record and
Reputation

I have been very successful getting external funding, but that's because I had already gotten my reputation and I was already able to make a case as to why this work was important. But to start a whole new project from scratch, no one externally wants to fund that. You need internal resources to start a new research agenda. —Catherine

for materials or supplies, time or salary for working on large externally funded grant proposals— either for individual grants or for collaborative, interdisciplinary proposals—or time and salary to revise or develop curriculum and instructional materials.

Small, internally funded grants can provide the foundation for building your track record (see Inset 7.1). Using seed money or time, you may be able to generate initial data or evidence that helps lay the foundation for a larger, externally funded proposal. Proof that you have the capacity is your track record to date: What have you accomplished with prior funding? What sorts of publications do you have related to this work? What do other team members bring to the effort?

Applications for internal funding are typically short, and the reporting requirements are minimal. You may write a report for how time was spent; provide evidence of grant proposal submission; or share copies of a syllabus, existing curriculum, or instructional innovation, being sure that the course modifications go through the appropriate curriculum approval process. The degree to which these applications are highly competitive usually correlates with the overall budgetary health of the university. When times are good and money is flush, more dollars are allocated to these sorts of activities and they are less competitive, with lots of faculty getting funded. When funds are more scarce, these internal grants are more difficult to receive.

As you think about applying for internally funded grants, consider how you can leverage them for publications or externally funded proposals. Have these longer-term goals in mind before you even apply for the internal grant. Then be intentional about moving from goals and activities to results with the internal grant, documenting your outcomes along the way so that you can make your best case to an external funder. As you do so, you are also building your own track record for productivity, something that can help you both with future grants and the tenure and promotion process.

Our suggestions for writing a competitive grant are the same whether you seek internal or external funding. Just keep in mind that internally supported projects are generally less competitive than externally funded ones, are usually shorter in terms of the application itself and the duration of the funding, and typically involve fewer people in the review process. Internally funded projects tend to be easier to navigate postaward as well.

External Funding

The two broad types of external funding are private foundations and public funds. The funding types have similarities and differences, as Table 7.1 shows. Typically, with external funding you are writing a proposal to match a specific priority or agenda held by the foundation or agency. In these cases, you need to do your homework and be sure that what you are proposing is a reasonably good fit for priorities of the organization offering the funds.

While our suggestions for writing the grant proposal are similar for internal and external funding opportunities, we focus next on the process of submitting a proposal for externally funded grants because the process is more complicated. Some of the steps are the same whether you are seeking private money or public money. Regardless of the type of funding, do not start writing a proposal in a vacuum. You need to go through many steps and various levels of approval. Start the process early so that you can get the approval to submit a request.

Preaward Activities: Preparing a Strong Externally Funded Proposal

Drafting a competitive grant proposal takes time, patience, persistence, and attention to detail. In this section, we walk you through our suggestions for crafting an effective proposal. While some of this process is linear—for example, you should get approval to submit a proposal before building a budget—much of the grant writing process is highly iterative in nature, and different components need to happen in parallel. For instance, you might develop your ideas and plans, draft a budget, and then realize you need to return to the narrative to scale back those ideas and plans. Also plan on gathering letters of support, CVs, and other materials. Begin the proposal planning process as early as possible to ensure that you have time to write the strongest possible application.

Develop and Align Your Idea With the Funding Priorities

Most of us have heard stories of someone who had a great idea for a grant, developed and submitted a proposal, and then learned that the proposal did not meet the funder's strategic priorities. Other stories include faculty

TABLE 7.1
Summary of Preaward Activities

Activity	Government Agencies	Private Foundations/Funders
Application process	• Request for proposal, generally open to all to apply. • Sometimes there is a required intent to submit or a preliminary application, after which you can submit a full proposal.	• You may need to be invited to apply. Sometimes you will do a short program overview, which, if successful, leads to an invitation to submit a full proposal. • Foundation staff may play a significant role in helping to shape the final proposal.
Campus permission to submit	• Talk to grants and contracts or sponsored programs office staff. • Determine allowable indirect rates. • Complete intent to submit forms on campus.	• Consult with an on-campus development officer. • You may need to meet with officers or trustees from the granting organization. Dress appropriately. • Determine allowable indirect rates.
Predesign phase	• Begin sketching out your ideas. • Consult with colleagues, dean, chair, and others to assemble your team and to get permission on key details (e.g., assign time).	
Budget and budget justification	• Identify the budget template required by your sponsored programs office. • Outline your projected expenses, gathering specific and detailed estimates. • Complete justification as you complete the budget. • Complete these steps early to allow for review.	
Project description and narrative	• Write proposal—reading and rereading the RFP as you go. • Be sure to address all elements of the RFP. • Be sure your program aligns with the funder's mission and vision or strategic plan for the program. • Talk with the campus development officer or program officer for clarification.	
Letters of support/ collaboration	• Create draft letters that your partners can tweak to make their own. Be sure that individual letters vary. Collect them early.	
CVs from key personnel	• Follow format provided by the funders (usually one or two pages). Collect them early.	
Submission process and clearances	• Complete internal clearance process—approval of budget and proposal. • Work with sponsored programs or the development office to submit your proposal. Sometimes the proposal needs to be submitted by such an office, not you.	

who might have had great ideas that a funder would have loved to support, but the professor did not move forward with the idea because he thought it would not fit the opportunity.

Before you start writing, you need to be clear about what you are proposing and what you want to do. We have known people who find appropriate RFPs to meet their scholarly agenda and others who find any old RFP and write proposals just to get the money. Colleagues in the latter group are less likely to have a cohesive scholarly agenda, and they sometimes lament the fact that they have to do research or a project about which they are not passionate simply because they received the money. As part of authoring your career, we encourage you to be in the former group. Know what you want to do and see how you can find funding to support it.

If you are thinking about submitting a grant proposal, we encourage you to do three things right at the start. First, if your idea involves others as part of a team, reach out to them immediately. Find out if they are interested, engage them in developing the idea, and secure their commitment.

Second, take the time to sketch out your ideas in very rough form. What are the goals? What kinds of activities, equipment, or research would this grant support? How many people are being supported? This step can be done in a very preliminary, brainstorming way, but doing it now makes the budgeting and writing processes far easier.

Third, if you have any question about whether your idea is aligned with the funding opportunity, find out. Your campus may have a grants specialist who can help you decipher the RFP and see if your idea aligns with it. You can also reach out to a program officer or foundation staff member, share your idea, and ask if that person sees it as aligned with the opportunity. Remember, these individuals want to fund projects and are looking to secure the best ideas. They are happy to help you.

Secure Intent to Propose Permission From Your Campus

Many state and federally funded programs limit the number of proposals from a single campus. Moreover, your campus likely does not want multiple proposals competing with each other for funding, which means you need to get clearance to submit your proposal for a given RFP. In all likelihood you will need to file a document that states your intention to submit a proposal, which is like calling dibs on the RFP. This step is important because faculty in different departments might be interested in the same call for proposals; for example, education and social work faculty might both want to pursue funding related to truancy, but the campus may only be allowed or wish to submit one proposal. When multiple parties want to submit a proposal that has a limited submission restriction, you need to make a case why your proposal should be the one to go forward. Your campus likely has a procedure in place that allows for a short, internal competition to see which faculty member(s) may submit a proposal. Your campus, as we have discussed, likely has an office of sponsored programs or a grants and contracts office. Meet the preaward people and figure out how the internal clearance process happens on your campus. You can do this well before you start thinking about your first proposal or are in the throes of writing it. They can walk you through the intent-to-submit process as well as other steps such as budgeting, clearance, and so on.

A final word of caution: Do not file an intent-to-submit document unless you are actually planning on submitting the proposal. Doing so prevents others from being able to submit on the same RFP. If you are selected to be the campus person who is allowed to submit the proposal and you fail to do so, you should anticipate some sort of penalty. This may be in the form of losing the right to compete for future single or limited submission funding opportunities.

Campus Indirect Rates

When you meet with your sponsored programs staff, ask about the campus rules for indirect rates. This rate is the percentage of the grant money the university gets. The money is meant to support the university's research infrastructure, covering costs such as your office, phone and computer, lab space, and grant support staff salaries. The allowable rate has been negotiated between your university and federal agencies (e.g., the National Science Foundation, the National Institutes of Health), and these rates can run up to 45% of the budget or higher.

If the proposal you are submitting allows for "full indirect" of these negotiated rates, then you build that amount into your proposal. You do not have a choice. Other granting agencies (e.g., foundations, the U.S. Department of Education) or even specific grants may have a limit on the allowable indirect rate. In those situations, your campus is allowed to charge only the published indirect rate on the RFP, and the campus needs to approve your moving forward under this rate as part of reviewing your intent to propose. If you have a grant that provides little or no indirect money, the funds required to support the grant need to come from somewhere—hence the need for permission to submit for a proposal that does not include indirect, or only allows a lower indirect rate.

You need to know what the indirect amount is because it affects the budget and your request. For example, suppose your university has an indirect rate of 40%. If you need $100,000 in direct costs to complete the project, you would need to ask for $140,000 (40% of $100,000 = $40,000 for indirect expenses). (Direct costs represent the money that supports your project specifically whereas indirect costs support your project via overhead, such as campus infrastructure and support.) This gets tricky is when the granting agency has a cap on what you can request. Suppose that the maximum you can request is $100,000. With a 40% indirect rate, you would be able to request only $71,428 in direct costs. Be sure that you are able to complete the project with the amount of money you are requesting.

We caution that this discussion, as well as that in Inset 7.2, is a vast oversimplification of the indirect rate and its impact on your budgeting. There are far too many nuances to how campuses and grantors mandate this rate, far too many to cover here. Quite simply, you need to be in early and regular contact with your sponsored programs office and be very clear on the rules and expectations for each grant opportunity.

With the indirect rate clear, you can begin planning your budget. We recommend doing this while drafting your narrative because the two are closely connected. It is worth knowing that your budget and budget justification both need approval from multiple people on campus.

Budget and Justification: Doing Your Homework and Planning

While starting the budget process as early as possible is important, you cannot get a real sense of what sort of budget you need until you know your project's scope, which means you have to do a bit of juggling.

Inset 7.2.
Strategies for Success:
Being Aware of Indirect Rates and Return to Faculty

In many cases, a portion of indirect money is returned to the faculty member or department to support research activities.

Campuses—and colleges and schools on a single campus—have different policies about how the indirect rate moneys are used and allocated. On research-intensive campuses, the indirect monies are often kept at the institutional level. At a research-intensive campus, you are supported in your research and scholarly work at higher levels than teaching-intensive campuses. You may have smaller teaching loads, larger annual budgets to support research, and so on. As a result, the institution may not feel the need to give back the indirect money.

On less research-intensive campuses, some of the indirect money may find its way back to you, your department, or both. This money is to be used to support your scholarly work and provide gap funding between grants. Campuses that return indirect money to the faculty member do so because they do not have the infrastructure of the more research-intensive institutions.

Ask about how and if indirect funds are distributed and allocated on your campus.

You need to work on the proposal—the narrative of what you want to do, the budget, and a budget justification—all at the same time. Have three files going at once. As you come across a program element that has costs associated with it, add it to the budget and jot down the justification for how and why it is needed.

When compiling a budget, think about all the elements needed for you to succeed in the project. You will also have your own institution's budget spreadsheets and likely a grant-specific budget sheet to complete. (If you are fortunate, your sponsored programs office can provide extensive support. Check with them because you may complete the institution's template, and then this office translates your work into the grant-specific budget template for you.) You will have annual budgets and an overall budget. Each of those budget sheets has its own categories, but as you think about the project, you also need to consider generic budget categories. Think about the fact that your budget needs and requirements change over the course of the project, with the project's start and end having different activities and different budgetary needs. The following are some categories to consider:

- *Personnel.* Who is involved and how much of their time will you need to purchase? Is it buyout from courses, summer salary, overload salary? Will student salaries be involved? What is each person doing? For the different personnel there should be clearly defined roles that align with the goals of the project and sufficient time to carry out the tasks. You will likely need to pay benefits in addition to salary, and your budget planning should reflect it.
- *Supplies and equipment.* What sorts of things need to be purchased to implement the project successfully? Include smaller items such as printer cartridges as well as the bigger-ticket items like equipment and data collection.
- *Travel.* Will you need to attend conferences or meetings to disseminate your findings? Work with researchers at other sites? Must you attend project-specific meetings in other locations? Will there be local travel?
- *Printing, postage, publications, websites, and telecommunications.* Are there newsletters or project publications that need to be developed and distributed? Mailings to participants? Questionnaire distribution costs? Photocopying associated with the project? A need for a graphic designer or website developer? Page fees for publication?
- *Meeting support.* You may need to budget for food (not always an allowable expense), parking, and meeting materials.
- *Stipends and salaries.* You might need to pay a stipend to an advisory board member or for people's participation in the project. There may be salaries, scholarships, or stipends for student participants.

- *Research and evaluation.* Your project may require costs for an evaluator, data entry and analysis, or even a research assistant salary.

Prioritize your list. In all likelihood, your ideal budget will be much greater than you are eligible to request. What on your list is a true need versus things that you would like to have? Does your institution give some of the indirect cost money back to faculty? If so, what costs can you cover with those funds? Are there other ways to get costs covered by the institution or is leveraging funds from other grants and projects an option?

Talk with your department chair early in this process, especially if you are planning to buy out some of your teaching time or hire staff, or you need additional space or have extensive travel considerations. These budget items impact the department in terms of your availability for teaching classes. Keeping your chair and others in the loop not only helps them plan and know what you are doing but also keeps them more informed when the budget and proposal pass through them on their way to final campus approval and clearance.

You also need to have a justification to go along with the budget, so keep good notes on your budget decisions along the way. These notes help you make the case for why you need a graphic designer or someone to translate your program materials into other languages, for example, or specify how much of your time is going to the project.

Budgeting takes a lot of time, planning, and high attention to detail. You want to be sure the budget reflects everything you want to do. Receiving funding and then realizing you have forgotten to include printing costs or transportation costs is painful.

The budget and budget justification are key components of the internal clearance process, which has to happen before you are able to submit the proposal to the funding agency. Be sure to allow time for internal clearance, when chairs, deans, and others review the budget and give their approval. This process takes time, as it is sequential. Your dean will not approve it until after your chair has approved, for example, which is why we suggest starting the budget approval process as soon as you have the budget finalized.

Writing the Proposal

The next piece of advice sounds overly simplistic, but it can be a deal breaker: *When writing the grant proposal, follow the RFP guidelines.* In fact, you should read, reread, then reread the guidelines again before you even begin writing; then, keep reading the guidelines as you write. Be sure that you know the nuances of the call for proposal—what is and is not allowed. Sometimes the granting agency has links to previously funded projects. Look at them.

Beyond just the content, follow directions. Give the funder whatever is asked for, using the correct number of pages with proper-sized fonts and margins. With so many proposals to review, grantors do not need much of an excuse to discard an application; do not let this happen to you.

The Abstract

While the abstract is the first thing reviewers read, it ought to be the last thing you write. You cannot know what to include in the abstract until the grant is fully thought through and written. When you write the abstract, keep to word or page limits, but make sure you highlight all the key and innovative components. Be clear without including too many details. Bold, underline, or italicize key points to make them stand out. If the granting agency requires certain items in the abstract or project description, by all means ensure their presence. Call them out and be explicit; for example, the National Science Foundation requires proposals to include a statement about the proposal's broader impact and intellectual merit. Do not make your reviewers hunt for this and do not try to couch the impact or merit in opaque language or terms.

Project Description

You need to make a compelling case for your project, because many of your peers are also applying for this limited pot of money. Make your proposal stand out by being clear about what you want to do. Write about it so that reviewers can easily understand your project while recognizing the value of the work. Again, use the funder's language when possible. Your track record as a scholar also comes into play here, as does the strength of your proposed work and, if relevant, the strength of the partners involved in the project. If you are working on a proposal with colleagues, you may be writing different sections of the grant. Be sure to coordinate your efforts so that your budget includes all the required components. Also make sure that the different components fit together. The proposal needs to come across as a single, cohesive project instead of a piecemeal project with somewhat related but uncoordinated components.

Making the proposal easy to navigate helps your reviewers make sense of your project. Remember that they are reading multiple proposals, all of which are as long as yours. By making it easy for them to read and remember, addressing all the required components, and being clear about the project and its outcomes, your proposal has a better chance than if the reviewers have to struggle to figure out what you want to do. Headings, bold or italicized sections, tables, and charts all help with readability, as does clear, concise writing.

While graphics, tables, and timelines can be important additions to a proposal, use them with care. Sometimes a half- or full-page graphic shares more information than several pages of text; a picture really is worth a thousand words. When you have a limited number of pages to make your case, a succinct graphic can be really helpful. You can include project activities, a timeline, and measurables or deliverables in a single chart in a way that lays out everything. On the other hand, sometimes that half-page graphic could be stated in one sentence and takes up precious space. Be careful and intentional in how you use these tools.

Project Outcomes, Reporting, and Evaluation

A good grant proposal has clearly articulated goals and outcomes, as well as activities (e.g., data collection, events, services) related to these goals. Be as specific as you can in the proposal about what you promise without painting yourself into a corner with unrealistic goals and deliverables. As you develop your grant's outcomes and goals, think broadly about the program's impact. What need are you trying to meet? What questions are you trying to answer? What constitutes success on this project, and how will you know you have been successful? There are some outcomes you are obviously aiming for, but what are some other impacts of the project? Are they measurable so that you can collect that data and report back?

All grants require some sort of reporting where you share your findings and outcomes with your funder. At a minimum, you need to describe what was developed and produced, probably via an annual report. You might be expected, for instance, to document activities done, number of publications that resulted from the work, number of students impacted by the project, or number of community members who participate in trainings or activities. You and your colleagues should be able to handle this kind of reporting on your own.

Some funders require an evaluation of the project as it moves forward. If so, you may need a formal evaluation component to the grant; some RFPs actually have an evaluation section on the proposal. Such a formal evaluation is especially true of programming proposals. These sorts of grants often require an evaluator apart from project personnel to observe the program in action, document activities, collect and analyze data from project staff and participants, make program improvement recommendations, and so on. Read the RFP carefully or check with your program officer so that you are clear on the standards for evaluation. As a rough rule, evaluation for major projects should constitute at least 10% of the budget. This amount shows that you are serious about evaluation and is a reasonable amount to enable you to secure a worthwhile evaluation to help you improve the project.

Letters of Support and Collaboration

You will likely want to provide letters of support and collaboration from your institution and your partners. Not all granting agencies allow for letters of support, which typically include praise for you (as the grant applicant), since they rarely get useful information from these "cheerleader" letters. Most agencies, however, want letters of collaboration, indicating institutional leaders' awareness of the project and willingness to participate if funded; these letters should convey institutional commitment to the project and speak to how the project fits with other institutional goals and priorities. Some agencies or funders even provide a template for the kind of language they expect to see in the letter. Following are some tips to consider regarding these letters.

- Give people enough time to actually think about the letter and get it back to you. Ask early and give them a deadline that still gives you time to collect and collate the proposal.
- Provide a draft of the letter to individuals for them to edit and make their own as opposed to expecting them to craft a letter from scratch. People are busy, and this step saves a huge amount of time.
- If you are providing your partners with a draft letter of collaboration to the grantor, make each letter unique. What does each specific partner add to the grant and bring to the endeavor? In addition, what benefit does the partner derive from the grant (it helps convince the grantor that there is buy-in if the partner receives some benefit from their participation with you)? How are you and the partner positioned for success? Having identical letters from each partner makes reviewers wonder about the true nature of the partnership.
- If a letter of support is allowed, the letter from your chair or dean should say something about your qualifications to complete the proposed project successfully. As with advice to read the RFP carefully, you should also read to see if a letter of support is allowed. As we noted, there might be a form for collaborators and administrators to sign that indicates awareness and collaboration.

If you have subcontracts as part of your grant, meaning that other entities will be receiving money from the proposal, you need letters from them also, along with their budgets and budget justifications. Subcontractors would appear as a line item in your budget.

Biosketches or Mini-CVs

Most proposals want a one- or two-page abbreviated CV for all named personnel in the project. Granting agencies, including the National Institutes of Health and National Science Foundation, often have a specific format to follow, and the instructions are included with the RFP. You can request these mini-CVs from collaborators and prepare your own early in the process. Include features from your CV that most closely align with the work of your proposal, which is another way of demonstrating to the grant reviewers that you and your collaborators have the required skills, expertise, and track record to complete the proposed work.

Before You Submit

Before starting the final submission process, read through the full draft of the proposal with the RFP open next to it at least one last time. Be sure that you have addressed all the required elements. If you have sufficient time, find someone you trust to read the proposal and give you feedback. You are often so immersed in the proposal that you cannot see the problems. Your critical friend has fresh eyes and can let you know what is unclear, where more details are needed, or what reads like jargon but does not really say anything.

Your proposal likely needs to go through internal clearance before it can be submitted. This process is hierarchical, usually beginning with you and extending through your chair and the dean, and then up to the senior administrator responsible for research on campus. They review the budget and the project to ensure that the institution can commit to it. Plan for this internal clearance on your timeline, considering the time restraints of the people involved.

Submitting the Proposal

Anticipate that submission is going to be more complicated than it should be, take longer than you imagine, and lead to glitches you did not foresee. Do not wait until the last minute or even the last day to submit the proposal. Collaborate closely with your sponsored programs office colleagues to manage the process and timeline; they may even be responsible for the final submission, so their partnership is critical.

Read carefully and well in advance how to submit the grant. Is it online via Grants.gov, Fastlane, or some other portal? Are hard copies required by a certain date and time? Must they be postmarked by that date or arrive by the date? If you are submitting online, remember that lots of other people will be submitting at the same time, so 4:55 p.m. on the due date for proposals due at 5:00 p.m. will have lots of Internet action and uploading will be slow. You do not want to put in all the work and effort of writing a good proposal and not be able to submit it. Plan on submitting early: Aim for a week ahead of time.

If this is your first proposal to submit online, give yourself even more time. Ask for help as needed. Your colleagues in the sponsored programs office should be able to walk you through the process. Remember, though, that they work with everyone on campus, so your emergency does not necessarily translate to their emergency—another reason to give yourself lots of time.

A Word on Grants From Philanthropies and Foundations

If you are hoping to get money from philanthropic organizations or foundations, you want to speak with a development officer on your campus for approval to approach the organization. Many times an organization supports only one or two proposals from a campus. If someone else on campus is ahead of you or has a tradition of getting her project funded from that group, you may not be allowed to make an ask. If it is a private funder and the university or college has been working with that funder for a while—perhaps working toward a large gift or grant—and you go asking for something different, you may undo the progress that has been made to set up a major gift. The university is not going to want you to ask for $50,000 when its advancement team is hoping for a six- or seven-figure gift elsewhere on campus from the same funder. There is a protocol for how each campus works with private philanthropies, and you need to be sure to follow it. Another point with private funders is that you may need an invitation to apply for funding.

Responding to Grant Reviews

The granting agency will contact you after reviewing your proposals. This process can often take months, particularly for governmental funding. If you are funded, congratulations! While getting money to support our research or other projects is great, it also brings a great deal of additional work. Grants are not bank accounts that we can use as we wish. They are contractual agreements between us and the funding agency to complete a given project.

If your proposal is rejected, take a moment to grieve, and then carefully read the reviewers' comments. Remember that getting funded is much more difficult than it used to be, and most of us are not funded the first time. Many times, funding agencies have RFPs on an annual cycle. You may be able to modify your proposal to address the concerns and resubmit the following year. Concerns of reviewers often vary. You may have been unclear, you may have missed a required element of the grant, you may not have clearly articulated measurable outcomes, or you may have lacked sufficient detail. You may also have totally missed the mark on what the RFP was asking for; for example, you wanted money for your project, and you shoved it into a proposal for something else, hoping you would still get the money. If you decide in retrospect that there was not really a good match between your project and their funding goals, seek other funders. If you conclude that it was one of the other issues, learn what you can, then revise and resubmit—just like with your other scholarly work.

Recognize that a different panel of reviewers does each round of review, which means you may address the concerns raised during the first submission only to find that the next panel of reviewers has an entirely different set of questions the following year. Talking with your program officer before you resubmit can provide you with insight. Clarify concerns raised in the first round of reviews to see if they still seem on target with the program officer's vision for the program. Inset 7.3 encourages you to take the opportunity to serve on review panels when you can; it will help you write better proposals!

> **Inset 7.3.**
> **Strategies for Success:**
> **Serving on a Grant Panel**
>
> Should you ever have an opportunity to serve on a grant review panel, seriously consider it. While a time-consuming process, it is incredibly useful. You will be able to see how a panel reads and reacts to different proposals, what makes for an easy-to-read and understandable proposal, and almost as importantly, what makes a proposal difficult to decipher. You will hear the sorts of discussions a panel has about a proposal and its alignment with the RFP, project goals, the feasibility of meeting said goals, and more. All of this exposure positions you to write a stronger proposal.

Postaward Activities

Once you have been funded, it is time to implement the project. You need to address compliance issues, consider reporting requirements, and work with the postaward staff on campus who help you with the fiscal side of the grant. The postaward staff processes travel claims, reimbursement requests, purchase orders, time cards, and so forth. Every transaction that takes place related to the grant goes through you and to the hands of multiple other people; plan on lots of paperwork and administrative speed bumps. None of us writes grants to fill out forms, but failure to do the paperwork correctly means your work is slowed down and your reimbursements and payments are also delayed. Your department or college may have a staff member devoted to helping faculty with this financial paperwork; if not, your sponsored programs office likely does. You still need to be involved, however. Set aside time regularly (e.g., every week, every two weeks) to deal with the paperwork. Get good at it and ask questions when you need help.

Inset 7.4.
Words From Early Career Faculty:
Navigating the Campus Grant
Bureaucracy

*How do you deal with the budgeting
aspects in terms of how to track what
you can spend? I thought that the
people who worked in Foundation
or Research and Sponsored Programs
really dictated what I could and
couldn't spend, but my colleague was
like, "No, you tell them what you need
to spend." If they don't approve something, you go argue with them. [The
granting agency] gives you money to
do your research. If Sponsored Programs can't figure out how to make it
work, that's their job. So if an administrator says, "No, this isn't right," you
have to go explain why. Sometimes
you have to fight them and push.*
—James

The paperwork aspect of grants
and contracts is frustrating. Sometimes we have items in our budgets
that are cumbersome or problematic
for sponsored programs to make
work. For example, you might be
compensating participants with gift
cards. This was part of your research
design, explained in the budget and
the budget description, but questions arise when the time comes to
spend the money as you envisioned.
As James points out in Inset 7.4, you
may need to push back to be able to
spend the money in approved man-
ners. Having frank conversations
with budget staff during the grant
writing process can prevent some
later frustrations.

In terms of grant activities,
be diligent about data collection,
program development, budgetary
expenditures, and project bench-
marks. Keep good records about
what you do, why you do it, and what obstacles you encountered. You have
annual reports to write and may need to participate in larger data collection
efforts. Being organized and staying abreast of deadlines and project activities
helps you meet these requirements. You probably had a tentative timeline in
your grant proposal that can be a starting point to help you stay organized
on the project.

Skills needed to run a project are different from those needed to be a
successful faculty member. For example, most of us are good at overseeing
ourselves and maybe students in our research groups, but we are not used
to hiring or managing staff. Being responsible for others, ensuring that they
have work, knowing what to do, and actually doing the work are different
skills than planning and teaching classes. You may need to ask for help in
learning what to do. This situation is a great time to rely on your professional relationships (see Chapter 4), so be sure to tap your mentors, senior
colleagues, department chair, and others.

Your project may include research or program activities, data collection
and analysis, and communicating your findings or achievements to others, via

a traditional research paper, presentation, book, or other venue appropriate for your field. In all you do, remember to recognize your funders. Acknowledge them in press releases, and keep them informed as you move forward. Stay in touch with the grant officer or program officer associated with your project. Since life rarely works exactly as we propose it, your budget may well need adjustments over the course of the project. Your granting guidelines specify how much flexibility there is in moving funds within the project; bigger adjustments to the budget or requests to carry over funds from one year to the next require you to be in touch with your program officer. Maintaining a relationship and being on time and thorough in your annual reports help you with these requests, your productivity, and your reputation.

As we hope is clear from the preceding pages, writing proposals for and managing grants and contracts represent a team effort. For any given proposal or project, multiple colleagues on a campus (staff, administrators, other faculty) are involved in the process from beginning to end. It is not an individual achievement, nor is managing a grant an individual endeavor, which is yet another reason why the professional relationships we discussed in Chapter 4 are so critical to you as resources. In Inset 7.5, we summarize some of the key institutional resources that you should plan to tap into through your grant writing career.

> **Inset 7.5.**
> **Resources for Success:**
> **Campus Resources to Support Your Grant Seeking**
>
> - *Sponsored programs staff.* There may be different staff to help with preaward processes and postaward activities. Get to know them and talk to them at all stages so that you are clear about their expectations and needs.
> - *Department chair.* Your chair should be able to provide you with some guidance about grant submissions and administration on your campus. He or she may be able to help you with the process; give you names of people on campus; provide you with input on the proposal; be a critical friend to give feedback from the proposal; and write a letter of support, if allowed, for the proposal.
> - *Departmental colleagues.* Department colleagues who have submitted—ideally, successfully submitted—proposals to the same funding source can be invaluable resources for the proposal writing and submission process. Others who have administered a grant can help you in that area as well. There is nothing like experience when looking for guidance and help.

(continues)

Inset 7.5. (*Continued*)

- *Senior administrator for research or grant writer.* There may be people on your campus whose role it is to assist faculty with identifying and writing grant proposals. Find them, take them to coffee, and pick their brains. Ask what exactly they do and how they might be able to help you. In some cases, it might simply be finding possible funders. Perhaps they can actually help you compose the proposal. Sometimes there will be campus-level or college-level boilerplate language that describes your institution or college that can be used in proposals, saving you from having to look up that data.
- *Development office staff.* These people are more aware of foundations and private donors whose goals and mission align with your work. Get to know the director of development and allow staff to learn your scholarly work, which could lead to future funding.

Concluding Thoughts

After reading this chapter you may wonder if submitting grants is worth the time and effort. Some of our colleagues have very productive, successful careers and have never written a grant. That said, many of us want or need funding to carry out our work. Depending on campus or department expectations, you may have to submit grant proposals; some campuses require you to submit a proposal to be eligible for tenure and promotion. Universities do not have the resources to fully support all faculty work. For us, having the financial support for equipment and supplies, time, personnel, and so forth means that we can be more engaged and invested in our scholarly pursuits. Approaching the grant writing process with open eyes, a clear idea for the work being proposed, and a plan of action for carrying out the work puts you in good stead as you take your first steps into the world of funded research and scholarly work. Pulling together an easy-to-navigate proposal and keeping your project goals front and center help your reviewers understand your work and more easily evaluate it.

Exercises

Following are some exercises that might be useful to you in building your knowledge and skills regarding the grant writing and submission process on your campus.

1. Identify sources that might fund your work, then bookmark or store the information.
   - What internal sources of funding are there? What are the timelines for their proposals?
   - What governmental agencies and foundations might fund your work?
2. Map the structure on your campus for securing and managing external funding.
   - Who leads and staffs the sponsored programs office?
   - Who from your college or unit is responsible for development work with foundations and private funders?
3. Find and read the website for your campus's grants office or sponsored programs office.
   - What information is there?
   - Who are the staff support people for preaward? Is there a specific person for your discipline?
   - Are there grant writers on campus to help you create a proposal?
   - What are the steps required to submit a letter of intent or notice of intent?
   - Are there campus forms for budgets and budget justifications?
4. Make an appointment to talk with a preaward staff member.
   - What information does the staff member want faculty to know before considering submitting a proposal?
   - What things should you learn how to do before submitting a proposal?
   - Which faculty members in your college do a good job with the administrative side of grants—preaward and postaward?
   - Get advice on the best way to develop the budget (e.g., with the staff member, on your own, with a budget analyst).
   - Are there guidelines for how to hire students or staff?
   - What sorts of training do you need in order to submit a grant proposal? (IRB training if working with human subjects, IACUC if working with animals, safety trainings, etc.). Can some of those trainings take place after rather than before submitting the proposal?
5. Take a grant-savvy colleague to coffee or lunch.
   - Tell her you are thinking about submitting a proposal for the first time on campus. What should you know going into the process?
   - Ask what you should do with the grants or sponsored programs office to help facilitate the preaward process.
   - What do you need to know about the postaward process? How easy or challenging is it to navigate the postaward requirements?

8

SHAPING YOUR CAREER AS
AN ACADEMIC CITIZEN

S ometimes we read an article that stays with us. The ideas resonate, and
we come back to them later in our career. A commentary by Milton
Greenberg in *The Chronicle of Higher Education* (1993) is one such
article. Written by a former provost who had recently returned to the faculty
ranks, the piece looked at how faculty account for their time. His main point
was that most of what faculty members do is voluntary. We need to teach
and hold office hours at set times—even those are often negotiated with our
department chair—but when and where we do our scholarly work, the field
we choose to study, and the type and quantity of our service activities are up
to us. This freedom is one of the great joys of our job: We are able to chart
our own course and have a great deal of flexibility in our work life. However,
Greenberg points out that this reality is difficult for an administrator, who is
basically working with a group of volunteers.

Faculty probably feel most like volunteers when we think about service.
Of the three staples of our job, we are usually least sure about what is involved
and required in regard to service. As Michael points out in Inset 8.1, the
understanding of what and how much service also varies by department.
Teaching and *scholarship* are well-defined activities, and we have spent years
becoming well-acquainted with them. Like us, you were once a student and
you may have worked as a teaching assistant while a graduate student, so
you have a sense about teaching. You spent years earning a terminal degree
and may have done a postdoc, so your understanding of research and scholarly work is likely fairly sound as well. Service, however, is something all
of us were shielded from as graduate students. Our graduate advisers went
to meetings and reviewed manuscripts, but that was not as visible as other
aspects of their work. Early career faculty usually enter into this part of the
job without really understanding a large portion of it.

The expectation of service or academic citizenship exists throughout the history of academia. Consider the colonial colleges, where faculty members were tapped to serve as president, or present-day campuses, where faculty contribute their talents and time for shared governance to move the work of the institution forward. The expectation of faculty service evolved with the founding of land-grant, city, and state universities. The government provided the lands and funds with the idea that faculty members would provide service to help run the institutions.

> **Inset 8.1.**
> **Words From Early Career Faculty: Learning Service**
>
> *What exactly is* service? *How much service is there? What kind of service? I always heard about those departmental obligations, but nobody actually tells you what those are or what you are going to do before you actually get in there. And plus, each department and each place are different. If I were to compare our department to somebody else's department there would be a whole different set of things to consider.* —Michael

Universities function as well as they do in large part because of faculty service. Faculty serve their department, college, campus, and community in ways that foster the mission of the university and show commitment to students and the profession. Each campus and each department have different expectations, but all expect some level of service. We are all expected to be good citizens of the institution.

In this chapter, we explore the nature of faculty service. Service takes place at multiple levels inside and outside the institution. After exploring types of service, we examine ways to chart your own course as an academic citizen, navigating the complexities of making choices and doing the right level of service. We also discuss what you can gain personally and professionally from the experience. Notice that this chapter is one of our briefest. By no means do we intend this as a reflection on the importance of service in faculty work. The brevity is simply because what we have to say is, we think, fairly straightforward.

Types of Service

The wide variety of service opportunities ranges from serving your department to your campus and your local community to your profession or discipline. Service to your department and campus can take place at multiple levels, from as small as a program or specialty area to the institution as a whole. Service to the profession and community takes place more broadly, through associations, accreditation work, and engagement in the surrounding community.

Campus Service

Service to your institution or campus takes place at multiple levels over your career. However, the typical faculty member's journey for service starts locally, at the department level, and expands from there. Your early department service might include activities like course development, student advising (sometimes part of your instructional load), or helping to organize colloquia. Over time, as you get more established, you are likely to be elected to committees (faculty governance), asked to serve as a coordinator for a multisection course, or get involved in curriculum development. It makes sense for your first meaningful campus service to take place at the department level. This is your academic home, where people know you best and where you are most comfortable with content and colleagues.

With time and experience, however, your service expands. For example, perhaps you join the college curriculum committee or volunteer for an important campus task force. Maybe you are elected to the campus general education committee that oversees that critical component of undergraduate education. When these broader involvements happen is up to you as well as the norms in your college; sometimes faculty start getting involved in service during their pretenure years, while other times they are protected from campus- and even college-level service until after tenure. That said, be careful about taking on too much service too quickly, and be thoughtful about which service commitments you accept. In Inset 8.2, Michael speaks to how he sees service as a way to be involved and get to know colleagues.

Depending on your campus and discipline, you may be expected to provide service that links the campus and the local community—perhaps finding industry internships for students, providing professional learning opportunities for the community, or teaching service-learning courses that have a community engagement component. These sorts

> **Inset 8.2.**
> **Words From Early Career Faculty: Service as a Way to Become Involved on Campus**
>
> *One of the best things about campus life is that you have the chance to be as individualized as you want to be or you can be part of a group as much as you want to. I know a lot of people hate committees, like their own little thing, work on their own grants, their own projects, or whatever, and that's good for them. I like to serve. What's better for more people at the same time? What can I contribute to more people?* —Michael

of activities and relationships take some time to cultivate. Do not be shy about asking more seasoned faculty to help make introductions or recommend people whom you should meet. Our experience is that these activities are rewarding and enhance your courses or programs while providing good opportunities for students.

Service is part of being a good colleague and citizen, and pulling your weight is important. The work needs to be done, and you can earn goodwill and make a positive difference by serving. The work furthers the mission of the university. In fact, a question you can ask yourself as you sit on a committee is "How does this committee's efforts help students learn, graduate, become engaged, and so on?" Some work helps keep the lights on, but even that can trace back to serving students. Think about the type of colleague you want to have and want to be to help you make some of your service decisions.

Service to the Profession and the Community

In time, you also engage in service to your discipline and the profession via professional organizations. You may choose initially to do nothing more than pay your dues, attend conferences, and write for journals, but eventually you will probably do something else to support the profession. You might be on a conference committee, help review proposals or manuscripts, serve on a standing committee, or run for a board position. You might, after you have been promoted, serve as an external reviewer for someone's RTP file or on review teams that are part of the collegial process of accreditation for academic programs. We noted earlier that campuses function because of the volunteers who run them; the same is true for professional organizations, which have few paid staff. Volunteer contributions keep the organization alive. In addition to meeting more people, you learn about their work, get new ideas, and feel more passionate about your contributions because you are helping your field directly.

Service to your community is another dimension of faculty work. Perhaps most common in the professions—for example, education, social work, and nursing—faculty lend their expertise and knowledge to the broader community through this work. Service to the community might mean giving interviews to the press, consulting with government agencies on policy, or commenting for news programs; for instance, think of historians who appear on television to comment on elections or big moments in history. However, community service might entail a longer-term commitment such as developing new programs to support teachers helping students learn to read. This kind of service can be immensely rewarding and benefit you, your campus, and the community.

Charting Your Course for Service

As an early career faculty member, you should not venture too far into service commitments until your teaching and scholarly life are in hand. The work you do for service can be incredibly rewarding, but it can also take a great deal of time and energy. As James points out in Inset 8.3, doing too much service too soon can affect your other work. Of the three traditional roles for faculty, service is the least valued on most campuses when it comes to tenure decisions. As a result, our advice would be to start slowly and do so in ways that help you get involved incrementally.

As you might have inferred already, we recommend that you start close to home—in your department—and be a little selfish. Look for synergies between your service work and other areas of work to benefit both you and the department to support your professional journey. For example, you might agree to coordinate curriculum revision or course oversight for a class you teach. Although there may be a high workload associated with this task, there is also a direct benefit to you as you teach the course. In fact, some of the work you do for the revision or oversight might be work you would have to do anyway as the course's instructor. Or you may coordinate and help organize the department's seminar or colloquium series. This certainly takes time, but it also allows you to make connections with area scholars and get known in the area, and the service may even earn you an invitation to another campus to present your research. If you use lots of technology in your teaching, consider getting involved with the academic technology committee. Alternatively, you might want to serve on a committee that meets once or twice, completes a task, and is done. While perhaps less

Inset 8.3.
Words From Early Career Faculty: Being Judicious With Service

I wouldn't mind doing more service, but I'm fine with the service that I do. It seems like a lot of these committees meet [just] to meet. I think that some make important decisions that affect both faculty and students, so I don't think that decisions they make should be taken lightly. I don't feel like I know enough or have been in the university long enough to have the historical knowledge I would need in order to contribute to these communities. So, I'm an alternate for something—who knows if I'll get on? I'll just keep putting my name in the hat and see how that goes. —Sarah

So a colleague of mine has had difficulty with the tenure process and essentially did way too much service. He liked service and finds a lot of value in it but was clearly punished for that because it affected the other things he did. —James

synergistic with other work, such service allows you to contribute but in a clearly defined way.

Be wary throughout your pretenure years of getting elected or appointed to committees such as budget or policy that require institutional knowledge. For one, you are less able to contribute to this sort of committee; for example, you cannot be a good member of the Nominating Committee if you do not know anyone on campus. Moreover, such committees may also be politically charged and not a good place for an untenured faculty member. You may not want to be on the committee that decides how university resources should be allocated before you understand how the campus works and whose toes you are stepping on to make financial decisions. It also seems obvious that, prior to getting tenure, you might not want to be making policy decisions that your senior colleagues do not like. We would hope your colleagues would not let that affect their judgments about you, but better to avoid being put in that situation. We had one colleague who, we think unwisely, chaired a department curriculum committee during a controversial proposal. Her service alienated colleagues and required so much time that her other work suffered. Consult with your chair or a more senior mentor to make smart decisions about committee service.

Keeping track of service beyond noting committees and dates can be hard, but you want to start thinking about this early as you consider your RTP file. One suggestion is to track the outputs of the committee's work to which you contributed. For example, if you are reviewing faculty proposals for mini-grants or summer research money, note the number of applications reviewed. If your committee produced a white paper to which you contributed, note that and keep a copy of the paper for your file. If you served on a search committee, list the person hired in your notes so that you can include comments in your RTP narrative; you may also want to note the number of applicants and describe the work involved in the search process, such as presentations, interviews, and meals. Jot down the data and information associated with service work as it happens rather than trying to resurrect them at a later point. You may not need it, but it is easy enough to list in an RTP file you should keep updated, as discussed in Chapter 9.

Finding the right service balance takes time. As you become more comfortable in your role as a faculty member, you are able and expected to take on more service duties. There is widespread recognition that new faculty should initially focus on establishing teaching and scholarship. Some campuses go so far as to actively protect untenured faculty from engaging in too much service.

That said, you may find that you really enjoy service. You not only are at the table to make decisions and move the mission of the university forward but also get to meet colleagues from across campus. In addition to helping shape policy or be part of the decision-making team, you learn about your institution and gain insights as to how your campus functions (Royles, 2014a), which can be helpful in both the long and short term. If you find yourself enjoying service, do your best to select activities that overlap or positively impact your instructional activities or scholarship; find the sweet spot. Spending lots of time on service means you are spending less time on those other areas, so get more bang for the buck and have your service provide new lecture material or be fodder for a grant, project, or article.

What Happens If You Find Yourself Doing Too Much Service?

If you find yourself doing too much service or always being asked to serve on committees and task forces, you need to ask yourself the following questions: Do you enjoy the service and is it something you want to do? Can you manage that level of service and still do what is needed for teaching and scholarship? If you answered "no" to either of these questions, you need to find ways to decline the service offers politely and figure out which service opportunities are ones you should select and which you should decline. Some tips are as follows:

- *Talk to your chair.* If you have too many offers, ask for help deciding which are worth your time and effort, and how to decline or step away from others.
- *Think about your own identity and how it may affect the service choices you make.* There may be committees or tasks that are personally or professionally meaningful to you, which should factor into your decision making. Chapter 13 provides more insight about integrating your identity with your professional life.
- *Consider why you are always being asked to serve.* Are you one of those people who says yes to everything, so you are an easy ask? Do you have good leadership or organizational skills that people on committees value? Are you a good worker, such that people know that if you are tasked with something, it will actually get done? Is your identity an added bonus for the committee and the members were looking for someone like you (female engineer, Latinx accountant, LGBT journalist)? Do you have good interpersonal skills that enable you to bring together warring factions? Just because you are what the nominating committee is looking for does not obligate you to serve. But if you think you have something to offer, consider your role and how much you can commit to the work.

Why Do Service?

You might walk away from this chapter with the notion that service does not count that much for tenure decisions; it takes time away from teaching, research, and scholarly endeavors; and it can be time-consuming and work-generating. So why would anyone actually want to do service? Allow us to explain.

For many of us, service is personally and professionally rewarding. Here are some of the good things about service.

- *Have a voice.* You get to be at the table when big decisions are made; you help chart the course for your department, college, or university.
- *Be known.* It is often through service that we build the positive professional relationships we discuss in Chapter 4. People need to know who you are, build trust and respect in you, and know that you can be counted on. Serving your academic community is a key way to become known and nurture those relationships for your long-term success.
- *Build your network.* Life as a faculty member can be isolating or lonely. On campus, working with people on a committee for a shared purpose is a nice break from working alone in your office. Within your discipline, you have the opportunity to create a network of colleagues across the state and nation that is helpful when you need collaborators for grants or projects or need to see syllabi for a new course you are developing. Additionally, many faculty find mentors via their service, as you are put into working contact with others from across a spectrum of disciplines and experiences.
- *Gain satisfaction and value.* Some service work just makes us feel good, and that may be motivation enough. We often receive public recognition for our work in the community or professional organizations while most of our daily work does not garner any. Minoritized faculty report that race-related work provides great personal benefit and can bring a sense of community they may not otherwise have on a predominantly White campus (Baez, 2000). What we as faculty contribute through service is unique and is of value to the committees on which we serve and the institution. The committee benefits and you feel valued for what you add.
- *Be a team player and good citizen.* As we noted at the start of the chapter, without faculty doing service, much of the academic work of the university would not take place. Service is a way to pitch in. The work needs to be done, and you want to be doing your part (Misra, Lundquist, Holmes, & Agiomavritis, 2011). Doing so can earn you

the appreciation, respect, and goodwill of your colleagues, which can pay off in other ways in the future.

- *You support students.* For many of us, working with students is one of the most appealing parts of the job. Advising and mentoring students is rewarding as we watch them mature and flourish. Advising and mentoring, however, take a great deal of time. If we wanted to do only research, we could do that in a venue other than a university. The process of supporting students through our service is fulfilling and something on which we enjoy spending time, but there is a caveat if you find yourself doing too much advising/mentoring or other race-, gender-, or identity-based service. Faculty in a department who are one of a kind or one of a few of a particular race, gender, or other characteristic often find themselves as de facto advisers or mentors to students of like identity. If you find yourself in this position, keep track of the data. Names, dates, and some brief comments about the interactions can be powerful information to bring to your chair or administrator to request that you are compensated for the time. You are providing an important service for students, but you need to be sure that you are not doing so in a way that disadvantages your ability to stay at that institutions as a faculty member to provide this sort of service and support long term. If this advising and mentoring load is large enough, you may be able to get some units for the task (i.e., release from a course) or you may be able to get the department to recognize this as your service contribution during reappointment and tenure decisions. The data you collect help in this regard.

Concluding Thoughts

The world of service, or academic citizenship, is far more varied and complicated than most early career faculty are aware of when stepping into their role and something they are generally not well-prepared for during graduate studies. We hope we have conveyed our sense that service is not just an obligation; it can be professionally enriching as well. Faculty often find synergies between their teaching or research interests and providing service at various levels. While you need to be cautious about double-dipping—counting the same activity twice, a topic we address in Chapter 9—service that aligns with other aspects of your career and self goes a long way to helping you navigate your self-authored career path and can make for a compelling story in your RTP narrative.

Done without intentionality, service can be time-consuming, interfere with our other faculty work, and strain our collegial relationships. When done well and thoughtfully, though, service can be a professionally enriching experience that helps us to learn about and make substantive contributions to our institution as well as build a vibrant professional network on and off campus. Service can be a way to live and enact those professional commitments that O'Meara and colleagues (2008) discuss.

Exercises

Following are some exercises that might be useful to you in building your knowledge and skills regarding service.

1. Take a colleague to lunch or coffee and ask the following:
   - What are some of the most important committees in the department? The school or college? The university?
   - What committees have some of the highest workloads? Lowest workloads?
   - How did you get elected to your first committee?
2. Learn about your institution's committee structure (this information can often be found in by-laws or constitutions on faculty governance websites).
   - What are the committees in the department, school or college, and university?
   - What is the charge or purpose of each committee?
   - On what committees can untenured faculty serve?
   - When is the schedule to be elected to committees?
3. Identify one or two department committees on which you might want to serve. Contact the chair and ask if you can observe a meeting. (These meetings are usually open. They might be surprised to have someone interested in observing, but it will show them you are doing your homework.)

Goal-Setting Activity: Shaping Your Career as an Academic Citizen

Here we provide a step-by-step process for you to start thinking about the kinds of things you might want to accomplish as a citizen during the next several years of your career.

1. Brainstorm several goals or things you would like to learn or accomplish as an academic citizen in the next three to five years.
2. Try to arrange those goals in some kind of order. For instance, does one lead to another, or could one be accomplished in a year or so while another goal might take two to three years to accomplish?

3. Now for each goal, ask the following:
   - What are some challenges I might encounter in reaching that goal?
   - What resources (e.g., people, information, skills) do I have access to that will help me reach that goal?
   - What specific steps will I take, and by when, to reach that goal?

You might consider using a chart like Table 8.1 to help you think about these questions. We've used the first row to give you an example.

TABLE 8.1
Shaping Your Career as an Academic Citizen

Goal	Challenges I Might Encounter	Resources I Have	Steps I Will Take and by When	Accomplished? When?
1. Identify one committee to serve on at department level	• *Lack of knowledge of committee structure* • *Not known by colleagues, so may not be elected* • *Committee work might take too much time*	• *Department chair* • *More senior faculty in department* • *Website with constitution, bylaws*	• *Talk with others to identify appropriate committees, workload* • *Observe at least one committee meeting* • *Be visible so that colleagues know me*	
2.				
3.				
4.				
5.				

Some other goals you might consider for service include

- being elected to at least one committee before retention review,
- finding one opportunity to demonstrate some leadership (e.g., chair a low-intensity committee or a short-term task force), and
- identifying service opportunities that support the community and that seem interesting and aligned with other aspects of your professional life (e.g., the local community, your professional community).

PART THREE

NAVIGATING CHALLENGES AND CREATING YOUR SWEET SPOT

9

MAKING YOUR CASE
AND THRIVING IN THE
RETENTION, PROMOTION,
AND TENURE PROCESS

Being evaluated is a constant feature of academic life. Our students evaluate our teaching, letting us know if we are successful in helping them learn. Professional peers judge grant proposals, manuscripts, and other scholarly and creative products that shape the direction and impact of our work. Our campus colleagues evaluate our overall performance for retention, tenure, or promotion. This last example is the most significant evaluation process as our jobs hang in the balance.

The RTP process, which we described in Chapter 3, is remarkably similar across campuses. The details about how the process works (i.e., timeline, what counts for evidence, process of evaluation) may vary, but the goal of the process is similar in that you are required to make the case that you have successfully met the institution's expectations for a productive, contributing faculty member. Most campuses have a tenure track for their faculty, although some campuses do not.

In this chapter we demystify the RTP process. We describe the types of reviews and the typical review process, and we offer suggestions for how to put together and maintain a file that showcases your work. At the end of the chapter we address some common RTP-related questions and give you suggestions for how to survive the process. All of this evaluation and review is something you can manage; it ought not dictate your life or make you run from the profession.

Understanding the RTP Process on Your Campus

Earning tenure is a multiyear process, and your institution is making a multimillion-dollar investment when it awards tenure. As you start your

155

faculty career, you want to learn how the review process works on your campus. There are two major aspects. First is the timeline for the submission and review of your documentation. Second are the criteria by which you will be judged. While not a checklist, the criteria indicate the sorts of things you need to achieve by the time you submit your file. Many times we focus solely on the criteria as they can be viewed somewhat like a to-do list, and checking off items brings us comfort. Losing track of the timeline, however, can have dire consequences, so be mindful of both.

RTP Timeline

The review process includes two different types of reviews: formative, check-in reviews and summative, decision points. Some universities also require you during your first or second year to write a professional development plan covering goals for your first six years. In addition to helping you chart out milestones for scholarly and creative work, grant submissions, and teaching and service obligations, you can create your own timeline to keep you on track for earning tenure. (If your campus does not require you to do this, make yourself do it.) You should also receive some general feedback on this plan to ensure that you are on the right track.

Early career faculty have multiple formative reviews. In many cases, the required documentation for these evaluations is less onerous than for the summative reviews. You might submit an updated CV and short narrative without any of the artifacts to back up your claims. Alternatively, you might submit artifacts associated with the past year or review period. No employment decisions are made as a result of these reviews, but they are important because of the feedback you receive. The committees reviewing your file during these lower-stakes reviews should comment on your progress toward meeting tenure expectations and give you guidance on what to do to be successful.

Your summative reviews will likely come in year three (retention or reappointment) and year six (tenure and promotion).[1] Year three will likely bring a reappointment decision—whether to retain you and for how many years—while year six typically involves tenure and promotion decisions. At each summative stage you submit a file, usually much more extensive than for formative reviews, and your file is reviewed—including, in some cases, by scholars external to your campus. The reappointment or retention review is followed by additional formative assessment reviews before the tenure and promotion decision. If you have been awarded service credit, your timeline will be compressed. Service credit is time served in other positions that is applied to your tenure clock, with products developed during that time counting toward tenure. For instance, you might negotiate one year of service credit for a prior position. Another factor that will influence your timeline is if you opt to temporarily stop the tenure clock. Inset 9.1 shares some ideas about when and why you might want to pause your tenure clock.

Some of you may decide that you would like to apply for tenure and promotion earlier than required. Inset 9.2 will help you weigh this decision. While tempting to want the promotion, prestige, and pay raise that come with early tenure, the stakes are high and you should be thoughtful when making that decision.

For formative and summative evaluations you receive feedback from each committee level of review. Depending on the type of review, the feedback comes from department, college, and university committees; your chair; the dean; and even the provost or president. Bring the feedback home and read it over a cup of tea or glass of wine. You likely need to sign the report indicating that you have received and read it, although your signature does not mean you agree with it—only that you have read it. The information you receive from the reviews leading up to tenure or promotion should influence what you do moving forward and what you write about in later reviews. We share how to use the information in future reviews when we write about constructing your file.

Inset 9.1.
Strategies for Success:
Should You Stop the Tenure Clock?
Most campuses have policies that allow you to stop or adjust your tenure clock if circumstances impact your productivity. Perhaps your building is being torn down, your lab moved, and you are sharing an office temporarily. Or perhaps you must care for a child or parent. Maternity and paternity leaves give time off from classes, but you may opt to formally stop the clock for this as well.

Findings about stopping the clock conflict (Williams & Lee, 2016). Pausing the tenure clock means you are delaying potential salary increases, but it may also be a requirement if there are issues outside your control that will prevent you from being productive. Consider the pros and cons, and explore your options with trusted colleagues and senior administrators.

Inset 9.2.
Strategies for Success:
Should I Apply for Early Tenure?
Typically, the people considering early tenure are strong candidates. They have demonstrated early on that they are productive and successful at meeting campus expectations for faculty. They likely have met the requirements for tenure ahead of schedule; the lure of a pay bump coupled with a desire to be granted early tenure can be strong. These colleagues would likely sail through the tenure and promotion process when

(*continues*)

Inset 9.2. (*Continued*)

applying at the normal time. However, the expectations for early tenure and promotion are significantly higher on most campuses. So while they would easily get tenure at year six, they may not get tenure early.

People may know this and convince themselves that they will be okay if they do not get early tenure because they will just apply again later. Many, however, are kidding themselves. In our experience, those who do not get early tenure are disappointed and angry, which often ends up badly for the candidate and the university. A candidate who was really strong and on the path to an exciting career ends up unhappy and may look elsewhere for employment.

Know yourself. Can you honestly say you will not be upset if you do not get early tenure? If so and you believe you have met the higher expectations for early tenure, go for it. If you think you will be upset if you do not get tenure, wait.

As you consider applying for early tenure, talk to a mentor, department chair, or someone who has served on the RTP committee and knows your file well. Do not take advice from colleagues who do not know the full scope of your file. The friend who likes you but has not seen your CV is not the right person to ask. Even getting encouragement from your chair or mentor is no guarantee that you will get early promotion and tenure. Approach this decision with care.

On rare occasions, you may feel the need to respond to comments or statements in the reports that are not accurate or with which you disagree. There should be a clear process by which you can respond to or rebut claims made in the various reports along the way. We will share strategies for how to do this at the end of the chapter; at this point we want simply to point out that there should be a clearly articulated process for doing so that you can review.

RTP Criteria and Expectations

You should know as much as you can about the evaluation process. First, read and review RTP policy documents on your campus to understand the formal written guidelines and criteria. Second, consult with your colleagues about their understanding of and experiences with the RTP process.

RTP Guidelines and Policy Documents

The RTP criteria and process should be spelled out in department-, college-, and university-level RTP policy documents. These documents represent a contract between you and the institution, laying out what you are expected to do in order to get tenure and promotion. The criteria are not meant to be a surprise. The document's level of specificity varies from department to department and campus to campus. The intent, however, is for you to be evaluated objectively on the evidence you provide demonstrating that you have met the standards of performance in your assigned duties and scholarly and creative endeavors. Knowing what is expected of you helps you plan your first six years as a faculty member. Review the RTP policy and document *before* you accept a job offer.

The tenure and promotion guidelines on most campuses are public, and the process should be transparent. That said, faculty of color are much less satisfied than White faculty regarding the clarity

> **Inset 9.3.**
> **Strategies for Success:**
> **Tips for Understanding RTP Process and Expectations**
>
> 1. Read the policy.
> 2. Talk with senior colleagues, members of the department, or the college RTP committee.
> 3. Talk with recently tenured colleagues and those just ahead of you in the pipeline.
> 4. Understand your role in the documentation and recommendations for external reviewers.
> 5. Be aware of timelines.

of tenure expectations (Trower & Bleak, 2004), and early career faculty as a whole are often frustrated at what they consider ambiguous or unclear tenure expectations (Austin & Rice, 1998). Inset 9.3 has some overarching tips for understanding the process.

RTP documents have guidelines for instructionally related activities, scholarship, and service. *Pay attention to all three areas.* While we urge you to craft your own career trajectory, do not ignore this document. Just as the timeline for the review process impacts when you might need to accomplish certain tasks, the requirements themselves can help you prioritize activities and efforts. Here are just a few examples of ways in which deep knowledge of RTP criteria and expectations can help you be strategic:

- Suppose you need to publish four peer-reviewed articles to get tenure. Those articles need to be submitted in sufficient time that they can be reviewed, revised, resubmitted, and perhaps even printed by the time you submit your file for tenure. If your campus requires external evaluation of your file, the deadlines for submitting manuscripts will likely be compressed, because those articles need to be sent to external reviewers. You must plan with this information in mind.
- If your department RTP guidelines indicate that you must publish a book to be tenured, with peer-reviewed articles as enhancements to the file, then you know you must spend time working toward a book contract and release.

Inset 9.4.
Words From Early Career Faculty: Being Strategic About Earning Tenure

I need to be more strategic about my own research. . . . We have two categories. So you have to have three in a peer-reviewed journal and then there's this whole other set of categories where it needs to be a [peer-reviewed] book chapter. . . . I'll be able to write and say, "Look here are the categories you set and I did all of these things. I also did other stuff, too, but I did at least the bare minimum in every single category and in some categories I exceed the expectation."—Sarah

I'm prioritizing one set of data that's kind of frustrating to work with because a student helped generate the data so I can honestly put their name on the paper [a requirement for tenure in the department]. —Carl

Having a well-thought-through plan also helps keep you focused. You will be asked to serve on committees, invited to collaborate on grants and projects, asked to participate in outreach activities, and more. The opportunities might be wonderful and career enhancing; however, if they do not align with *your* career plan, they may pull you away from your goals and keep you from doing the work you must do in order to keep your job. Sarah's and Carl's comments in Inset 9.4 show how they strategically used the RTP document to decide what sorts of activities to focus on next. After meeting criteria for having one or more book chapters published, Sarah shifted her emphasis to meet the criteria in another area. Carl, knowing he needed to have papers coauthored with students, spent time on that data set even though other data were easier to work with. Having a plan kept them both focused and gave Sarah permission to say no in a thoughtful way to things like an invitation to coauthor another book chapter.

As we noted in Chapter 1, knowing institutional context is crucial to deciphering expectations. Minimum expectations for tenure and promotion vary across institution types. Knowing what is expected of you helps you plan your first six years as a faculty member. If you are at a research-intensive university, expectations for scholarly outputs are greater than if you are at a teaching-intensive university (Inset 6.2 and Table 6.1 can help you determine scholarly expectations). The emphasis placed on service varies by campus and department as well. Additionally, the level of specificity in the document detailing what is required to earn tenure varies from department to department and campus to campus. The intent, however, is for you to be evaluated objectively on the evidence you provide demonstrating you have met the standards of performance in your assigned duties and scholarly and creative endeavors. A careful reading of the RTP document can help guide you.

Recognize also that, whatever the institution, people are rarely promoted and granted tenure for their outstanding service contributions. The balance between teaching and scholarship is unique to each campus, but you need to meet minimal standards in both to get tenure. If it is a choice between getting an article or grant submitted and serving on a time-consuming committee, the scholarly work is probably a better choice.

Uncovering Unwritten Expectations: Talking With Your Colleagues

Almost as important as what is written in the RTP guidelines is what is not written. Some of this ambiguity is understandable—you cannot put every detail in a document—but some of it is driven by the personal inclinations of senior faculty or administrators or the slow ramping up of expectations over time. While the ambiguity is not ideal, and is frustrating for many early career faculty, it may be the situation within which you must work.

In addition to reading the document, you also need to gauge the culture of your department and campus; this is where talking with your colleagues can be invaluable. As you think about who to talk with, we recommend respected senior colleagues in your department, colleagues who have recently served on RTP committees, and department colleagues who are slightly ahead of you in the RTP process. Colleagues outside your department, college, or school are generally less useful as expectations may vary considerably. Senior colleagues who have not served on an RTP committee and who received tenure long ago are also less useful as they are less likely to be familiar with current expectations, as Carl alludes to in Inset 9.5.

Talk with a variety of people. Pick their brains about what counts, what is important, and where you can best put your energy. However, take all suggestions with a grain of salt. Your faculty colleagues do not know your entire story nor your complete file. When they compliment you and say you are a slam dunk for earning tenure, they do so with good intentions and incomplete information. While nice to hear, it may not be

> **Inset 9.5.**
> **Words From Early Career Faculty: Changing Expectations**
>
> *The younger faculty are thinking that this should be more like a research university where research is prioritized. And then my understanding is that a lot of the much older faculty think teaching is the most important role. Apparently, there is this big cultural change in this department now; whereas previously all the thought had been on teaching, and now it's like you're shifting more toward research.*
> —Carl

reliable feedback. Therefore, talk with them, listen to them, but corroborate your understanding by asking lots of colleagues in your department, including your department chair.

In Chapters 5, 6, and 8 we offered suggestions for uncovering unspoken expectations related to teaching, research, and service. Here are some examples of questions that might not be addressed explicitly in the RTP policy but could have some bearing on your experience:

- If peer-reviewed research articles are required, must one (or more) be in a certain type of journal, or is *any* peer-reviewed publication acceptable?
- Must you be sole author on articles? If you collaborate, how important is lead authorship?
- Should you be coauthoring with students?
- How acceptable are online publications?
- Should you be using data collected in your current position rather than in a graduate student or postdoc role?
- Must your instructor evaluation ratings be excellent, merely close to the department mean, or show growth over time?
- Is experimenting with new pedagogies and strategies in your courses encouraged, or should you be more conservative before tenure?
- Where should you focus your service for retention and, after that, for promotion and tenure? Do you need service at all three levels?
- How is consulting work reported and counted?

Then chart your own course. Remember that *only you are responsible for your career*. A scary thought? Perhaps. But also a great opportunity and presumably part of the reason you pursued a faculty career.

The RTP Process and Players

Each time you submit your RTP file, it goes through multiple levels of review. To begin the process, your file is usually read by tenured colleagues in your department or college. If your campus uses external reviewers, your scholarly work is reviewed by colleagues in the field at this level as well (more about that later). Figure 9.1 outlines the typical levels of review for a file going through a summative (reappointment/tenure) review. Note that some levels may not be present on every campus, and you do not necessarily go through all levels every year; the most thorough process is for your reappointment/retention and tenure reviews. At all points along the process, the RTP guidelines inform the ultimate recommendation that reviewers make.

Figure 9.1. A typical RTP file's journey.

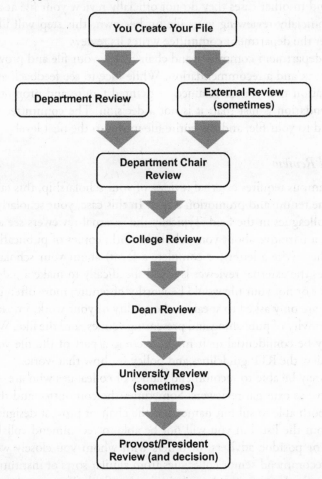

Department-Level Review

The first level of review, by department colleagues, is usually the most important as the people at this level are closest to your field. Higher levels of review take these first reviews seriously because of this proximity. While you may be engaged in a unique line of inquiry within your department, the colleagues at this level are most likely to understand the jargon and language of your field. They are also closest in terms of knowing about the courses you teach and service you perform. They are the reviewers with the most intimate knowledge of you, your field, and your department's RTP policy.

Department chairs play multiple roles in your professional life, and they might be required to review your file. Sometimes department chairs serve on the department RTP committee, sometimes they write an independent review, and in other cases they do not officially review your file at all. If the chair is officially reviewing your file on her own, this step will likely take place after the department committee writes its review.

The department committee and chair review your file and provide written feedback and a recommendation. While nice to see feedback and a recommendation that you be retained or granted tenure and promotion, that recommendation is just that; it is not a decision. The committee feedback gets added to your file, and the entire file moves to the next level.

External Review

If your campus requires external reviews of your scholarship, this takes place only at the tenure and promotion stages. In this case, your scholarly work is sent to colleagues in the field. Typically the external reviewers see a copy of your CV, a narrative about your scholarly work, copies of publications, and so on. They write a letter (or complete a form) about your scholarship. In some cases the external reviewer is asked specifically to make a judgment as to whether or not your file would be worthy of tenure; more often than not, reviewers are only asked to speak to the quality of your work, impact on the field, selectivity of publishing and presenting venues, and the like. What they write may be confidential or it might become a part of the file you get to read. Review the RTP guidelines and policy for how that works.

You may be able to recommend names of colleagues who are appropriate to serve as external reviewers. Sometimes the committee and the candidate are both able to submit names and the chair or provost designee selects names from the list, but you will not be able to recommend collaborators, graduate or postdoc advisers, or others with whom you closely work. You want to recommend senior colleagues from similar sorts of institutions who have recognized expertise or knowledge in your field. (You may also get to list people who should not be sent the file.)

A point to keep in mind: If your campus utilizes external evaluators or you request external evaluators, your file needs to be completed earlier than if you are not having external evaluation. Files are typically sent for external review in spring of year 5, while your file goes through the on-campus review process fall of year 6. Pay attention to the deadlines!

College-Level Review

The next level of review is usually a college committee. This committee comprises tenured colleagues—typically full professors—from across departments in your college. You will have at most one person from your department serving on this committee; in larger colleges, probably no members of your department will be serving on this committee. The college committee reads your file and reports from earlier reviews. The committee then composes its own response and adds another recommendation to your file. The committee's job is not to rubberstamp earlier reviews; rather it is to conduct another level of review.

Dean Review and Beyond

Next the file goes to your dean. The dean also reads, reviews, and recommends. At some universities your file then goes to a university-level review before finally going to a senior administrator on your campus. Then either the provost or president reads the file and all the reports and recommendations from earlier levels of review. This decision is the one that ultimately matters. When the provost or president recommends reappointment or tenure and promotion, you can celebrate.

Updating Your File While Under Review

Your accomplishments may change while people are reviewing your file. For example, you might have listed an article as *in review* on your CV and be pleased to get a letter from the journal noting that it has been accepted. Your campus or department RTP policy probably addresses the question of adding information to the file after it has been submitted. Be sure you understand the policy and whether, if ever, you are allowed to add something to your file.

Often, if something is added, the file must go back to the beginning and start its way back through the process, which means extra work and time for all levels of review. We do not say that to dissuade you from adding to the file, but we might suggest you only consider trying to add to the file if it makes a big difference. If this happens during a formative review (as opposed to reappointment or promotion/tenure), it is likely not worth adding the letter noting journal acceptance, for example; you will have the opportunity to add to your file during your next review. If it is a summative review and could make the difference between meeting expectations or not, then you likely want to try adding it. If you have already far exceeded expectations for scholarly and creative work, you may opt not to add the letter at this point; you can save this letter for your next review—promotion to professor!

While going through this process, you naturally want to read the tea leaves, so to speak. What can you glean from the recommendations at various levels? Obviously, if you get positive recommendations at the department, college, and dean levels, you will likely have a positive recommendation from the provost. Similarly, if you receive consistently negative reports and recommendations as your file goes up the chain of review, the provost will not be likely to overturn that decision and grant you tenure. Having conflicting recommendations at different levels is more complicated. In this case, predicting the final decision can be difficult.

Documenting Your Career: Creating Your File

In this section we address strategies for assembling your file for reappointment, tenure, or promotion; the more formative reviews we described earlier are far less involved.

The typical file includes a copy of your CV, a narrative, and documents providing evidence of your accomplishments in the three areas of faculty work: instructionally related activities (teaching), research and scholarship, and service. These three components of the file should be tightly integrated to tell a compelling story about your accomplishments.

For some of us, the idea of putting together a file of our accomplishments feels like bragging and is an uncomfortable task. Doing so may even bring forward the feelings of being an imposter that we discussed in Chapter 2: you may feel like the accomplishments you describe are not really yours, that others will not believe you, or that what you did will not be good enough. Others of us might not trust the process. These feelings may cause us to document every single thing we have done in our professional life, resulting in an unbearably large file. Such a file taxes us and the committees that review it and can result in high-quality work getting lost in the mix with less valuable efforts and contributions. We encourage you to fight that temptation. Build a file that shows your best work.

CV

Your CV is like the overview or broad catalogue of your accomplishments in your current and perhaps prior roles. You should be updating it often, so it should take little energy at this stage to include it in your file. Your campus may ask you to make it clear on your CV which activities were completed during the review period (e.g., since you arrived on campus or during the last three years). Even if it is not a requirement, clearly delineating the entries under review is helpful to your review committee and helps decrease the impression that you are trying to get credit for things that are not covered in the current review period.

Narrative

Your RTP narrative is your chance to tell your professional story. The narrative provides the readers with an understanding of your professional work that a CV alone cannot do. In Chapters 5, 6, and 8, we talked about your teaching philosophy, scholarly and creative agenda, and service. You write about all three of these areas in your narrative. Here you explain how and why you made the professional decisions you have, how your line of inquiry fits into the broader discipline, and how you are crafting your career—that is, you should show reviewers that you have a scholarly agenda or research agenda. As you lay out your story, the committee can see that you have an overall plan as a teacher or that you are doing more than just cranking out the required number of papers or projects in a haphazard fashion that might end as soon as you are granted tenure. A good narrative tells a story and shows the reviewers how you are thoughtfully crafting your career even as you lay out the case for meeting their expectations for tenure and life beyond it.

Your narrative should be written for intelligent readers, but not filled with jargon or insider language. Remember that most of your readers will be outside of your discipline, so you probably need to educate your colleagues via the narrative. You may be the only medieval historian or biomechanical engineer in the department. Part of your task when writing your narrative will be to position your accomplishments within a larger context (e.g., what unique contributions you are making in the scholarship, why you are selecting particular pedagogies), hence the need to provide some background information to situate your work. There may be page limits on this narrative, so know that you cannot write about everything. Whatever you write, however, should be tightly integrated with the exhibits you provide as evidence.

Writing the narrative is challenging. Some of us have a hard time tooting our own horns, fearing that we will come across as bragging or be outed as imposters. Our advice: Do not write about yourself; write about the work.

As you put together the narrative, pay attention to two documents. As noted earlier, the RTP guidelines are crucial. In addition, you should also look at the form the RTP committees must fill out after reviewing your file. Anything you can do to organize your narrative in ways that help the committee fill out their form, the better.

We encourage you to organize your narrative sections around the main categories by which you will be reviewed. For instance, you might have a section on instruction, with subsections related to teaching philosophy, approach and strategies, and student response—*if* these are categories as outlined in your RTP document or the committee's evaluation form. Structuring your narrative and your evidence files in this way helps you be organized and helps the reviewing committees with their work, which often leads to a much happier committee. If you have developed a multiyear plan for your goals (see Chapters 5, 6, and 8), it may serve as an organizer for how you structure the narrative and you can refer back to it as you describe your accomplishments.

Inset 9.6.
Strategies for Success:
Crafting a Compelling Narrative

- Make the document as easy to read and review as possible.
- Use language from the RTP document in your narrative to show how you have met requirements.
- Be aware of the template or format of feedback that the RTP committees are required to use. Then be sure that your narrative addresses all those areas, making it easy for the committee to evaluate your work.
- Text boxes, judicious use of bolding or italicizing, and graphics can make the document more readable.
- Explicitly refer to comments in past reviews and show how you have addressed earlier concerns.
- Use an appropriate font size and margin; white space is okay!

Inset 9.6 provides some pointers for crafting your narrative.

Using language from the RTP policy can also enable you to show how you have met certain criteria. For example, when writing about your scholarly efforts, you might say, "The department RTP document requires faculty to have three peer-reviewed articles and at least one conference paper/poster/ presentation every other year. In this past review period I have published four peer-reviewed articles and presented seven times."

In earlier chapters, we discuss creating the sweet spot where your faculty work categories overlap (see Figure 9.2). In your narrative, make the case for how different artifacts demonstrate your performance in instructionally related activities, scholarly and creative pursuits, or service.

Be transparent and make a case for how each component fits in a particular part of faculty work. While some activities might address two or three of the primary areas (e.g., a service-learning course fits into instructionally related activities and service), *you* need to decide if you want to use this as an example of your teaching efforts or service, or both, and then explain carefully. For example, in the case of a service-learning course, the teaching strategies and course structure are part of instruction and teaching, while the connections and outreach to the community might be service.

If you are using the same activity as evidence for both teaching and service, be sure to delineate how distinct aspects of the work fit each category. Do not try to count the same parts of the work for two different areas. You want to be efficient and find ways to describe synergies in your work, but you do not want to give the appearance of double-dipping. As James points out in Inset 9.7, you get to choose how to categorize the contribution (so long as you can defend it), so put it where you need it.

Figure 9.2. Integrating faculty work to create your sweet spot.

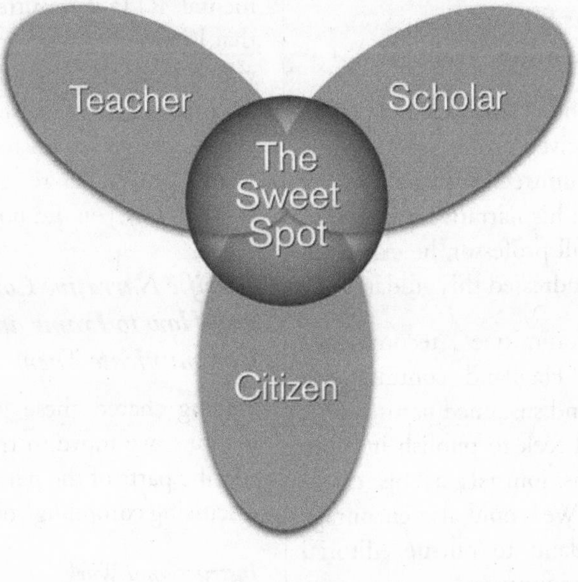

Do not feel compelled to write about every entry on your CV. Be selective. However, CV entries that you discuss in your narrative might need to be matched with artifacts in your file, so be intentional about this. Check with your colleagues and review the RTP document for expectations.

If the prior reviewing committees have done a good job, you will have received actionable feedback (e.g., do less service, adjust a particular aspect of teaching, get a publication that includes student coauthors, submit a grant proposal). Remember the advice we gave about looking at your teaching evaluations and not dwelling on the negative comments? The same sort of advice works here. Look at the things you are doing well and celebrate them.

Then, pause and look at the feedback that identifies areas for improvement. Inset 9.8 shows feedback Haviland received in his tenure review. It is in your best interest to respond to it both in action and in the narrative for your next review round. Doing so allows you to showcase how you have tried to improve. Be explicit about this. For example, you might say, "In

> **Inset 9.7.**
> **Words From Early Career Faculty: Strategically Crafting Your Narrative**
>
> *I had to meet with our department [RTP] committee ahead of time and I said, "Well, where is this going? Is this service? Is this research? If I'm not going to publish the data, is it service if I wrote a report for them?" . . . You can really choose whichever area you think it is.* —James

Inset 9.8.
Resources for Success:
RTP Committee Feedback

Here is some feedback that Haviland received from the college RTP committee during his tenure review. In his narrative for promotion to full professor, he explained how he addressed this guidance:

"The committee recommends that Dr. Haviland continue the focused and sustained nature of his work and seek to publish in more prestigious journals as his career matures. We would also encourage Dr. Haviland to pursue editorial journal assignments."

my third-year review the departmental RTP committee indicated that I needed to work more on providing feedback to students. I have attempted to do this by. . . ." If you choose not to act on recommendations from earlier reviews, make a case for why you did not.

Specific Narrative Components and How to Frame and Communicate Them

Having shared these general suggestions, we move to tips for more specific parts of the narrative before discussing compiling your evidence.

Instructional Work

In Chapter 5 we discussed articulating a teaching philosophy. Now, in the narrative, explicitly make the connection between your teaching philosophy and what you actually do in classes, how you plan for classes, and how you shape assessments and use assessment data to inform your practice. Consider addressing questions such as the following:

- How does your instructional philosophy impact your instructional decisions?
- What evidence do you have beyond a syllabus, course exams, end-of-course grade distributions, and student evaluations that showcase your accomplishments and growth as a teacher? You may consider providing samples of student work and the type of feedback you provide, so be sure to collect samples as you go along. (If you use student work samples, you may want to see what policies regarding the practice exist on campus. As a rule of thumb, it is nice to ask your class if they are comfortable allowing you to use copies of their work in your RTP file. We suggest asking the entire class and then selecting the samples you want, as opposed to asking individual students. This approach allows you the flexibility to showcase strong and weak students and the feedback you provide them to help them improve. We also recommend removing student names from the work samples.)

- What sorts of feedback do you provide to students? How do you know if it works?
- How are assessments aligned with the course's student learning outcomes, and how have you used assessment data to inform your practice?
- What sorts of professional learning opportunities related to teaching have you attended? What impact have they had?
- If your course has changed, can you document this via changes to syllabi and assignments? What is the rationale for those changes?
- Have you tried something new and had unfavorable results? Own it, talk about what you changed (and why), and explain what you are continuing to change to improve instruction.

Your faculty development center should also have resources relating to documenting instructional effectiveness that might be helpful to you.

Scholarly Work

Faculty are often challenged to document how they have met the requirements for scholarly and creative achievement. As we said in Chapter 6, it is up to *you* to explain your goals, trajectory, and the importance of your scholarly and creative work. It is in your best interest to provide clarification in your narrative whenever questions arise about a publishing venue or authorship. Online journals and open-access journals are increasingly prevalent. However, reviewers are unlikely to know which are peer-reviewed and high-quality or pay-to-publish sorts of journals of questionable merit; reviewers may be overly suspicious when, in fact, the journal is quite reputable. Gathering data such as impact factor, journal acceptance rates, and the like—and providing the sources of that information within your narrative—helps your reviewers make informed evaluations of your work.

If you collaborate with others, we suggest getting letters from coauthors indicating the levels of your contributions. This is imperative if all of your published work is multiauthored or the pieces you are citing as having met the minimum criteria are collaborative endeavors. The committee reviewing your file wants to know that you made a substantive contribution to the work. Letters from collaborators indicating your contributions (and theirs) help substantiate claims you make in your narrative.

STEM and lab-based fields often require that you publish with data gathered at your institution, not with postdoc or graduate school data. Again, be clear in the narrative about this if it is an expectation. Anytime you make the review committee guess, it increases the chance for misinterpretation.

Service Work

As with the other sections of your narrative, you set the context in discussing service. If you made strategic decisions for how your service fits into a larger plan, describe those decisions. For instance, perhaps you wanted to learn about curriculum development and how to propose a new course, so you joined the department curriculum committee. If you were an opportunistic service provider (i.e., you served on a committee because it was required to keep your job), do not turn it into something it was not. A committee where all you did was count votes once per semester or you were a marshal at graduation is a smaller level of commitment and work than chairing a committee or taking a major role in a committee's work. You did the service and received the credit, but do not make it seem bigger than it was. You need to write about what you contributed and, if appropriate, gather documentation that corroborates your claim. Remember that your colleagues are reviewing your file and they are familiar with many of the service opportunities. Exaggerating service contributions can cause reviewers to wonder what else you are exaggerating.

If it seems like keeping everything organized is tough, you are right. Inset 9.9 provides suggestions for organizing and maintaining an electronic version of your file and artifacts. Being organized as you start your career will save you time as you progress through the ranks and compile your various files.

Compiling Your Evidence

Now, to your evidence file(s). We have said you probably cannot and should not include everything you have produced in the time under review. You may have limitations on how much evidence you can include. Being judicious in what you include increases the amount of time reviewers spend on the good stuff. So how do you decide?

First, your campus may require certain artifacts (course syllabi, sample assessments, student work

> **Inset 9.9.**
> **Strategies for Success:**
> **Tips on Maintaining an Electronic File of Your Evidence**
>
> - Have digital folders for teaching/instruction, scholarly/research, and service easily accessible and stored in the cloud. As you get new artifacts, scan them and put them into the appropriate folders.
> - A good calendar can help you remember what you did during the past year. Keep your calendar electronically for safety.
> - Build your file as you go. Scan or save documents for use as artifacts in your file as they come in.
> - Title the artifacts in ways that you know what they are without having to open them.
> - Keep a copy of your CV on your desktop and update it as you go along.

samples, summaries of student evaluation results). Obviously, include the required elements. Then check with colleagues to know what is expected and typically included. Sometimes you may be required to submit minutes from meetings to show that you were present, for example, but it may be sufficient to include a committee roster or a memo from the committee chair that notes your attendance and participation. Asking to see the files of those who are just ahead of you in the process is a great way to get ideas both for evidence to include and how to organize your file. Second, be sure that your evidence is tightly integrated with your narrative so that readers can see and read both in parallel. Creating a clear, easy-to-navigate file makes it easier for the reviewing committees to read and evaluate your information. Inset 9.10 provides some suggestions for creating a clear file.

It is better to include fewer high-quality artifacts than a large number of insignificant artifacts mixed in with the high-quality ones. Remember that your goal is to provide evidence that demonstrates how you have met or exceeded the requirements for retention, tenure, or promotion, so choose your evidence accordingly.

Inset 9.10.
Strategies for Success:
Building Your Evidence File

- Have a clear and consistent labeling system. Use tabs in the notebook so that reviewers can find things.
- Use the same labeling convention in your narrative and evidence files. For instance, if in your evidence files you have a syllabus under "I-7" (for Instruction), then include that reference mention in your narrative.
- Include a table of contents.
- Include page numbers (you may want to paginate each section separately—for example, I-1, I-2, I-3 for Instruction; R-1, R-2, R-3 for Research; S-1, S-2, S-3 for Service).
- Do not put papers into page protectors.
- Follow your campus guidelines about electronic files. (These are often not allowed as it is hard to control access to and editing of the files.)
- Check to be sure that you have included all the required components (CV, narrative, course evaluations, syllabi, etc.).

Responding to Feedback

We mentioned earlier that it is important to respond in subsequent reviews to past feedback from RTP committees. However, at least two other scenarios may be less clear. For instance, perhaps you have read the committee feedback and believe they missed key portions of your narrative or evidence, resulting in a faulty assessment. Alternatively, perhaps you feel they reviewed all of the material but you disagree with their conclusions about your performance. While both of these scenarios are rare, they do happen. How you respond when faced with negative feedback says a lot about you as a professional. Here we outline some ideas as you deliberate whether and how to respond.

The RTP Committee Missed Key Information

If you believe the committee misstated facts or missed something important, there is usually a process that allows you to respond. Typically you are not allowed to add new documentation to the file at this juncture, but you can clarify or point to evidence within the existing file to inform the next level of review of the error or oversight.

In considering whether to write a response, do so with care. Consider whether a response is really necessary. For example, if you have a strong positive review but the committee made an error in reporting the number of committees you served on, a formal response may not be appropriate—especially if the number they reported, while low, is above the minimum threshold or did not appear to affect their assessment. A response in this scenario may look nitpicky. But if some errors do or may negatively impact the RTP decision, a clarification may be appropriate.

If you choose to respond, be careful in your language. Stick to the facts and avoid emotional wording. Wait at least 24 or 48 hours before submitting anything, but do be aware that there are timelines for submitting a response. For a situation like this, you are merely pointing out the error. You can do this rather succinctly and you should include data from the file or CV that supports your claim. For example, simply state that the committee noted service on four committees, but in your narrative and CV you have identified six committees, including one role as chair. This response should not be adversarial in tone or intent. In fact, you should be sure to thank the committee for their hard work. You might also ask your chair or a senior colleague who is not involved in the RTP process to review the letter. This response then becomes part of your file as it moves through the rest of the review process.

You Disagree With the RTP Committee's Interpretation of Your File

Trickier than a report with factual errors or errors of omission is a situation when the committee comes to a different conclusion about your work than you do. They acknowledge the artifacts and work but interpret its importance less positively. In that case you may feel more compelled to set the record straight. This scenario may be even more delicate than the previous example, as you would be rebutting a committee's interpretation.

As noted, be careful in your language; stick to facts and avoid emotion. You must respond in a manner that is respectful and clear as to how you came to a different conclusion. We suggest you use the reviewers' language about which you are in disagreement, as well as language in the RTP policy, and start from there. Where do their thinking and logic differ from yours? What evidence in your file supports your interpretation? What language in the policy, taking your accomplishments into account, supports your interpretation? If you have a trusted colleague or two, you can ask them to give you feedback on your response before submitting it.

Survive and Thrive: Strategies to Keep You Sane

As efficient and effective as we hope these tips are, maintaining, compiling, and submitting your RTP file is still a stressful process. The logistics alone are challenging. Then add the ambiguity of the process, self-doubt that arises, and general angst about the preparation for and process of review. With these factors in mind, we offer the following reminders and suggestions:

- *Seek allies.* See if those who are at or near the same career stage would share their files with you, allowing you to see what they included, how long their file was, and so on. Know that no two files are alike, but seeing someone else's can be helpful as you think about what yours should look like. It can be helpful to see a file from someone in a closely related department, but keep in mind their guidelines may vary. Find a colleague, read each other's narrative drafts, and provide feedback; look at each other's evidence. Doing so with people outside your department can also be helpful; if they can understand what you wrote, so will RTP committee members outside your department.
- *Reach out to your peer network.* Your graduate school friends are on the same timeline as you. Are you still close to your graduate adviser? These people know you better than most. They have seen how you survived the dissertation process, so they may have some suggestions to help you live through this process also.
- *Write about the work, not about yourself.* One of us got the advice when writing our file to convict yourself of tenure. This made the process of writing easier. It is about the product and process, not about you as an individual.

- *Take your time.* Do not try to compile materials or write the entire narrative at once. Work methodically and in brief regular sessions (Boice, 2000), just like you would on teaching and scholarship. Work on sections and come back to the project over time. Done this way, it is actually kind of cool to see all that you have accomplished.

Concluding Thoughts

The RTP process should not dictate your life and all your academic decisions. Do not live and die by the RTP list of required artifacts. You certainly cannot ignore the requirements for gaining tenure, but you want to chart your academic pathway to be more than just meeting a checklist. You are building a career that will be significantly longer than six years, so map out a plan that will have you being productively engaged in a course of action that makes you happy while meeting your institution's guidelines. The RTP file you put together is just a way of sharing that story with others.

Note

1. Tenure and promotion may not always go together. Some campuses decouple them, with faculty going up for tenure one year and promotion the next, for example.

Exercises

Here are some ideas for exercises that might be useful to you in building your knowledge and comfort level around the RTP process.

1. Find your department's RTP document.
   - What are the expectations in the department regarding your narrative?
   - What are the expectations for teaching and instructionally related activities to earn tenure? What sorts of documentation are required?
   - What are the expectations for research and scholarly related activities to earn tenure? What sorts of documentation are required?
   - What are the expectations for service activities to earn tenure? What sorts of documentation are required?
2. Find the guidelines or reporting requirements used by the RTP committees.

- What prompts must the committee write to in regard to your overall file?
- How is the committee required to report its review of your teaching-related activities?
- How is the committee required to report its review of your research and scholarly related activities?
- How is the committee required to report its review of your service activities?

3. Chart out how your department's RTP document and the RTP committee's document align and keep track of what you have done to satisfy requirements to earn tenure. Table 9.1 provides you with a format you can use.

4. Visit with early career faculty in your department and college (recently tenured or soon to apply for tenure). Ask them about the process from their perspective.
   - What are the norms in the department regarding documentation and evidence for your file?
   - What advice do they have for you starting out in the process?
   - Would they be willing to share their narrative or file to give you a sense of what one looks like?

TABLE 9.1
Tracking Your RTP Progress and Institutional Expectations

	RTP Document		RTP Committee Document	Your Work	
	Expectations for tenure	Required documentation	What the committee needs to report	Completed work products to demonstrate you have met the goal	Work in progress to meet this goal (anticipated date of completion)
Instruction					
Scholarship					
Service					

CREATING BALANCE IN YOUR WORK

One of the greatest challenges for faculty members is finding a balance between their personal and professional lives. Often as graduate students, a day might consist of two or three main tasks, perhaps coursework and research. Early career faculty members are often surprised at the variety of tasks they face as professors on any given day, from teaching and scholarship to student needs, committee work, and surprise requests from the dean or department chair.

Adding to this challenge, faculty members can, for better or worse, work anytime and anywhere; much of our work is portable. Student papers and exams can be graded at home or in the local coffeehouse; reading or data analysis can happen in the office, on the couch, or at the beach. While this may be somewhat less true for scientists or artists—who may need to be present in their labs or studios or out in the field—even these professors have more flexibility in their work schedule and setting than many professionals. Buddle (2012) examined his own work patterns over the course of a week and among his observations was a point familiar to many faculty: he worked at odd hours (sometimes late at night, sometimes early in the morning) and often a bit on the weekend.

This kind of flexibility is a double-edged sword. For many faculty, the flexible work schedule can be an appealing aspect of the faculty career. A person who writes best in the evening can work on the latest article from 9 p.m. to midnight, sleep in, and then teach the next afternoon. Flexibility can also allow faculty members to handle child care issues, run errands, and take care of family needs in a way many professionals cannot. However, flexibility also poses challenges. It can lead many, particularly early career faculty members, to work more hours than the average 40-hour workweek. Moreover, working additional hours, coupled with the demands of the job, can contribute to stress and anxiety as well as strain personal relationships.

One of the important skills for being a successful faculty member and, more importantly, having a successful life is having a sense of balance in what you do. Boice (2000) calls it "nihil nimus"—or the need to moderate our work. Our goal in this chapter is to give you strategies and tools that you can use to find balance in your work as a scholar. We begin by continuing our discussion, started in Chapter 1, of how much and where faculty work, as well as some of the consequences that can come from common work patterns. Next we examine advice from others about why seeking balance is so important—and what it looks like—as well as why it can be so difficult to achieve. As with the other topics in this book, our goal is to help you take ownership of your career and be an agent in choices about how you spend your professional time. Therefore, we conclude by offering strategies for being effective and efficient at finding balance.

Perspectives on Balance from Experienced Faculty Members

We have noted that faculty members typically work more than the normative 40-hour week and that the flexibility of our work can be a blessing and a curse. The result is that faculty members at all levels feel like they are continually swimming upstream against the current. A common feeling is that you have more work to do than you can reasonably accomplish (Colbeck, 1998), and time is a perennial challenge. Inset 10.1 provides a quote from Karen in her second year as she struggled with balance and considered other career options. Similarly, the early career faculty interviewed by Austin and Rice (1998) reported difficulty with balance; a sense of guilt for not working; and making choices to neglect their personal commitments, including children. Nearly two decades later, the problems continue. Sangaramoorthy (2015) described an ultimatum from her husband to tune out work and tune in family when with their children. Trower (2010) reported that early career faculty consistently said time was their most precious resource and time management their greatest challenge. In reviewing the literature on faculty careers, O'Meara and colleagues (2008) point to multiple studies indicating that women faculty experience greater challenges than men in balancing career and family in academe. Whatever your gender, the consequences of this struggle to find work-life balance can include stress, interference of work with life,

Inset 10.1.
Words From Early Career Faculty: Seeking Balance

I love what I do. I love research and I enjoy the aspects of teaching, but, you know what? My social life suffers. Is it worth it? Can I find the balance I want somewhere else?
—Karen

Inset 10.2.
Words From Early Career Faculty:
Balance Starts Now

Your life is happening right now, and you can't wait to start your life until you finish these other things. —Sarah

strained relationships, and health problems (e.g., Olsen & Sorcinelli, 1992).

The idea of sustaining and achieving balance may seem like a luxury. "Yes, balance is good and fine," you may say, "but I have lectures to prepare, papers to grade, data to collect, grants to submit, and tenure to earn. Balance can wait." We have been there, and Sarah speaks to this point in Inset 10.2. Remember that a faculty career is just that—a career; it is *part* of your life, a fulfilling part we hope, but only part.

In case we have not convinced you, let us share wisdom and advice from colleagues—some senior and some relatively new—about the importance of balance, what it looks like, and some things to keep in mind.

- *Family first.* Robert Sternberg, a professor at Cornell University and a past president of the American Psychological Association, shares pointed advice in *The Chronicle of Higher Education* (2015). His very first point: "Put your family first." He reflected on his early career:

  Like many academics, I was more concerned about getting than about giving, and giving to my family always seemed as if it could wait another day. The trouble is, the family really can't wait. Intimate relationships can grow rusty, and children just grow up. . . . I've seen many academics wait too long to attend to their family relationships. . . . You can't count on your publications and awards to take care of you. You need your family now, and you'll need them more later. More important, they need you now. (Sternberg, 2015, paras. 2–3)

- *Self-care.* Sternberg (2015) offers a "close second" piece of advice: take care of yourself. As you age, exercise is increasingly important to taking care of your body, and it is a key to managing stress. Kirk (2013) and Nel (2015) both target their advice directly at pretenure faculty and echo Sternberg, urging them to eat well, exercise, and get rest, while Curzan (2015) speaks to the importance of hobbies and interests outside of academe.

- *Be okay with being okay.* Most faculty are used to being high achievers, and the push for tenure surely plays to that instinct. However, experienced faculty caution against trying to be exceptional all the time. Kirk (2013) notes that you cannot be 100% successful in all areas of your work all of the time. Similarly, Laura Krystal Porterfield

(Royles, 2014b) encourages her early career peers to accept being okay as a teacher in some class sessions if it helps you save time and energy. Sarah also speaks to this point in Inset 10.3. Think about your work as a *career* that unfolds over time rather than feeling like you must accomplish a life's

> **Inset 10.3.**
> **Words From Early Career Faculty: Being Okay**
>
> *Well, you know . . . so this is now round two of not the best lecture in the world. Or I wish I had another video for that, or I would do things differently. But you know, it's good, it's good enough.* —Sarah

work of quality and quantity before you earn tenure. No single event, or even a small group of events, will make or break you.

All of these bits of advice, from both senior and junior faculty members, point to the importance of finding balance in your life and being careful to not let the demands of your career push out other important aspects of who you are.

Work-Life Balance: Chasing a Unicorn?

Finding work-life balance can be a challenge, even for those who believe in pursuing it and have experience in the profession. Many faculty members are not content with this state of affairs. Schmidt (2009) reported on a study by Kate Quinn and James Soto Antony that looked at generational differences among a national sample of faculty. Among their findings was that Generation X faculty (the newer faculty at most universities at that time) placed more importance on finding work-life balance than on money or status compared to their more senior counterparts. However, while early career faculty want to find balance, they rate work-life balance as one of the weakest areas of their professional experience (Helms, 2010; Trower, 2010).

If faculty members, particularly early career faculty members, are looking to find this balance, why does it seem so difficult to achieve? Is chasing work-life balance, as the heading for this section suggests, akin to seeking a unicorn? While it certainly feels this way, we do not believe so. Before turning to strategies for finding this balance, we think it is important to identify at the outset what may contribute to our sense of imbalance.

First, there is no doubt that professional pressures are often greater for early career faculty members than their more experienced colleagues. As we noted in Chapter 1, academics are not well-prepared for the full range of faculty work (Gaff, Pruitt-Logan, & Weibl, 2000; Golde & Dore, 2001;

Rice et al., 2000), which means that much of what we experience in our first years of work is brand new. We are often engaging in multiple new course preparations, trying to start a research or scholarly program, and navigating service and relationships with new colleagues while learning about politics and the institutions where we work. This all takes a great deal of time. It also creates significant anxiety and requires emotional energy as we are pulled in multiple directions, learn to manage numerous new relationships (with students and colleagues), and adjust to a new locale. Finding work-life balance does not just *feel* hard for faculty, it actually *is* hard to achieve.

Second, societal forces shape our work practices and perceptions. As Gappa and colleagues (2007) note, for example, the academic workplace is increasingly governed by pressures to be accountable to stakeholders (via learning outcomes, graduation rates, etc.), and technology means that faculty are seemingly expected to be accessible to students 24 hours a day, 7 days a week. These modifications have changed the nature of faculty work compared to what it was even 30 years ago, adding new dimensions, tasks, and pressures to the work. Perhaps even more importantly, societal changes have resulted in the disappearance of the "ideal worker" (Gappa et al., 2007, p. 25). This (male) worker was able regularly to work more than 40 hours per week, took limited vacation time, could count on household duties being taken care of by someone else (usually a wife), and seemingly did not need or desire family or parental leave time.

Those days are behind us, as both partners in a relationship usually need to work, putting pressure on two people to balance professional and household duties. Academic couples might have partners working in different cities (whether both work in academe or not), adding stress and straining relationships. Couples may have children, elder care, or other responsibilities. In heterosexual relationships, men are generally shouldering more of the housework, including child care, today than 50 years ago; however, it is still the case that women do more hours of housework and are more likely than men to be engaged in the care work that goes with a family (Bianchi, Sayer, Milkie, & Robinson, 2012; Ward & Wolf-Wendel, 2004). As suggested previously, men and women both feel the pull between academic careers and family (Grant, Kennelly, & Ward, 2000), with some studies (e.g., Armenti, 2000, 2004; Ward & Wolf-Wendel, 2004) highlighting the tensions that women in particular feel.

Third, and amplifying these pressures, the academic culture rewards and celebrates the idea of long hours of work. In graduate school, most aspiring academics are socialized to read more, write more, and collect more data. The push to publish before having earned your degree, in an effort to be competitive for increasingly scarce tenure-track positions, leads many to work nights and weekends, pushing issues like health and hobbies to the side. Once in faculty positions, we often experience what one of our colleagues calls the *throw-down culture*, where we get into a verbal back-and-forth in competition over who is busiest. In the hallway, one harried colleague regales another with how late she was working last night and all of the tasks (grant applications, papers to grade, data to collect or analyze) that remain, then the other colleague responds in kind, creating a competition for who is busiest and works the hardest. (Inset 10.4 offers some strategies to avoid being drawn in to this competition.) An October 6, 2016,

> ### Inset 10.4.
> ### Strategies for Success: Avoiding the Throw-Down Culture
>
> To avoid conversations where you appear to "compete" for busyness, try the following:
>
> - Volunteer one thing that you are working on that you are excited about, but do not share *when* you have worked on it
> - Smile and listen, nod with understanding, but do not share the details of your weekend
> - Agree that you have been busy, too, but do not go into details

post from the Shit Academics Say Facebook page captured this culture in a humorous way: "I was just wondering if you had time to grab a coffee and discuss how busy we are" (2016b). Indeed, a major theme of Shit Academics Say is to identify the guilt faculty members feel when they are not being productive. As a result, we learn early and often that it is important to let our colleagues know that our attention is seemingly always focused on our work; we feel the pressure to work as much as everyone else appears to, even if we do not know exactly how much that is.

Recently, commentators have begun to question how many hours per week faculty actually work, as well as the wisdom of working so many hours. Duffy (2015) has sought to debunk the idea that it takes 80-hour workweeks to succeed in academe. She noted that while she surely *felt* she was working this much early in her career, she tracked her time and found that it worked out to about 60 hours per week at most. Duffy (2015) quoted one of her blog's readers, who was in a consulting job for nine years and had to track his time by the hour for billing purposes. Even at his most frenetic, the reader reported working 60 hours per week as an upper limit in the role; he argued that 80-hour weeks were almost impossible.

Arguably even 60-hour weeks are not sustainable over the long term: Duffy (2015) has noted that she might be able to sustain two or three weeks of 60 hours of work, but ultimately returns to her 40- to 45-hour workweek out of necessity after that. Nelson (2015) has noted that, at most, she can sustain 55-hour weeks for a couple of months. The point is that 80-hour workweeks are not necessary to succeed in academe—and probably do not even happen much, if at all (Duffy, 2015), a point supported by data earlier in this chapter and in Chapter 1. We heartily concur and worry that, to the extent this myth is perpetuated, it dissuades talented potential professors from coming to academe and causes great stress and pressure for the early career faculty in the role.

Fourth, most academics love what we do. We must love it; we needed deep commitment to our fields to sustain us through long days and nights in graduate school; ups and downs with our scholarly and creative activities; and arduous, highly competitive searches for a faculty position. But as Curzan (2015) has observed, this passion can often drive us to work more and more, filling our time with work-related activities. That same passion can even be something that leads us to think about work even when we are not working, adding to the perception that we work all the time.

The fifth and final element that can make it feel difficult to find balance in our work and professional lives is ourselves. For instance, while we may take advantage of the flexibility of our positions to take Friday afternoon to attend a child's soccer game, we may also forget that we did so while grumbling about having to work on Sunday afternoon. In addition, as noted earlier (and suggested by Duffy [2015]), we may overestimate our time spent working. For example, we might think we are working but are not as productive as we might think (a confession: As this very page is being written, Haviland has checked e-mail and social media a couple of times, extending "work" time without producing anything!). Other times, our stress or anxiety about the job can lead us to feel like we are working more, without actually engaging in any productive activity. And it could just be that we are not always working efficiently. A post from Shit Academics Say captures this sentiment: "I'm very busy. On an unrelated topic, I have questionable time management skills and difficulty saying no" (2016a). This is a point Boice (2000) makes, albeit more gently, when he notes that his quick-starting early career faculty focused on the more important tasks and took less time to do them than those faculty members who struggled in their early years. At times, we may be our own worst enemies when it comes to finding the balance we seek.

Of course, we know from experience that most faculty do work a lot. And no matter how much we love our disciplines, our colleagues, and our students, finding ways to moderate our work (Boice, 2000) is key to finding balance. Working too much is tiring and creates stress, both of which result in declining rewards for the amount of work. This begs the question, of course, of what faculty members can do to achieve this balance.

Strategies for Achieving Balance

Much like doing high-quality scholarly or creative activity, finding professional and work-life balance is not achieved by doing any single thing. Rather, balance comes from an ongoing series of choices and strategies, as well as a mind-set that is both disciplined and optimistic (believing that pursuing these strategies will pay off both personally and professionally). With that in mind, in this section we offer strategies to help you achieve work-life balance. Remember, of course, that just as the faculty career is a developmental process, so is finding balance. You will want to revisit and fine-tune your approach as you learn more about how you work, as your career evolves, and as your life changes.

Set Clear, Specific Goals and Priorities

The foundation for having a manageable career is having clear goals and priorities. The exercises in Chapters 4 through 8 should help. Start by thinking about what you want and need to accomplish in your first five or six years on the job, taking into account what you know about tenure and promotion expectations (Chapter 9). What are your goals as a teacher, scholar, and colleague? If there are expectations for a certain number of publications before tenure, or certain types of products, break these out over the years. For example, perhaps you need or want to write a book or compose a specific piece of music before tenure. Then break these larger goals down further into annual goals and specific tasks. Next, start scheduling those tasks into specific semesters or even months (e.g., write Chapter 1 for book proposal in January, submit proposal by March). Just as importantly, think about your personal goals. What kind of partner or parent do you want to be? What hobbies do you have or want to have?

Set Your Own Standards (Trust Yourself)

Closely related to the previous point is this one: As you seek to establish work-life balance, keep in mind that the only standards you need to follow are your own. We do not mean you should disregard the advice of senior colleagues or standards for tenure. However, a core part of authoring your faculty career is taking responsibility for and making your own choices in the context of advice and existing standards. Thus, we encourage you not to get distracted by the throw-down conversations about how much others work, but rather to set your own standards and make your own choices (Nel, 2015; Rockquemore, 2015b). *There is no one path to achieving tenure.* Choose your goals and priorities, and then trust your own instincts and have faith in your

Inset 10.5.
Words From Early Career Faculty: Managing Tasks

I like to do things. . . . I have half an hour—how much stuff can I accomplish? Can I knock out page 1 of all my midterms in half an hour?
—Michael

own strategies (based on what you are learning in this book and elsewhere) to achieve these goals.

Schedule Your Priorities

Experienced scholars (Kiewra, 2008; Rockquemore & Laszloffy, 2008) stress that it is up to you to control your routine. If you want to accomplish the important things, then you need to schedule the important things; your goals can guide you here. As we noted in Chapters 5 and 6, Boice (2000) recommends working in brief regular sessions on class prep and scholarship (e.g., this paragraph is being drafted during a planned 30-minute session). Michael speaks to this in Inset 10.5. You can schedule those times and then protect them. If you need to be writing or researching, then schedule that time and tell others who ask to meet with you then that you have a meeting at that time. Look at your syllabus, figure out when assignments are due, and block out grading time on your calendar (Jenkins, 2015). A rough rule of thumb might be to imagine that, on a given day, with meetings, e-mails, and other activities, you likely only have time to do two or three really substantive things (like writing or grading) well. What do you want those things to be?

Manage Tasks, Not Time

Boice (2000) has said that the challenge faculty face is not managing time, but rather managing *tasks*. Specifically, early career faculty in particular spend too much time on tasks, especially teaching, and reach a diminishing marginal return on their effort (Boice, 2000; Rockquemore, 2015a). There are things you can do to manage your tasks and make life easier:

- *Set aside a specific amount of time to do a task, do it, then move on.* Could you craft a beautiful e-mail in 20 minutes? Sure, but we suspect minutes will do. Rockquemore and Laszloffy (2008) recommend multiplying your estimate of time by 2.5 to allow for unexpected demands; that might be appropriate for scholarship, although we think over time that you will become more refined and accurate in your assessments. Commit to preparing for class for a certain number of minutes, or spending no more than 15 minutes on each student paper, and honor that. Your initial estimates might be off the mark, but you will get more accurate with time, and setting limits helps you prioritize.

- *Evaluate how much time something should take.* On our campus, 3 course units (a typical course) equates in theory to about 8 hours per week of work. Thus, we know that if we are regularly spending 15 hours per week on a class, we need to rethink our efforts. While there will be higher demand times than others, having a sense of how much time you should be spending on something is key to managing your tasks and time.
- *Limit e-mail use.* Do e-mail no more than two or three times a day. Set aside designated, preferably low-energy times, to read and reply to e-mails. Inset 10.6 offers some tips on how to manage your time with email.

Inset 10.6.
Strategies for Success:
Making E-Mail Work for You

1. Triage e-mails. Respond to those for which you can easily reply in one to two minutes.
2. For e-mails that require more time, move them to a designated folder for the day on which you will reply.
3. E-mail is for sharing or getting information quickly. Keep e-mails to two to three points at most.
4. Have templates for e-mails you will send often (student inquiries, advising information, etc.).
5. Disable all notifications (bells, chimes, etc.) on your e-mail client.

Inset 10.7.
Words From Early Career Faculty:
Quality Time

Now we almost never come home and sit and watch TV. . . . Last night we played Scrabble. . . . Sometimes we'll just go for walks. —James

Plan Your *You* Time

Again, if it is important, schedule it. Like going to the gym? Then plan when you will go. Need time for leisure reading? Carve it out. The same is true of time for your relationships. We know colleagues who choose one weekend day to never work and use that day to maximize quality time with family and friends. In Inset 10.7, James describes how he and his wife worked to maximize the quality of their time together. Also, know the difference between self-care and soothing (Cale, 2015). It is quite likely that things that distract us or are habits (like social media) may soothe us for a moment but not actually reduce our stress or anxiety. Nelson (2015) points out that she can recharge with just a 15- to 30-minute break at points during the day. Carve out time for things that refresh and rebuild you.

Protect Your Time

Once you have scheduled what is important to you, you have made a commitment. Protect that time! If you have scheduled teaching prep time, then you have a meeting with yourself. Keep it and do not book something else.

Decide Where and When You Will Work on Tasks

For some faculty, particularly those in the sciences and arts, it may be that you need to be on campus on a daily basis to be in the lab or studio. However, for others, the flexibility of faculty work means that you can work in many places, so it bears some careful thought about where you will work best and on which tasks. Will you keep all your work on campus in an effort to strike a balance between home and work? Do you write best in coffeehouses with ambient noise? Will you grade and write at home, but do teaching prep and service work on campus? When are the best and most useful times to be on campus (i.e., when your colleagues and students are around), and when can you easily slip away? Remember from Chapter 3 that being clear on the department culture is key, so what are the expectations of your department culture? Are all faculty expected to be present and visible each day?

Inset 10.8
Strategies for Success:
Organize Your Workspace

1. Set up work zones. At the least, have a computer zone and a non-computer zone. Consider a zone for where you will meet with students.
2. Keep out on your desk only those supplies you need on a regular basis (e.g., stapler, Post-it notes).
3. Recycle. At least weekly, purge paper you do not need to keep.
4. Consider scanning and creating electronic files for paper documents you have received.
5. Leave 10 minutes at the end of each day to clean up (file, recycle) your workspace.

Organize Your Workspaces

Having an organized workspace is key for at least two reasons. First, as Rockquemore and Laszloffy (2008) note, it projects your image to colleagues and students. As an early career faculty member, a messy office indicates disorganization, poor management skills, and inefficiency. (Only after you establish yourself can you lay claim to being a quirky academic.) Second, a disorganized office means you have trouble finding things and are working through clutter; in other words, it means inefficient use of precious time. Inset 10.8 offers some strategies for organizing your workspace.

File Management

Set up a system for your electronic files and documents. Your filing system on your computer should mirror the filing system for your e-mail account and your paper documents (right down to the hierarchy and naming conventions). For instance, Haviland has a single section (or electronic folder) for teaching. Within that teaching folder he has a folder for each course. Then, within each course folder a main file for each semester a course was offered, with items such as the syllabus, grading sheets, and so on. He then has a separate folder for each week of the class, with readings, assign-

> **Inset 10.9.**
> **Strategies for Success:**
> **Organize Your Digital Life**
>
> 1. Have the same file structure for electronic files and paper files (e.g., keep all teaching files in one group; structure for e-mail, computer, and hard copy filing is the same).
> 2. Use a consistent naming convention for your files.
> 3. Include either the date or version number (e.g., "v2") in document names.
> 4. Use a capital letter or underscore to show breaks between words. Avoid spaces in file names.

ments, and lecture notes. In this manner, files from one semester can be easily copied for a new semester and modified. We highly recommend using a cloud service for your files (e.g., Dropbox, Box, OneDrive) to ensure that your files are backed up and accessible at all times. Name files and documents consistently so you can find them each year. Inset 10.9 offers suggestions on staying organized digitally and on naming conventions for electronic files.

Be Strategic About Using Your Energy

Some faculty work demands our best energy and thinking (e.g., writing), while some can be done in more relaxed and casual moments (e.g., checking off homework in front of the TV while sipping wine). Try to engage in the work that requires the most energy at the time that is best for you. For instance, if you write best in the morning, carve out time each morning to do so. Similarly, find ways to save your energy in some tasks and apply it to others, as Catherine (described in Chapter 5) did when she discussed her discovery of active learning in the classroom as a way to save her energy for other things.

Work With the Future in Mind

Most of your work is work you will continue in the future. You will likely teach the same course multiple times; you may be able to adapt and build

Inset 10.10.
Words From Early Career Faculty:
Planning Ahead

How have I changed? Well, for teaching, I definitely try to . . . design my classes so that I can teach them the second time easier. —Carl, asked about what he had learned over time.

Inset 10.11.
Strategies for Success:
Weighing Your Options

1. *Always* thank the requestor for the opportunity.
2. Tell the requestor you need one to two days to review your calendar and commitments before responding.
3. Then consider the following:
   - Is the work aligned with your goals and commitments?
   - Is it politically wise to say yes?
   - Can you easily fit the work in with your current work? OR
   - Can you identify something you will drop or reduce time on to fit in this work?
   - Can you learn something new and worthwhile from the project?
   - Would the opportunity connect you with colleagues you want to know or enjoy already?

on components of your research projects in future efforts. Try to balance limiting your time on teaching preparation with being intentional as you prepare materials. Carl speaks to this point in Inset 10.10. The more thought out something is the first time, the easier it will be to replicate in the future, and you will inevitably learn things along the way as well. Take time at the end of each class to make notes on your lesson plan about what did and did not work. Do the same at the end of each semester about what worked and did not work in the course.

Say No . . . Sometimes

The advice on whether and when to say no is ambiguous. Seltzer (2015), speaking specifically to women, cautioned that women are more likely to say yes (particularly around teaching and service work) and should say no to small things so that they can focus on what is important. Others, like Nel (2015), have said their best growth has come when they said yes to unexpected opportunities.

Our best advice is to think carefully before saying yes to a request, no matter how big or small, and consider how it fits with your professional identity and goals. Indeed, Nelson (2015) talks not about thinking before saying no, but being deliberate before saying yes, and having a plan in place for how she will find balance in life in the wake of a new commitment. Inset 10.11 speaks to criteria for weighing your options, while Inset 10.12 provides some tips on how to say no.

Saying no is fine, provided it is done with tact and care. We have each turned down opportunities (e.g., courses, committees, book chapters) and all earned tenure and promotion. Remember our caution in Chapter 4 that being liked and respected are important components of your overall success; thus, saying no is an exercise in image management. You should say no in a way that leaves your colleagues with a sense that you appreciate the opportunity, have respectfully considered the request, and are too busy (but not overwhelmed).

> **Inset 10.12.**
> **Strategies for Success:**
> **How to Say No**
>
> Tell the requestor the following:
>
> 1. You would love to do something like that in the future, but that you are not able to take on the commitment at the moment.
> 2. You spoke with your chair, who said that you are not able to do it at this time (talk with your chair first so that you can be sure this is true!).
> 3. You cannot take on the full role at this time, but would be happy to take on a smaller piece (offer some ideas).

Concluding Thoughts

The academic culture, the fact that many faculty are very driven, and the anytime, anywhere nature of our work can make finding balance with faculty work a challenge. How much is too much? That is very much an individual decision, one that you must make based on your own life situation and in consultation with those around you. However, finding whatever that right balance is requires intentional effort. Thinking about the kind of faculty member you want to be—your goals, commitments, and priorities—can help you make smart choices about where and how to invest your energy. Similarly, using some of the strategies in this chapter can, we hope, help you make optimal use of your time. Remember, your faculty work is just one part of your life.

Exercises

Following are ideas for exercises to build your work-life balance.

1. Conduct a weekly time analysis to see how you actually spend your time.

- Decide on categories to track your time. You might consider categories like teaching, class prep/grading, other student contact, writing/creating, and service.
- From the moment you get up, pause at the top of each hour and record how you spent your time in the prior hour, perhaps in 15- or 30-minute increments.
- At the end of the week, total up the time spent in each category.
- Consider if this represents your desired balance among activities or whether you might make some changes.
- Do this at the beginning, middle, and end of the semester to see how times compare.

2. At the start of the next workweek, identify the two or three things you want to accomplish each day. Put those things on your calendar, blocking out time specifically for those goals. (You might even do so for some goals on a monthly basis.)

3. Pick one of your goals this semester or year (e.g., developing a new course, drafting an article, doing a proposal). Then do the following:
- Break the goal into discrete tasks or to-dos.
- Arrange the tasks in logical order and assign each task an estimate of how many hours or days it will take to complete.
- Schedule each one of those tasks on your calendar.

4. As you plan for a new semester, create a table with each of your courses as a column and each week of the semester as a row. Use the grid to list where assignments (and therefore grading) are due for each course.
- Make adjustments to your due dates to try to spread out your grading load.
- Block out time on your calendar for grading after various assignments are due.

II

MANAGING DILEMMAS

In preceding chapters we have identified strategies for addressing issues that might arise appropriate to the topic of each chapter. For example, we shared how to respond to negative feedback in your RTP evaluation process (Chapter 9) and explored strategies for saying no (Chapter 10). We regard these kinds of issues as dilemmas, for there is no single right way to address them; each situation is unique, and navigating it requires reflection and tact.

However, some dilemmas that early career faculty face transcend clean categorization. For instance, you may consider leaving your position early in your career or may be in an uncomfortable or even hostile work environment. In this chapter we identify some of the most significant dilemmas you may face early in your career. For each dilemma, we first define what the problem might be. Then we explore some possible strategies, approaches, or considerations as you go about solving the difficult dilemma.

Managing Macro- and Microaggressions

The Problem

Derald Sue and colleagues (2007) define *microaggressions* as "brief and commonplace daily verbal, behavioral, or environmental indignities, whether intentional or unintentional, that communicate hostile, derogatory or negative racial slights, and insults toward people of color" (p. 271). This definition is now commonly extended to other nondominant social identities such as gender and sexual orientation. If you are a woman, you might be experiencing microaggression if someone in your department consistently interrupts you at meetings but seldom does this with his male colleagues. Or perhaps, if you are a younger faculty of color, a student in your class continually challenges you while praising the White faculty in the department. If you frequently advocate for students from your social identity group, a colleague giving you the eye roll may be not only showing a lack of respect for your position or what you might be saying but also trying to shut you down. These can all be considered microaggressions.

Of course, there are also *macroaggressions*, a parallel word representing what is commonly known as *discrimination*. Such discriminations are not subtle, but actually distribute advantage to those from dominant groups and disadvantage to those from nondominant groups. For example, you may always be assigned the class sections no one else wants or be given multiple preps when folks newer than you are getting fewer. Perhaps colleagues are extended invitations for funding or collaboration and you are continually left out. If those getting the advantage are from dominant groups and you are not, then you might be experiencing discrimination. Further along the continuum, you might experience sexual or racial harassment.

Possible Strategies

Addressing microaggressions and discrimination are difficult because our first reaction is to look internally and ask, "Maybe it's me?" That is part of racism, sexism, and homophobia's job; they make you, as the receiver or target, believe that the fault lies in your hands, rather than the perpetrator's. Following are suggestions for ways to protect yourself and change that narrative.

- *Name it; call it what it is.* It is likely not you! If you are experiencing these slights and insults, especially if they consistently come from the same person in similar contexts and circumstances, recognize the behavior as a microaggression or discrimination. Even if you decide not to talk about this with anyone, knowing what this is can be helpful in building your internal defense mechanisms.
- *Find an ally.* Unfortunately, as an untenured professor, you also need to be aware of how your colleagues perceive you. Thus, you may not want to launch into an educational campaign to enlighten them on the presence of microaggressions in the department or classroom. It is important to find an ally to discuss what you are experiencing. It is great to have a place to vent, but also to have someone strategize with you. This ally can come from on or off campus. Chapter 4 offers ideas for how to find this critical support.
- *Be realistic.* Not everything is a microaggression. Because members of minoritized groups have likely spent a lifetime dealing with microaggressions and more, it is easy to apply that lens to many situations. But sometimes that senior colleague is just a jerk who belittles or bullies all of the new people. Maybe that student has disrespect for authority in general. Looking at the behavior you are

experiencing more broadly may be a constructive way to diminish its impact on you.

- *Take formal action.* If you continue to experience microaggressions from the same person over a period of time, taking action may be indicated. If the behavior is in the form of discrimination or harassment or if it has escalated to the point of creating a hostile work environment, then taking action is a must. Your campus has adopted explicit legal definitions of *harassment,* and you have specific rights to work in a nonhostile and harassment-free environment. The institution has specific responsibilities and processes that it must honor and engage when you report that you are experiencing harassment. It also has a reporting unit, such as an Office of Equity and Diversity. After receiving your complaint, it conducts an investigation by interviewing relevant parties and yourself. That unit will come to a decision and recommend sanctions. This is a serious matter. Use your ally to help you make the decision to file a complaint. If you have a positive relationship with your department chair or dean, discuss this action with that person before you take it. If you feel as if any situation may go this route, keep copies of all your e-mail correspondence and enter incidents in a log or journal, noting as many specifics as you can—what was said, time and date, and so on. If you are dealing with a student, in addition to taking notes, you might want to ask colleague to be present when you are meeting one-to-one with the student. Follow meetings up with a short e-mail of what was discussed and agreed. With this level of documentation and caution, if you make the decision to file a formal complaint, your chances of successful resolution increase dramatically.

Wanting to Leave Your Institution After a Year or Two

The Problem

Kerry Ann Rockquemore (2015a) noted in a commentary that some faculty arrive at their new position, are immediately disillusioned, and consider leaving at the end of their first year. Perhaps you have experienced this situation. You may not feel like you are fitting in with your colleagues, or you may not like the students with whom you work. Perhaps you do not like the campus or the larger community in which you live; perhaps you even feel some combination of these things. Whatever the cause, you have started to think that maybe this institution, this job, or both are not for you. Should you stay or should you go?

Possible Strategies

To help consider strategies, we pose the following questions and ideas that may be useful to you:

- *Pause and ask, "Are these growing pains?"* We do not want to minimize your concerns; however, it is very human to have such experiences (e.g., insecurities about teaching, loneliness) and to translate those very real concerns into larger issues about the job or the institution. We recommend having honest conversations with yourself about the root of your concerns. Then, assuming you determine you would still like to leave your institution . . .

- *Ask, "Could I stay two more years?"* If you are considering leaving in your first year on the job, and are in and want to stay in a tenure-track position, it is unlikely that you could move to a new institution the next year because the searches for those positions are already well under way. While you could go on the market in your second year, it might help if you wait to do so until your third year. For one, your perceptions in year two may change as you become more familiar with the institution, the courses you have taught, and the nature of the work. Also, faculty at most institutions undergo a detailed third-year review on their way to tenure. If you are able to wait to apply for new positions in your third year, and you do good work along the way, you can use the reviews from your current institution to point to your successful track record as a faculty member as you go through other search processes.

- *Do good work.* Whatever you decide about the timing of your search, be sure to continue your scholarship and your good work as a teacher. If nothing else, you can use your work in your current position to point to your ability to succeed as an independent scholar.

- *Seek out feedback.* Consider whether you can voice your concerns to anyone at the institution. You might not need to tell others that you are considering leaving. Perhaps you could share that you are feeling like you do not quite fit in or are not sure how to work with the students. Remember that this institution hired you and is, or should be, invested in your success. If you feel like there is someone you can trust to have this conversation with, he or she may help you discover some strategies or some perspectives you had not considered.

Whatever you do, reflect carefully and be judicious in your choice of actions. Pausing to reflect on the real nature of your unease and then acting in accord with that is critical. You most certainly do not want to stay in a position or place where you are unhappy. At the same time, you also do not want to begin a pattern of moving from job to job. Ultimately, our disciplines are very small fields, and you want a reputation as someone who honors your commitments. So pause, reflect, and then make choices when you are ready.

Not Making Adequate Progress to Tenure

The Problem

Perhaps it has become clear based on feedback from your RTP reviews that you are not meeting expectations for tenure. Often this comes up in the retention review (usually in year three), but it could come up at any point. While this is difficult news to hear, you need to be realistic. Read the reviews and be honest with yourself. Ask yourself, "Can I really do what is expected of me to get tenure? Do I want to do that work? Am I able to devote the time and effort needed to meet the expectations?"

Possible Strategies

- *Take stock of the situation.* The feedback you get is serious, and failure to meet the tenure expectations comes with huge consequences. It may be tempting to blame others, but blaming the RTP committee will not change the situation or magically get you an additional publication. Own this problem and the situation. Read carefully the feedback from your reviews. What are the feedback and the RTP document(s) telling you that you *must* do to be successful? Sketch out a list of things that you would need to do to meet expectations.

- *Talk to people.* Do not talk with just anyone; consult with people who know you, your file, and the department expectations. Start with talking with your chair, and consider speaking with your dean or a mentor. Share with them *your* assessment of the situation and ask them for theirs. Ask them for advice and suggestions about what you need to do to make tenure happen. This is not the time to complain. This is the time to go in with an open mind and a willingness to hear hard truths.

- *Be honest with yourself.* Having an honest conversation with yourself at year three can save you heartache at year six. Can you do what is needed in the time you have to earn tenure? Do you *want* to do what is needed? If not, you may need to consider an exit strategy. Perhaps you need to be at a different type of institution (with different expectations, students, etc.) or leave academia altogether. It may be better in the long run to change jobs now, well before the crucial sixth year. Honestly considering what duties and responsibilities you like and excel at can help you decide what to do next. You will likely have a much easier time getting a new job if you have not been denied tenure at your institution.

- *Prioritize!* If you decide that you can do what is needed and wish to do so, create a clear plan, put it in place, and push aside other priorities. Keeping your job *is* your priority. It is usually scholarship that prevents someone from getting good reviews; sometimes teaching is the problem area. Either scenario means you can push service to the side as you focus on getting publications out the door or improve your teaching to satisfactory levels; we recommend you consult with your chair as you make these decisions to get support. You will need to make sacrifices as you spend more time on the scholarly work (or teaching) to meet expectations. Identify and seek out resources, such as the faculty development center, to help you. Review Chapter 5 (teaching) or Chapter 6 (research) for suggestions for becoming more efficient and successful in those areas, as well as Chapter 10 (time management).

Job Searching

The Problem

While you may not decide you want to leave in your first year on the job, it is possible that in the course of your six years on the tenure track, you will think about leaving your institution. Perhaps you receive a nomination letter for another position. Maybe a position closer to your friends and family finally opened up, or you might want to move up in the institutional hierarchy. Possibly you want more money. Whatever the reason, deciding to go on the market, or even applying for one position, brings anxiety and a bevy of questions. Do you tell others? Who? When? Would you entertain a counteroffer from your current institution?

The Strategies

First, as we said earlier, carefully assess your situation. If you were made the right offer, would you be willing to leave? You need to be sure that you would be willing to leave, so be honest with yourself. If your answer is yes, then the following can help you navigate this tricky path.

- *Continue to do your best scholarship.* No matter what your next move is, you will be in the strongest bargaining position if you continue to be productive in your scholarship and research. Even nonacademic positions value productivity as they show you are developing expertise and a reputation in the field.

- *Only apply for positions you would actually take.* This is not the time to do the blanket job search you did when you were coming out of your doctoral program or postdoc fellowship. Be selective. Know that every time you submit your materials there is a whole new group of people who know you are on the market, and this situation poses a risk to you because you need to. . .
  - *Be as discrete as possible with others at your current institution.* When your campus colleagues discover you are searching, it can strain your relationships. We recommend telling only your department chair or dean and doing so at the point you are actually going on a campus interview. Only accept campus interviews for jobs you would actually take. Like it or not, when your colleagues know you are seeking another position, and they *do* find out, there will be a perception that you are not happy at your institution, you think you will not get tenure (if you are searching at a less prestigious institution or for a nonacademic position), or you think you can do better.
  - *Be careful with counteroffers.* Getting another job offer may be the only way we can renegotiate salaries or other support (see the "Negotiating" section in this chapter for more advice). The institution that has offered you the new position likely knows that if you have been doing your best, your home institution will probably counteroffer. This is a great position to be in if you have been honest with both institutions, are willing to take the new position, but are also willing to stay since you have agreed to entertain a counteroffer. The caution here is that in your pretenure years, you can only do this *once,* so do it right. Do it a second time, and your home institution will not likely entertain it again, perhaps feeling that you are trying to take advantage. And once your field has seen this, your ability to do it again before tenure decreases. You do not want to get the reputation for jumping around to the highest bidder. Deans and presidents may or may not be angry with this kind of behavior, but your departmental and disciplinary colleagues surely will be.

Negotiating

The Problem

Academics tend not to be the best negotiators. We (your authors) are not from the college of business, so we imagine maybe they are better; but in general, especially at the assistant professor level, we are just happy to have landed a job. However, it pays to think about what you will need and want to be successful even in your very first position, and to ask for it. You want to feel like you and the institution have worked together to set you up for success. Or it might be, as we have suggested earlier, that you have become less satisfied in your current position. Perhaps you have learned that you make less than your peers or would like more support for scholarship or a different teaching load. Maybe you already have a counteroffer from another institution in hand. Depending on the institution, almost everything can be negotiable.

Possible Strategies

In this section we offer general strategies for negotiating and then focus on context-specific negotiations related to your first job offer, an offer from a new institution, the counteroffer from your current institution, negotiating at your current institution without a competing offer, or negotiating at a time of promotion.

- *Do your research.* Have your facts in hand. You need to know the range of salaries, research support, or other benefits that your colleagues across the university have negotiated to frame your own requests. Concrete examples and data are critical. If you are at a public university, salaries are public. On a campus interview, ask a few people, perhaps over a meal or during informal time, what support they negotiated in their offers. Continue to monitor this after you are in the job so that you may renegotiate your terms if needed.
- *Make your case.* You also need to make the case that the value you bring to the department, college, or university is worth the additional compensation or support. Be ready to outline your value to the institution. If you moved on, what would the institution lose? Talk to your mentors about how to do so succinctly.
- *Know what you need to succeed and be specific in asking for it.* If it is a graduate assistant, know how much that will cost and lead with that. More travel support? Ask for a specific amount. You may consider asking for more than you are willing to accept; that way the other person can feel like they gave a little and you gave a little, and you hopefully get close to what you wanted.
- *Be cautious with ultimatums.* Ultimatums work only if you are serious about acting on them, so do not make one unless you are willing to walk away if you do not get what you want.
- *Negotiate with respect and empathy.* Effective negotiation is about not only asserting your needs *but also respecting* the position of the institution and those with whom you are negotiating. There may well be limits or

conditions on what administrators can do. For instance, your dean may have to worry about salary equity. Know also that deans can sometimes offer nonsalary support (travel, research assistant, or equipment funds) or adjust the teaching load (classes or types of classes taught in your first few years, summer teaching load) with more flexibility and at less cost than, say, salary. Understanding what their constraints might be can help you shape your position and find compromise.

Having addressed some general negotiating strategies, we turn our attention to specific scenarios in which you might apply some of these strategies.

- *The original offer.* The initial offer sets your base salary, so try to get as much as you can. *Always* counter the salary. The department chair, dean, or provost expects a counter and has probably factored that in to the original offer. Because you will have done your research, you will know what others have been offered in recent years. Also ask for research support, a travel budget, equipment you might need for your research, or a commitment to summer teaching or salary if you want to augment your salary. Listen for signs that you are pushing your luck. If someone has offered to coach you, definitely accept that help. If you have another position on the table, do not be shy in sharing the details of that offer in hopes of a match.
- *The new position.* Perhaps you have been offered a new position and are tempted to leave your current role. You are negotiating a new base salary and you already have a job, so you can be a bit more assertive in what you are asking for in terms of salary and support. Also consider your tenure clock: can you jump to a tenure decision? If you are in year four or five, and you have a good record, consider asking to move the tenure decision forward as a part of the offer. The current faculty will likely have to vote on your case, but this is a great way to move forward more quickly. Also think about your sabbatical clock, especially if you are asking for service credit (counting the years in prior positions). You may not get both tenure and an immediate sabbatical; you should decide what is more important. If you are offered service credit, be sure you are honest with yourself about how productive you can be in the shortened time to tenure.
- *The counteroffer.* You have sought and secured another position, and you have the offer in hand. If you are actually willing to leave your current institution, but willing to stay if they make a strong counteroffer, you can gain a lot of ground on your salary and other benefits. In many cases, you will be asked to produce the competing

offer letter. Do not be shy about asking for your current institution to go above and beyond the competing offer when negotiating. Imagine that you are only doing this once, so demonstrate that you are making a commitment to your current institution by making it clear that you will not seek other positions for at least some defined period of time.

- *Negotiating without securing another position.* Perhaps you have been at your institution for some period of time and would like to negotiate some changes. If you have been productive with your scholarship, and are a good teacher and a contributing and well-regarded colleague, you can negotiate many things along the way. Do not be afraid to ask for a research assistant or other research support. You might be turned down, but there might be discretionary funds that administrators can access. If you believe that your base salary is below those of your rank, ask for an equity adjustment. Your institution, especially if unionized, might have mechanisms for a special review. Summer teaching assignments can also be negotiated in lieu of a base salary increase. In this scenario, timing is key. Whatever you plan to ask, seek advice on timing. When is a good time in the budget cycle? How long has it been since you requested something extra? Use your capital wisely.

- *Earning promotion to associate professor with tenure.* Yippee! You did it. Every promotion comes with some kind of salary increase, but this is also an opportunity to renegotiate your salary. In our experience, deans and provosts have great latitude in salary enhancements at this stage. Take advantage of your position. Articulate what you have accomplished and contributed over the years. Do your students graduate on time? Do they earn awards? How much grant money have you secured? Where are you publishing? Do or can you play a specialized role in your service responsibilities? No one wants to lose a newly tenured faculty member, so bargain hard.

Concluding Thoughts

Part of navigating and shaping your faculty career is understanding that you will face challenges and dilemmas along the way. Navigating these dilemmas, however, can provide you with significant opportunities for growth, development, and ongoing success. For example, negotiating strategically and professionally may help you shape your career in positive ways. The key is to remember to pause, think carefully about your needs and goals, and map out a strategy that is likely to help you build the career you wish to have.

12

TO DEANS, CHAIRS, AND COLLEAGUES

Supporting Your Faculty

T his chapter speaks directly to the department chairs, deans, and colleagues who are critical to the success of early career faculty. While the success of all faculty members is ultimately their own responsibility, it is also the responsibility of leaders and colleagues to support and encourage that success. Whether you have picked up this book on your own or it was given to you (in Inset 12.1 we suggest to early career faculty that they share this chapter), we hope in this chapter to provide some tips, strategies, and insights that help you support your early career colleagues.

O'Meara, Bennett, & Neihaus (2015) say it best:

> As the most recent hires, early career faculty reflect strategic decisions by departments about where they want to spend scarce resources to stay relevant and competitive in their field. Therefore losing early career tenure track faculty means losing a critical department resource for achieving these goals. (p. 270)

This is especially pertinent when we consider how difficult it can be for a department to be awarded a tenure track line. Taken in its entirety, every hire represents costs in the national search, moving and research start-up costs, and six to seven years of annual salary before tenure. Making a mistake in

> **Inset 12.1.**
> **Strategy for Success:**
> **Share This Chapter**
>
> Make a copy of this chapter and share it with your department chair and dean. If you are in a mentoring program, share it with your assigned mentor as well.

the hire or failing to support the new hire through tenure is a costly mistake in human and financial resources.

Two concepts frame our thinking in this chapter. First, O'Meara and colleagues (2015) use the concept of psychological contracts to describe the expectations that their participants had of their colleagues and institutions. Through the interview process these new hires developed a set of expectations based on what they learned and conversations they had during their interviews. Thus, when they came to their positions and their expectations were not met, they felt a sense of betrayal; the psychological contract was broken. In this chapter we share best practices for working with early career faculty, one of which is adjusting and managing their expectations so that they do not reach the place of disillusionment, like those in Reybold's study (2005), or experience a violation of the psychological contract.

Second, organizational justice is another concept that is appropriate to apply to the experiences of early career faculty. Ambrose (2002) addresses the connection between how one experiences organizational justice and how employees feel about where and with whom they work. Using this concept, when early career faculty members feel as though they are being treated fairly, their commitment to the university grows, their performance improves, and they form good relationships with their colleagues. Further, when they believe that they have value to the organization, they are less likely to feel like victims when things get hard. In August and Waltman's (2004) study, level of influence in their departments was the most important variable in predicting career satisfaction for nontenured women.

Bad feelings and poor behavior are hard to overcome; thus it is critical that we do what we can to be as transparent as possible in policies and procedures that affect early career faculty members and work to develop workplace climates that lead to a sense of belonging and satisfaction. This should not be considered coddling, but rather a sincere effort on the behalf of colleagues and administrators to honor the investment that has been made in the early career faculty member.

One of the primary roles that deans, department chairs, and senior colleagues can play is to protect their early career faculty from potential pitfalls, abuses, and mistakes. This requires us to dispatch the sink-or-swim mentality that is often a fact of life for faculty on the tenure track. When you think of early career faculty as investments, then protection makes sense. We all want to protect our investments so that they grow and prosper; new faculty are no different.

An ongoing theme in this book is faculty growth and development, and much of our advice and guidance is meant to empower faculty members by giving them information and tools to self-author their work and lives. O'Meara and colleagues (2008) propose the following dimensions of faculty growth: (a) faculty are lifelong *learners* growing into roles and changing over time; (b) faculty have *agency* where they can shape their environments and work; (c) faculty *relationships* challenge, inspire, and enhance, contributing to growth and identity; and (d) faculty make *commitments* to what they do, their institutions, and their professions (see the introduction for more on the faculty growth perspective). Your role in this effort is to help early career faculty stay on a path of growth and encourage agency. Further, you are key in helping them see obstacles in their paths and then strategize solutions using the resources at your disposal, including influence and persuasion.

Understanding the Social Context of Early Career Faculty Members

In Chapter 1 we provided general demographics about current faculty. Much has changed since many of us were assistant professors. Women are now nearly half of all faculty but continue to be severely underrepresented in several fields. Although there are far more faculty from diverse ethnic groups, their proportion of all faculty remains very limited and far below parity. Just 4.2% of the faculty are from Hispanic backgrounds, and only 5.5% are Black/African American. Although teaching is still the activity where faculty spend most of their time, time spent in research and scholarship has been increasing (Milem, Berger, & Dey, 2000). Multiple studies have continued to document that women spend more time engaged in service activities than men (Link, Swann, & Bozeman, 2008; Schuster & Finkelstein, 2006).

Higher education has changed in many ways since most deans and chairs were assistant professors. There were more resources at the state and national levels to support research. The public's ongoing critique of higher education has played a role in calls for greater accountability. Students' lives were less complicated. Tenure expectations and standards have likely increased. Tenure-track positions were more plentiful, so there was less pressure and more mobility in the event that change was needed. Technology has not only changed the way we teach but also where and how we do the other parts of our work. The job of an assistant professor may look the same, but it often does not *feel* the same. Therefore, your expectations of early career faculty cannot reflect your own experiences. Trower (2010) contends that younger generations want flexibility and greater integration of their home and work lives. They expect more transparency in the tenure process, more supportive and diverse work environments, and more frequent and more helpful feedback about their progress. Much has been written about the expectations millennials have of their work environment. Many early career faculty come from this generation with those expectations.

The complex lives of early career faculty members are also different than faculty lives in the past, especially those of very senior colleagues. The increase of dual-career academic couples often means that both are in the tenure process at the same time and sometimes living in different cities or states. And, if one of them is not yet on the tenure track, stability is even less likely. In the past, the advice of "letting relationships go" until tenure was common (Austin & Rice, 1998, p. 743), but more recently the narrative is to help early career faculty members achieve balance, as we advise in this book (see Chapter 10). Deciding if and when to have families has always been a challenge for early career faculty members, but now we see them also struggling with elder care.

A more diverse faculty also means that family and commitments are more diverse. It may be a challenge in some disciplines to accept that, because of contemporary gender roles, both parents may take maternal/parental leave. Even the ways in which one becomes a parent have changed dramatically (adoption, surrogacy, in vitro fertilization, parenting nieces/nephews, etc.), and these developments have an effect on tenure clocks and medical leaves, in addition to maternal/parental leave. Financial pressures are different as well. In most cities, assistant professor salaries do not allow for home ownership, especially on one salary. This is magnified by the student debt load most early career faculty members carry. We have seen this lead to them taking on extra assignments, summer teaching, and outside consulting—all of which impact balance and scholarly productivity.

Despite the relatively slow growth in the diversity of the national faculty, the increased presence of minoritized faculty has called to question dominant campus culture and the impact of chilly climates (see Chapter 3 for a full discussion). Whether our early career faculty feel a sense of belonging and whether we judge them to *fit* is all a function of culture and climate. Predominantly White institutions (PWIs) often are plagued with beliefs and attitudes that lead to the exclusion of minoritized faculty. Culture and climate operate at multiple levels: the campus, the discipline, the college, the department. Early career faculty, as we discuss in many places in this book, are affected by stereotypes, prejudice, and discrimination (all manifestations of culture and climate) in the classroom, in their relationships with their colleagues, and even in the research that they choose. This level of impact may be difficult for more senior members of the faculty to understand, as that was not their reality as early career professors. Further, many early career faculty, especially women or faculty of color, fear academic cloning by their senior colleagues (Light, 1994; Stanley & Lincoln, 2005). *Academic cloning* refers to the tendency to mentor according to our own values, experiences, and cultures, molding mentees into younger versions of ourselves. This is problematic when that self reflects a dominant culture that does not allow for minoritized faculty to bring their unique cultures, experiences, and values into their professional identity and ways that they want to conduct their jobs as professors.

Systems of Mentoring, Support, and Guidance

The changing context of higher education and the lives of early career faculty mean that support, mentoring, and guidance need to be different than in the past. Greater intentionality is needed, as leaving good mentoring and support up to chance is risky business. Just as we have worked to empower early career faculty members throughout this book, we hope to embolden you to do your best to promote their success.

The Importance of the Department or Academic Unit

In August and Waltman's (2004) study of tenured and nontenured women, the most significant predictors of career satisfaction were all elements related to their experiences in the department: climate, the quality of student relationships, advising, a supportive relationship with the chair (see also Cawyer & Friedrich, 1998), and level of influence in the department. The chair or dean is in the unique position of shaping the reality of early career faculty members by the mentoring, guidance, orientation, and training they provide.

Additionally, the leadership you show when orchestrating department faculty to also support new members can be a key to early career faculty success. Part of this guidance is helping these faculty members navigate relationships with their senior colleagues and interpret messages they hear from them (see Inset 12.2 for ways to encourage senior colleagues to form relationships with early career faculty). It is also showing them when they need to temper their angst in a system where people who are less productive than themselves decide their fate. Also, they may simply need to vent when they are not supported or if they are having difficulty staying motivated when they see some colleagues phone it in.

The department should be considered the primary unit of socialization (as noted in Chapter 3) and the primary social unit. Early career faculty members want to learn about how to be a professor at your university and how to be a scholar of a particular discipline as well as socialize with their departmental colleagues (Cawyer & Friedrich, 1998), talk to them about their personal concerns, support them, and feel their support

---

Inset 12.2.
Strategy for Success: Encouraging Senior Faculty Support of Junior Colleagues

1. Encourage them to initiate contact by inviting their early career colleagues to lunch, offering to read papers, or visiting classes.
2. Build into evaluations responsibility for nurturing new colleagues.
3. Create opportunities for formal collaborations: team-teaching, coauthoring, or curriculum work.
4. Recognize and reward their efforts.

Note. Adapted from Sorcinelli (2000, p. 11).

in return. The social/emotional support they find validates early career faculty in many ways—intellectually, as we discuss later, but also just in knowing that their concerns are real and they are worthy members of the team (Lindholm, 2003).

The department and college or school are also places where early career faculty find their intellectual home. Early career faculty who experience intellectual stimulation from their colleagues and who have colleagues who are interested in their work find that work is a fun place to be (Lindholm, 2003). Finding their intellectual home in the department is often harder for women and other minoritized faculty, but those in Lindholm's study (2003) were able to locate more support in research centers or other organizations on campus.

What can deans and department chairs do to make sure the closest academic unit is where the early career faculty members find the best fit, the most support, and the best launch pad for their careers? Although we address more strategies later in this chapter, here we focus on a few that are most directly related to the goal of fit, belonging, and support. First, a department orientation has been shown as the best predictor for satisfaction for early career faculty members (Cawyer & Friedrich, 1998). However, it would be shortsighted to think, that all orientation needs are met through orientation or mentoring programs. Inset 12.3 provides an example of a syllabus that a department chair might use to orient faculty over the first two years; all newcomers, not just assistant professors, can benefit from ongoing orientation.

Second, scheduling regular meetings with your early career faculty provides a regular time to touch base, normalize asking of questions, and ensure that all areas of the orientation syllabus are covered. We find that faculty may not use that time every week, but they feel secure knowing that time and space are on the books for even the

Inset 12.3.
Strategies for Success:
Two-Year Progressive Mentoring Plan
Each Semester:

1. Review CV and talk candidly about progress, especially in scholarship; suggest supports as needed; give specific feedback.
2. Review student evaluations; explain the confidential, formative, and summative components of the evaluation process; and give specific feedback.
3. Review faculty member's experiences, plans, and needs; celebrate successes.
4. Discuss faculty member's comfort and fit within the department, college, and university.
5. Review prior semester teaching evaluations and outline plans for improvement.

(continues)

smallest question. It structures the open-door policy so that all know the invitation is real. We recommend that chairs schedule one or two meetings a month for the first period of review, and then taper from there to ultimately a semester meeting once tenure is achieved. Assuming that a dean would have time for a similar pattern would be unreasonable, but deans should meet at least each term with their untenured faculty members. While the syllabus in Inset 12.3 is meant to guide the work of the department chair, deans can also use that as a guide and a check for understanding and consistency among their early career faculty in different academic units. Senior colleagues play a role here as well. While we do not recommend that they also schedule regular meetings with early career colleagues, it is good practice to ask them to coffee or lunch or stop in from time to time to touch base. The open-door invitation is made more genuine by these actions.

Third, department chairs and deans have a special role in making sure that early career faculty members are treated fairly by their colleagues. This role operationalizes the protection we spoke about early in this chapter. Making sure that their tenured colleagues are doing their fair share of (i.e., more) service is a place to start. Too often, early career faculty members raise their hands simply out of the discomfort of the silent room when the chair is asking

Inset 12.3. (*Continued*)
First Semester:

1. Orient the faculty member to the department: human resources and support, material resources, expectations, and overall culture.
2. Review campus resources.
3. Establish a safe listening space with the faculty member.
4. Suggest a mindful attitude of observation and data gathering before making possible service commitments.
5. Share the faculty member's own prior experiences, early campus experiences, plans, hopes, and personal well-being (e.g., social life, family, balance in lifestyle).
6. Strongly encourage a class observation by a program coordinator, department chair, faculty center for professional development, or a representative of another relevant entity.
7. Encourage the faculty member to attend workshops and other opportunities given to new faculty.
8. Introduce the faculty member to academic technology resources and library services.
9. Discuss RTP process, policies, documents, and necessary documentation.
10. Share funding opportunities at college and university levels. Offer to provide feedback on proposals. Share examples of proposals that have been awarded.

(*continues*)

Inset 12.3. (*Continued*)
Second Semester:

1. Help match the range of service possibilities to the faculty member's expertise and professional growth.
2. Discuss desired teaching experiences for the second year.
3. Coach through any reviews due that semester.
4. Review status of research and manuscripts. Offer to review manuscripts prior to journal submission or to coordinate a well-qualified senior faculty member to do the same.
5. Ask the faculty member to identify mentors on the faculty and in the field in general. If possible, facilitate a mentoring connection with the identified faculty mentor.

Inset 12.3. (*Continued*)
Third Semester:

1. Discuss annual review; review materials.
2. Discuss ways to connect with others outside the program and department.
3. Discuss ways to connect the faculty member with the scholarly community outside the institution. Offer to make introductions.

(continues)

for nominations or volunteers for committee membership. Tenured colleagues who continually shirk their service responsibilities are especially harmful to the progress of their nontenured peers. Chairs and deans need to be firm in confronting this behavior and holding tenured faculty to their obligations.

The more relational abuses that early career faculty may experience from their senior colleagues are more difficult to address, but it is even more important to do so, as they affect the newcomer's satisfaction and sense of belonging. Examples of these behaviors range from dress downs in meetings or group settings to microaggressions (e.g., eye-rolling, interrupting, calling them by the wrong name) based on minoritized status, to research collaborations that fail to honor contributions equitably, and even to bad-mouthing colleagues to students. Deans and chairs should not only be on the watch for this kind of behavior but also invite feedback from their early career faculty members by asking if they are experiencing any of these kinds of actions. If they are occurring, the chair or dean's responsibility is to follow up with the offending colleague to educate about and correct the behavior.

Building Networks Beyond the Academic Unit

Isolation is a very real phenomenon among early career faculty members and can occur for a multitude of reasons. If the department is very tenured, then there may be many gaps between the newcomer and the senior faculty. There are not only generational differences but also likely methodological or disciplinary differences based on the recency of the newcomer's training. Differences in the social context in which the early career faculty members are coming to the professoriate are also present, as discussed earlier in this chapter. The differences in the social identities (race, ethnicity, gender, sexual orientation) of the newer and more senior colleagues are key areas where early career faculty also experience isolation. Given the relatively slow diversification of the U.S. professoriate (see Chapter 1), it is not just in very tenured departments where faculty find these differences. If a chair and dean are working hard to attend to the issues raised in the previous section, then they are already working to break down barriers that result in isolation. However, while those changes are underway, the chair and dean also need to facilitate connections for early career faculty across departments and the university to lessen the isolation they may experience.

> **Inset 12.3.** (*Continued*)
> **Fourth Semester:**
>
> 1. Help the faculty member interpret the department review letter.
> 2. Guide the preparation of the retention review files. Offer to review the faculty's professional narrative for the RTP file.
> 3. Make clear the process for the retention review, including any external review processes.
>
> *Source:* Adapted from Farmer, et al. (2014).

Early career faculty who are striving for intellectual community and a place of belonging appreciate connections to networks across campus. They enhance the experience of all early career faculty and have the potential to contribute significantly to their retention at the university. As mentioned, many minoritized faculty need to find community outside their academic units because there are likely just not enough colleagues from their racial, ethnic, sexual, or gender identity to form community and support. Faculty whose research areas are unique or multidisciplinary are also in particular need of extending their reach to other corners of the university. Because tenure-track lines are decreasing, helping early career faculty connect to other assistant professors across campus helps to build their social support network. This may be especially important if your institution does not have a formal mentoring or faculty support program. Cross-campus connections can soften the persistence of limited resources in higher education. Research has shown that early career faculty are especially appreciative when their chairs and deans connect them with colleagues who are involved in extramural grant projects where they can learn the craft of getting and managing grants, as well as bring their recent training to new projects (see Inset 12.4; see also Thomas, Lunsford, & Rodrigues, 2015).

Considering an ecological approach, deans, chairs, and senior colleagues can also facilitate early career faculty in creating regional, national, and

Inset 12.4.
Words From Early Career Faculty: Facilitating Connections

One of the things I'm so disappointed with is the fact that we don't have these research [connections] so a junior faculty like me could work with a professor who has a grant. To introduce me to the happenings in my area because coming in as new, it's going to take me a very, very long time to get a chance to meet or interact or to have that kind of relationship with people in this area who are doing research or who have funding or who have a source of funding or how to get funding. —Nancy

Inset 12.5.
Words From Early Career Faculty: The Importance of the Department Chair

I find that my chair is the most supportive chair a person could ever hope to have, but in a very conscientious way; he doesn't want to cramp my style. But it's almost been too much sometimes, where it's like, "Just tell me what you think I should do," you know? I'm a new teacher, and at a new job you would want that. —Catherine

international networks. If your institution expects your faculty to become nationally known in their disciplines, then facilitating these connections is an obligation. However, regardless of institutional expectations, many early career faculty are interested in networks through their professional associations and disciplines or in maintaining networks established in graduate school. Ensuring sufficient resources for travel to professional meetings is an obvious starting place of support here. But you can also use your own networks to connect early career faculty, especially if you share a disciplinary home. And you can encourage their involvement in special programs that professional associations have to mentor early career faculty. Sponsoring a lecture series where your early career faculty invite stars from their disciplines is another way to encourage connections.

The RTP Process

Early career faculty work diligently as detectives to figure out what they need to do to get tenure and promotion in their new academic home. They are concerned that expectations are different for them than when their senior colleagues were untenured, they find that expectations are ambiguous and ever changing (even if they may not actually be changing), and they hear conflicting messages (Austin & Rice, 1998). In the Austin and Rice study (1998), participants also spoke of the importance of specific and explicit feedback in order for it to be truly helpful. In many ways Catherine, an early career faculty member (see Inset 12.5), not only demonstrates this need for specific feedback when she appreciates her supportive chair but also wants him to be more directive regarding her teaching.

Continuity of mentoring and guidance is key for faculty members who are still in the process of tenure and promotions, which includes associate professors as well. However, as Austin and Rice (1998) found, early career faculty members often experience turnover in department chair and deans. If you are a new chair or dean, it is still important to attend to the needs of your pretenure faculty, even if they have a longer history at the institution than you do.

Mentoring

Most colleges and universities have some form of faculty. support that may be considered *mentoring* programs. These programs may be as small as preterm orientation, a longer-term group mentoring program based in a college, or as large as campus-wide mentoring programs

> **Inset 12.6.**
> **Resources for Success:**
> **Characteristics of Good Mentor Matches**
>
> 1. Meet regularly.
> 2. Show enthusiasm and motivation for mentoring.
> 3. Demonstrate authentic compatibility.
> 4. Engage in helpful, supportive interactions.
> 5. Show reciprocity.
> 6. Arrange collegial contacts.
> 7. Interact to improve teaching *and* scholarship.
> 8. Mentor evidences own benefits from mentoring.
> 9. Mentee eventually shows interest in mentoring others.
>
> *Note.* Adapted from Boyle and Boice (1998, p. 164).

matching individual faculty members. Participants' experiences with success in these efforts are just as varied. In general, most research says that spontaneous mentoring is most effective—those relationships that develop outside formal structures. However, research has also found that those who benefit most from spontaneous mentoring are White men (Boyle & Boice, 1998). This finding is problematic for many reasons, as these mentoring relationships often result in a number of benefits, such as access to funded research and publication opportunities. Compounding this problem is that research does not paint a very optimistic picture of formal mentoring programs, and at times those who stand to benefit the most—minoritized faculty—are sometimes worried that their participation in these programs may be considered remedial or even fear that what they share may be used for evaluative purposes (Boyle & Boice, 1998; Denard, Lunsford, & Rodrigues, 2015). For those deans and chairs who are establishing mentoring programs, Boyle and Boice's (1998) study of a comprehensive mentoring program provides excellent practices, criteria, and dimensions of effective mentoring programs. Their bottom line is that these programs must be carefully structured and require ongoing supervision to keep them operating at optimum levels, as summarized in Inset 12.6.

Regardless of the type of mentoring, early career faculty report that they need mentoring on the following: (a) research and scholarship, (b) teaching, (c) promotion and tenure, and (d) collegial relations and politics (Boyle & Boice, 1998). One role that department chairs and deans can play in the development of good mentoring relationships for their early career faculty members is to make sure that those who mentor do it well. If an early career faculty member needs mentoring around teaching, make sure that advice is coming from your best teachers. If another is seeking mentoring around scholarship, be sure the mentor is an active scholar. We all know some colleagues who might be better kept out of the mentoring, orientation, or advising process in some areas, but who might be excellent in others.

Professional association mentoring programs are important for early career faculty for multiple reasons and should be encouraged and supported by department chairs and deans. These programs take many forms; for example, online mentoring programs, preconference workshops, and one-to-one matching programs that continue over time. These opportunities have multiple benefits for faculty members who are prone to isolation in their department due to social identity status, subdiscipline focus, or academic rank. Mentoring opportunities at this level promote the development of national networks where they start as mentees and then become mentors.

Supporting Good Citizenship Through Appropriate Service

Service is likely the most ambiguous of the three areas of responsibility for early career faculty. There is a good amount of anxiety when faculty are trying to figure out what to do, how much to do, and when to do it. They are also likely receiving conflicting messages from colleagues about service. "Learn to say no" or "protect your time" messages place them in a difficult place. They know they need to serve, and they may want to serve because they are genuinely interested in the work, as well as contributing to and developing relationships with colleagues and students. But they also do not want to be considered pushovers by saying yes or too often raising their hands to volunteer. Your guidance in helping them to choose and balance is invaluable. And in reflecting on the theme of protecting your investment, advocating for them through tapping senior colleagues for service is a key feature of your support.

We recommend that chairs, deans, and other mentors adopt a developmental approach to service responsibilities. Extensive service is one of the pitfalls that many early career faculty experience. In the first two years—usually before the retention review—service should be focused at the program or department level. After retention, opportunities can include low-risk service, meaning avoiding politically charged committees, at the college level. Later in the pretenure years, service can perhaps include program coordination (if it cannot be avoided prior to tenure) or service on nonpolitical university committees or other activities.

A consistent complaint of minoritized early career faculty members is that they are asked to serve on committees because their "diverse perspective is needed," essentially being asked to represent their ethnic, racial, gender, or sexual orientation group. This request puts an uneven burden on these faculty members, both in terms of time and, ironically, in their ability to develop a sense of belonging and commitment to the department, college, or university. While their perspectives may indeed be needed on many aspects of faculty governance, a better practice is to present all the options and allow the faculty member to decide the best fit, with your coaching around the appropriate amount of service and where they can best contribute without being at political risk.

The next piece of advice may seem counterintuitive to the last: Value identity-based service and train your RTP committees to do the same. The difference is that in identity-based service, faculty members choose to be involved in governance and service activities that align with one of their social identities. Examples of these might be advising an African American student organization, holding an office in the Latinx faculty association, providing workshops for the Women's Center, or leading a community mentoring program for LGBTQ teens. Often this kind of service is less valued than traditional service, such as on curriculum committees or the academic senate. However, for minoritized faculty, service in these arenas means they are able to contribute to their own communities and also develop important relationships that sustain their growth and provide concrete ways for them to actualize the sweet spot— a central theme of this book, where faculty members align teaching, research, service, and their identity.

Developing Outstanding Teachers

For most, the purpose of doctoral education is to prepare scholars in the field with the assumption that deep content expertise transfers to good teaching once the doctoral candidate enters the classroom. Although teaching-oriented professional development for graduate teaching assistants is offered at most research universities, the activity is primarily voluntary. Given the busy lives and scholarship focus of most doctoral students, elective how-to-teach programs are seen as tangential to their preparation, and thus, doctoral students think the time may better be used elsewhere. It would be erroneous to assume that your early career faculty know how to teach, and even more erroneous to believe that they are comfortable in the classroom. In this section, we address three ways in which you may best support faculty in becoming great teachers, namely, providing resources, limiting new course preparation, and offering support in the course evaluation process.

Few professors appreciate a blank slate when it comes to teaching a course for the first time. We assume that standard course outlines or syllabi are approved by the department, complete with approved required texts. Make sure that faculty have all of this material far in advance; even new hires can receive this information several months before their appointment begins. Assigning a senior faculty member as a teaching resource person for early career faculty members provides a venue for them to have easy access to someone from whom they can seek answers, share concerns, and receive sound advice. Also be sure that these early career faculty members know all of the technology resources available to them, as well as any departmental conventions concerning technology.

For many faculty, regardless of rank, it takes three years to master a course—the first to experience it, the second to revise it, and the third to perfect it. It is good practice to give early career faculty an opportunity to show improvement over time by not switching courses each year. In addition, limiting the number of unique courses allows faculty to economize their work. If possible, assign multiple sections of the same course in a semester. These strategies allow early career faculty to develop expertise and confidence in their teaching.

The whole issue of evaluation of teaching causes much stress for early career faculty members. As noted in Inset 12.3, department chairs should review course evaluations with their early career faculty as soon as the evaluations become available. In Chapter 5 we offer several strategies that can assist faculty members in digesting this feedback and moving forward with plans for improvement and changes. As you help faculty with these plans, you can connect them with resources and help to set a schedule for tackling needed change. Class visits, not for formal evaluation proposes, are also a way to support good teaching. So often, the classroom is the professor's private domain; newer instructors are thus learning to teach in isolation, relying only on student evaluations for feedback. In a class visit, the department chair or other senior colleague can provide feedback on what the faculty member is already doing well and make recommendations for specific improvement in other areas. Pay attention to things like overreliance on PowerPoint presentations, use of active learning techniques, student engagement, and other conventions that are important to your discipline.

Helping Early Career Faculty Achieve Their Scholarship Dreams

Due to the competitive nature of tenure-track searches, your early career faculty members likely join you with a record of scholarship. Of course, now they are working to establish their scholarly agenda and produce while taking on the full scope of faculty work. Therefore, in this section we focus on how you can help faculty, not so much with how to do their scholarship, but on how to maneuver the elements that complicate their efforts. We find that early career faculty need help in the following areas: (a) managing the notion of time to publication, (b) focusing in the face of competing demands and opportunities, and (c) coaching in the management of collaborative research.

The research and scholarly process is slow at best. Depending on your discipline, establishing labs, completing research projects, and designing creative activities all take time—not only in raw hours to get them done but also in terms of the processes they demand. Starting a research project today might mean that the conference paper is at least a year away, with the journal article taking as long as three years to get in print. When most assistant professors are up for retention in year three, it is evident that time management and project management skills are sorely needed. In Chapter 6 we offer strategies that early career faculty can employ to make wise choices and to move forward efficiently.

In your regular meetings with your early career faculty, be sure that you ask *specific* questions about their progress, not general questions like, "How is it going?" Ask if items are complete, if they have been submitted for review, and so on. We advise early career faculty to have items at different points in the pipeline. You can reinforce this suggestion by helping them estimate the time it will take to move a project to submission and by strategizing their timing—making sure that when they are in a waiting period on one project, they are working on another. You might also need to be firm in advising them on projects that may just take too long for the pretenure years, encouraging them to look at their career with a longer view. A complex longitudinal or multilayered project may be best saved for later.

Part of time and project management is guiding early career faculty in making decisions when they have competing demands and opportunities. If you have created a collegial environment in your department or college, a natural outcome might be that more senior faculty invite newcomers to join them in projects. Steer them in the right direction. Who are your excellent researchers, those who can model good work? Who will invite true collaboration rather than consider the early career faculty member as a seasoned graduate assistant? And by all means, if you see early career faculty members going in a wrong direction, do not hesitate to intervene. Likewise, if your faculty are involved in professional associations or national networks, you may need to help them choose collaborations efficiently as they are increasing the number of opportunities available to them.

Within collaborations, even with your best guidance, early career faculty likely need assistance with negotiating workload, boundaries, and authorship. Catherine, an early career faculty member, found her department chair to be incredibly helpful in taking advantage of grant opportunities by assuring her that he would take care of competing demands in the department (see Inset 12.7). These choices and conversations are especially difficult for your faculty

Inset 12.7.
Words From Early Career Faculty: Prioritizing Scholarship Opportunities

I'm sort of in the point of looking for postdocs and looking for funding to finish my book, and my chair said very clearly from day one, he's like, "I just want to let you know that from my perspective, I'm saying for the best thing for the program, the college, the university, is for you to get the money and do your thing. We'll miss you in the classroom, but that's not a factor. You need to do your thing." So that was pretty awesome, actually. And he's right. If you want to attract and keep good people you have to have that attitude. —Catherine

to initiate, so begin to talk with them early about these topics. You can role-play the conversations. You can give them suggestions about what work is worthy of first authorship and what is expected for second authorship. If problems have already arisen, role playing assertive conversations (not confrontations) can give them language and confidence to protect their interests in these collaborations. If you know them to be in scholarly collaborations, be sure to ask about these issues specifically in your regular meetings. You may also find it necessary to mediate problem situations, especially if the collaborators are within your department or college.

Concluding Thoughts

In Chapter 2 we propose that faculty are most productive and most satisfied with their careers and lives when their identities as teachers, scholars, and citizens intersect and express who they are as people. Early career faculty want to be at the aspirational place where they integrate the three areas of faculty work with their professional and personal identities. As you work with your faculty, you can help them see the integration and connections to their identities. Of course, to do this you will need to get to know them as people to learn what is important to them, what kind of careers they want to have, and what kind of professors they want to be. Then you can point out opportunities for integration that they perhaps cannot see. You can help them to see the overlap in what they do in teaching, scholarship, and service and teach them how to optimize the synergy of that overlap. Doing so represents the concept of organizational justice we introduced at the start of this chapter and honors the psychological contract between the faculty member and the institution. If you can help early career faculty grasp the opportunities to create the sweet spot, they will be more likely to love their work and where they do it—and they will more likely create a career and life at your institution, delivering the ultimate return on your investment.

13

PULLING IT ALL TOGETHER

Getting to the Sweet Spot

As assistant professors, we so often think of our work and careers as three distinct buckets: teaching, research, and service. We worry about having enough in these buckets and the quality of what is in there. We hope that, throughout these chapters, you have begun to get a sense of how to balance these buckets and to be successful in them. But more so, we hope that you are beginning to see yourself and your career as more than just a series of buckets defined by traditional performance expectations. In fact, we would add an even more important bucket that most early career faculty may not consider—*you*. And all of those buckets should overlap and come together to build not only a career but also a professional identity and life.

We contend that when your identities as a person, scholar, teacher, and citizen are well developed and well aligned, the synergy that results allows for a sense of *flow* in such a way that work in one area enhances work in another; that conflicts between who you are as a person and who you are as a professor are minimized; and that you ultimately study, teach, and serve in ways that enrich who you are in ways that benefit the students, discipline, and institutions you serve.

Faculty Growth, Identity, and Conflict

The larger concept of identity is one that encompasses all the different ways we define ourselves, our *history*, the roles we play in family and life, the values and ethics by which we live, how we interact with others and the relationships that result, and the way in which we make sense of the world around of us. More simply, King and Baxter Magolda (2005) think of a *holistic identity* as one that has intrapersonal (values, feelings, ethics), interpersonal (relationships and interactions with others), and cognitive (how we think, how we make meaning) dimensions. Given the multidimensionality of identity and how it connects to so many parts of our lives, considering it a cornerstone to how we function as professors seems appropriate.

Indeed, the faculty growth framework (O'Meara et al., 2008) positions faculty as *learners,* with sufficient *agency* to create their work environments. To have *relationships* that are both inspiring and challenging, leading them to make *commitments* to their work and institutions, this agency must be grounded in identity in order for it to work. As in all areas of life, the growth process is not always smooth. O'Meara's later work (with Lounder & Campbell, 2014) connects the growth perspective with the tension it may take to get there through a discussion of how sensemaking helps us protect what we see and feel about ourselves. In many cases, growth comes of conflict or dissonance, and the way we make sense of it may help us to maintain a positive identity while moving forward.

Returning to our idea of the sweet spot is useful. As Figure 13.1 reminds us, creating your sweet spot is a complex process involving interaction across multiple layers of self.

We are negotiating our personal identities and values; our professional identity; and the tasks of teaching, scholarship, and service. Add in the fact that we are trying to navigate and decipher institutional expectations (at

Figure 13.1. The sweet spot within your professional identity and self.

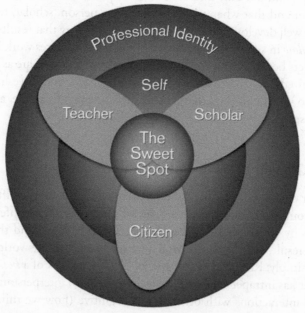

multiple levels) as well as relationships with colleagues and students, and probably settling into a new life in a new area, and internal conflict or dissonance is almost inevitable. However, this conflict is also the foundation for creativity and growth.

Cognitive conflict or dissonance is important because this is how we learn. Interactions with colleagues, students, and institutions provide the venue for that learning. Through challenges they offer, we examine our positions, values, and capacities and evaluate them to determine what improvement is needed and what changes need to be made. For example, in Reybold's study of early career faculty (2005), participants described how these interactions affected their experiences. Many felt disillusionment following a honeymoon period, and "disagreements with peers and mentors, frustration with students, and anxiety about tenure" (p. 112) caused some to consider leaving the academy. Those most affected by this kind of disillusionment were motivated by an ideal, and when that ideal was disrupted, they experienced dissatisfaction with their work. Others, who were motivated by accomplishment, resented disruptions that affected their productivity and focus—especially in relation to teaching and service assignments. In these cases, perhaps if faculty members had used these experiences as opportunities to examine and evaluate positions, values, and capacities in relation to the disruptions, they could more easily have reframed and taken ownership of these things that happen to them. Using Reybold's (2005) examples, a faculty member who is frustrated by how tedious, practical service interfered with productivity could instead accept that service is part of the job; having to do service allows him to do the research he loves.

The whole point of Reybold's (2005) findings is that perhaps disillusionment is a natural part of the process, calling us to see our jobs in new ways, define ourselves in relationship to our jobs, and confront the reality of the job itself. We resolve the conflict by accepting what it is and what it allows us to do, by changing as much as we can about the situation to get it as close to the ideal as possible, or perhaps making the ultimate decision to leave the institution or the academy all together. Indeed, Reybold concludes that those who "engaged the disrupting force through reflection and action" (2005, p. 118) reconfigured their professional identities and found an opportunity for growth. A good example for this is how a faculty member constructs the meaning and response to a tepid retention review. The initial response might be to blame the RTP committee for misunderstanding the quality or effort of his performance thus far. But by truly examining one's own work, by carefully reading feedback and reaching out for verbal feedback, the candidate is able to see himself differently, more accurately. Perhaps his professional identity changes from one that is founded on self-assessed achievement to one of a learner who is in the process of becoming more expert.

Resolving cognitive conflict in ways that are productive for our well-being and for our success as a professor and individual means developing an internal locus of control that lays a foundation for a career where we set and meet our own standards for excellence. We move from asking, "What do I need for tenure?" to asking, "What kind of impact do I want to have on my field?" Defining who we are according to our own standards is a pillar of identity, personal and professional. It is also critical in the development of self-authorship and the enactment of agency, which helps us to create the sweet spot. Through reflection, reframing, and taking action in all the dimensions of a professor's work, it is possible to move from a place of *letting things happen to us* to *making things happen for us*—authoring our work life.

In Chapter 10 we focused on finding and maintaining balance. We revisit it here because the sweet spot only becomes a reality when you are able to connect identity to your work—achieving intrapersonal balance. Sternberg's (2015) essay on reflections from an old professor, discussed in Chapter 10, supports this well. He championed being true to yourself, operating from your own standards, and making decisions that reflect your integrity. Most important, he advised placing your family (however you conceptualize that unit) first, and all else follows. From a self-authorship perspective, nothing works unless you are clear about who you are, what you value, and how your work as a professor connects to you as a person.

The academy, with its focus on objectivity and depersonalization, has not traditionally left much room for a professor as a person. Current forces reinforce this trend: increased competition for resources; fewer tenure-track positions, with no fewer candidates on the market; a push to run universities like businesses. These make it an employer's market, one where there is plenty of talent out there, where if a faculty member is dissatisfied or unsuccessful at fitting in, another candidate waits around the corner.

This dynamic makes much of what we advocate harder than ever, but so much more necessary for your work and life satisfaction. Each time you are able to take the parts of the job—teaching, scholarship, and service—and move them closer to who you are and what you value, the greater the chance that you increase satisfaction. Authoring and agency transform the place where you work (department, college, institution, discipline) into one that integrates all the spheres in your sense of professional and personal identities. By taking control of how work and place make you *feel*, your excellent performance follows.

In Chapter 2 we highlighted how making commitments to ideas, people, and institutions comes from identifying the things we care about most.

Done well, this process results in our ability to center our passions and work to integrate them into the multiple dimensions of our work and lives. It helps us develop and discover our own sweet spot. In the following sections, we get more pragmatic, with recommendations to help you actualize your passions in all the domains of the job, placing you and your identity at the center.

Grounding Teaching in Your Identity

Early in your career you may not have a lot of choice over which classes you are assigned. Over time this changes as you climb the seniority ladder, become recognized as expert, or as those who "own" the courses you want move on. For some, depending on the size of your institution and department, this may come quickly; for some it may seem like forever.

However, many times assistant professors are first assigned service courses that are distant from their disciplinary passion. What can you do? In terms of formal courses, we recommend two options. First, negotiate to have at least one course a year that is closest to your beloved subject matter. This may mean that you take another of those service classes, but if you start with asking for just one course in your area of expertise, the chances of getting it are greater. Second, find ways to build your subject matter into the courses you are assigned. If you are allowed to choose texts and readings, be creative in finding the connections to the course material and your subject matter. Perhaps the connection is in the assignments you create or in the examples you use in your lectures.

You can also teach your subject matter beyond the classroom. Offering a special lecture to students and colleagues is a smart way to find your intellectual community and work on having your colleagues recognize your expertise. Seeking out certain students to advise may be another strategy to connect your identity and passion to your teaching. If you are from a minoritized group, being an adviser may happen naturally, as we discussed in Chapter 8, or may be intentionally assigned. Think of advising as an opportunity to serve groups that are important to you and to develop mentoring relationships with students where you involve them in your research or advocate for them in department policies and practices. In these out-of-class experiences with students, you may be more likely to experience the interconnections between who you are as a person and a teacher. You teach students in different ways, through mentoring and involvement in your research, and provide important service to your department.

Grounding Scholarship and Creative Activities in Your Identity

If this is your favorite part of being a professor, it is likely that your identity is fairly well connected to it. You may already see yourself as a biologist or a sculptor, over all other professional identity choices. If this is the case, then your task is to make sure you have what you need to do the best research or creative work possible. For almost any discipline, the surest way to get the most time and resources to fund your work is through external funding, which is one of the reasons we devoted Chapter 7 to the subject. But external funding is hard to get, and in some disciplines, there may be very few grant programs.

Again, turning to our spheres and the sweet spot, there are ways to optimize your research time and resources by tapping into the other dimensions. Try to integrate research and data collection into course assignments. In essence, each student becomes a miniresearch assistant for you. As an example, one colleague constructed an interview protocol for his class and, for three consecutive years, had students interview participants as part of a group assignment. He retained the data (with their permission, of course) and now has a large qualitative dataset that would have been impossible to build on his own. You can also integrate research into the service that you perform. These can be action research projects, where participants are also part of the inquiry process and the findings directly assist a school, agency, community, and so on. Another example is a colleague who studies beach waste. He developed a children's book educating children about garbage's impact on marine life and a field guide for classes to collect data on local beaches. The teachers sent the data to him, and he amassed data he could not collect on his own while providing a critical educational experience for children.

Connecting research or creative activities with one or more social identities is another way to develop the sweet spot. Almost any discipline has applications to specific groups of people or communities. Finding ways for your work to enhance, improve, or change circumstances for communities you care about is immensely rewarding. Because almost all minoritized groups are understudied, if you are a member of such a group and an expert in your field, you have the potential to bring insights that have been ignored or overlooked. As an example, the University of Hawaii has implemented a program to recruit Native Hawaiian assistant professors in specific disciplines across the university. Bringing these perspectives to medicine, law, education, ecology, land management, and so forth has been instrumental in addressing critical needs in communities that have long been underserved. For these young scholars, an opportunity to give back through their scholarship has enabled them to connect research and service to their identities as Native

Hawaiians and then take that expertise into the classroom to complete the integration of who they are with what they do.

Grounding Service in Your Identity

In our experience and through our review of literature for this book, service is that dimension that most faculty say they try to avoid. However, our institutions, our disciplines, and our communities *need* us to serve. When service is connected to your identity, it becomes much less tedious and can become something that feeds your soul. The bottom line is that you have to do service regardless; our institutions may differ in how much service they expect and where it needs to be, but unless you are unusually successful at bringing money to the university, it will be required of you. The great thing is that, for the most part, the choice of how to serve is yours.

As we discussed in Chapter 8, all kinds of reasons influence your choice of service activities. If you are new to the area, choosing low-risk committees that introduce you to new groups of colleagues on campus is a great way to meet new people and may help you develop social ties that lead to a more balanced life. Becoming involved in a community organization that is connected to your disciplinary work extends your network beyond the university and opens opportunities for friendship and collaborative scholarship. If you find that your teaching assignments are not enabling the kind of interactions you would like to have with students, consider advising a student organization or volunteering for an alternative spring break or study abroad trip, especially if you also like to travel.

As in the other sections in this chapter, finding opportunities to connect your service to one or more of your social identities is a way to make service meaningful. Baez (2000) found that when faculty of color connected service to the needs of their communities, they had experiences with critical agency that helped them to resist and redefine academic structures that hindered their success. Gaining confidence and refining resistance skills has the potential to help minoritized faculty defend their choices and take action to counter microaggressions and discrimination when they occur. Serving their communities also gives them a sense of belonging and an opportunity to create research opportunities and partnerships.

Synergy and the Sweet Spot: Making It Happen

When your scholarship, teaching, and service are aligned with who you are and what you value, the act of making and defending those choices is easier. You seek research, scholarship, or creative activities that connect to your passion and purpose. You jockey to teach subjects that are the closest to your passion and purpose. You have a sound rationale for declining a request to be on a committee. Being able to do these things requires that you talk to colleagues about what you do and what you value. The more they know about your work and passion, the more likely you are to have these choices honored. Kelsky (2015) says that you need to "toot your own horn" and offers several ways to do so (she also stressed that men do this more easily than women). This horn tooting is a way you can get those around you to care about what is important to you, so that they see its value and support the decisions you make.

We would be naïve to think that aligning your work with your social identities is controversy free. Many colleagues question the legitimacy of such involvement, especially in the area of scholarship. Doing *me-search*, at times a derogatory term for researchers who study the experiences of their own minoritized social identity group, is often critiqued for being subjective, being nonrigorous, and lacking the objectivity that is a hallmark of good research. Despite nonpositivist research paradigms that contend that there is no objectivity in research, conservative colleagues, institutions, and disciplines still have growth to do in acknowledging the legitimacy of research conducted by non-White male scholars in non-White male communities. A recent essay by Victor Ray (2016) offers a strong counter to this way of thinking, noting that most research that is automatically deemed objective and rigorous is based on Eurocentric values and the universality of White culture and norms. If you are making the choice to engage in scholarship embedded in your social identity community, learning to defend your choice and provide a counterargument is wise. Ray's (2016) essay has a number of references that may be helpful if you are making this argument in your tenure narrative.

Part of self-authoring your career as a faculty member is making and truly owning your choices. Here, the push is being able to defend those choices not only to your colleagues or RTP committees but also to yourself. Letting go of externally imposed expectations and replacing them with your own can mean that you are opting out of long-standing expectations. When Ortiz left her position at a large research university for a teaching-oriented comprehensive university, the decision was questioned by many except those who knew her well. Their understanding of that decision was made easier because she had regularly shared what was important to her with her department colleagues. Thus, when an opportunity became available to move closer to home, to a community where she already had established ties, where there was a lot less winter and more people and resources from her cultural background, the move was not a surprise. It took her longer to accept the legitimacy of the decision. It is an example of what Rockquemore (2013) stresses: Early career faculty members need to map out their own career and define their own success, resisting—or embracing, if they choose—traditional expectations.

Conclusion: Building A Career Worth Having

Our goal for you is to create a job that you love, that supports your goals for not just a career, but a life. Your career will have twists and turns, successes and disappointments. As long as you attend to developing your life along with your career, setbacks are more manageable. Kirk (2013) says that if you cannot find some part of the job that feeds your soul, then please find something else to do with your life. Find your joy and have the strength to overtly commit to it. Be grateful for the parts of the job that you love. Let that joy help you to focus on what is going well rather than on the problems. Remember that a career is long.

To more concretely demonstrate the sweet spot, we offer illustrations of our career arcs. Our intent here is to show that these pretenure years are but a fraction of your career and that getting beyond them successfully with a full life is actually possible. They also give examples of how we have integrated parts of our lives so that the intersections reflect who we are as people and professors, catching a glimpse of how our identities are expressed throughout.

Laura Henriques's Journey

The early part of my time as a faculty member was less self-authored and more opportunistic. I started as a lecturer while finishing my dissertation and felt compelled to say yes to most of the opportunities offered to me. I wanted to be a tenure-track faculty member when I finished my doctorate and figured these opportunities would provide me with experiences to grow and be more competitive. It is only in retrospect that I could see a common thread throughout the experiences. I love science and how we can make sense of our world through that lens. I am passionate about helping others see that beauty. As I look across my 20-plus-year career, I can easily trace that common theme through my scholarship and service. My scholarship includes multiple programmatic grants to help students and practicing teachers become more confident and competent to teach science. I have been able to merge this professional passion with my personal core values by providing a science camp for homeless youth that is cotaught by prospective teachers. This has been my most fulfilling and rewarding professional project. I am service-oriented, and my service started at the local level and has expanded to be state-level service to support the implementation of high-quality science education. Findings from scholarly and service work impact my teaching as I seek to engage students in science learning. I strive to surround myself with like-minded people. I enjoy working with others to solve problems and make a difference. When I am in a community of similarly inclined people, there is a joy to the work, which compensates for the long hours. As I have matured in my career I find that I still have a tendency to say yes to too many things. I cannot help but see the opportunities present, but I am more discerning in what I agree to do. I need to feel strongly about the project and its outcomes, and I need to enjoy the people with whom I will be working.

Anna M. Ortiz's Journey

As my career has evolved over 20 years, I have found it more and more synchronistic. My initial work on ethnic identity development in college students led to work on other diversity topics, fortunately at a time when this became more focal in higher education. This not only allowed me to develop broad expertise from a scholarly perspective but also gave me numerous opportunities to engage in service at multiple levels where this expertise was needed. I was able to work on behalf of Latinx students, both in service and scholarship. That work fed my need to give back to my community and to better connect to my own ethnic identity. Along the way, my interest and commitment to supporting students of color transferred to supporting faculty of color. Many of the developmental strategies I taught also worked with my mentoring of new faculty. That work extended to faculty development in general, finding ways to help faculty, regardless of rank or level, reach their full potential and create their sweet spot. I took this on at a national level when I was asked to create the faculty division for my practitioner-based professional association. There are many more linkages and overlaps. At this point in my career it can be difficult to see where scholarship ends and service begins or imagine when teaching stood alone. More recently I have taken my favorite avocational interest—wine—and became a certified sommelier. I bring my work as a professor to that role, as I teach wine classes, write columns, and advise on wine-related travel.

Don Haviland's Journey

I am part of a dual-career academic couple, and we made a commitment to always live in the same location—taking whatever jobs would allow us to do so. While my wife immediately found a faculty job at a community college that she still loves, I spent eight years moving between jobs in educational research and administration, not even seeking a faculty career. However, as I write this, I am now completing my tenth year of a faculty career and could not feel more fortunate. I started to find my rhythm around year five, and my work and my professional identity have continued to merge since.

I have always had a personal commitment to making things work (thus my administrative work) so that students could succeed. My early scholarship was around implementing and supporting faculty work in assessment of student learning, to support faculty and student success. This work (and my own experience) sparked a deeper interest in the faculty experience, which led to longitudinal research on pretenure faculty (and this book!), as well as studies on non-tenure-track faculty. These inquiries reflected my personal commitments to student success, but also to equity and respect for all faculty. As I have matured as a faculty member, I have also been able to translate my interests into growth in other areas. My work in assessment and evaluation led to my involvement in the creation of a center for evaluation, evaluation studies that led to publications, and my service on institutional committees devoted to research to improve student outcomes. As a teacher I have grown confident enough to move away from lectures and toward active learning, discussion, and more class activity—all designed to help students learn the problem-solving skills I see as central to addressing issues in higher education today. And after 10 years, I am finally able to teach courses using readings that I use in my own scholarship and even use my own scholarship in those courses! I have loved the journey and look forward to more.

Although these statements make it seem like we are done, we are not! The faculty growth perspective shows that career building is a lifelong endeavor. Although we are all full professors, our careers continue to change. Our work continues to evolve, coming in even closer to the sweet spot. As we assume leadership positions, these roles may become a new sphere where what we learn there feeds back into and is informed by the other spheres. Surprises in our nonwork lives may give us opportunities to bring more into the sweet spot.

Our pretenure years were fraught with the same struggles you may or will be experiencing. Those six years just did not seem like they would go by quickly enough, and then they had gone by too quickly. There was the anxiety over fit, over legitimacy, wondering if we were doing enough. But as we moved to the associate professor years and beyond, what became clear is that it is possible to construct a faculty career that is humane and meaningful and honors all parts of ourselves. With guidance, we may have come to this conclusion earlier—and we hope we are providing you the guidance to do just that. In the Season 14 finale of *Top Chef*, after the final "chef-testants" presented their meals in the context of their life's passions, one of the judges proclaimed that when we perform at our absolute best, we ultimately find ourselves (Lakshmi, 2017). We wish you the best as you find your passion, integrate your identity as person and professor, and bring all those dimensions together to create your sweet spot. Enjoy the journey.

Background on Longitudinal Study of Early Career Faculty

I n summer 2009 we began a longitudinal study of tenure-track faculty members at a public, comprehensive university, as they have moved through the pretenure years of their careers, navigating (among other things) adjustments to faculty life, a new institution, and changing family situations. The goal was to follow these faculty as they progressed through the early years of their career and moved toward tenure.

Annual interviews with these faculty were conducted starting at the end of their first year and continued through until they either left the institution (as 2 did) or earned tenure. In total, 42 separate interviews, ranging from 60 to 90 minutes each, were conducted with 9 faculty members, resulting in nearly 1,000 pages of interview transcripts. Participants were from the professions, sciences, and social sciences.

The interviews used the same faculty growth framework (O'Meara et al., 2008) we have used in this book to explore these faculty members' experiences, challenges, growth, and learning. The faculty members were asked each year about their high and low points, lessons they were learning, actions and strategies they were using in their work, and their personal and professional goals. We talked about their work and personal lives, colleagues, spouses or partners, children, and friends.

Resources for Success
Books and Other Resources on Being a Faculty Member

In our work as faculty members and in writing this book, we have come across and used many sources. Following are some that we have found particularly valuable.

Books

There are many good books on how to succeed as a new faculty member. We have particularly enjoyed the five listed here, for various reasons. Boice's (2000) book is a classic and perhaps the one most grounded in empirical research. The others offer solid advice and great insights and serve as good reminders that you are not alone.

1. Boice, R. (2000). *Advice for new faculty members: Nihil nimus.* Boston, MA: Allyn and Bacon.
2. Lang, J. M. (2005). *Life on the tenure track: Lessons from the first year.* Baltimore, MD: The Johns Hopkins University Press.
3. Lucas, C. L., & Murry, J. W., Jr. (2011). *New faculty: A practical guide for academic beginners* (3rd ed.). New York, NY: Palgrave Macmillan.
4. Rockquemore, K. A., & Laszloffy, T. (2008). *The Black academic's guide to winning tenure—without losing your soul.* Boulder, CO: Lynne Rienner Publishers.
5. Watson, E. (Ed.) (2014). *Overcoming adversity in academia.* Lanham, MD: University Press of America.

Online and Other Resources

Myriad online resources are useful for ideas, support, and contextualizing your experiences. Following are some of our favorites:

- chroniclevitae.com—From *The Chronicle of Higher Education*, this site posts commentaries and advice, has online communities, lists jobs, and includes a syllabi database.
- chronicle.com/blogs/profhacker—ProfHacker is a jointly edited blog hosted by *The Chronicle of Higher Education*.
- insidehighered.com/blogs/gradhacker—GradHacker, hosted by *Inside Higher Ed*, offers advice targeted to graduate students that is still quite relevant to faculty.
- insidehighered.com/blogs/mama-phd—Mama PhD, also hosted by *Inside Higher Ed*, is written by mothers balancing parenthood and academic life.

REFERENCES

AAUP. (2016). *Collegiality as a criterion for faculty evaluation.* Washington, DC: American Association of University Professors. Retrieved from https://www.aaup .org/report/collegiality-criterion-faculty-evaluation

Alexander, P. A. (2008). Yes . . . but: Footnotes to sage advice. *Educational Psychology Review, 20,* 71–77.

Ambrose, M. L. (2002). Contemporary justice research: A new look at familiar questions. *Organizational Behavior and Human Decision Processes, 89*(1), 803–812.

Anderson, K. J., & Smith, G. (2005). Students' preconceptions of professors: Benefits and barriers according to ethnicity and gender. *Hispanic Journal of Behavioral Sciences, 27*(2), 184–201. doi:10.1177/0739986304273707

Armenti, C. (2000). *Women academics blending private and personal lives.* Unpublished doctoral dissertation. Ontario Institute for Studies in Education, Ontario, CA.

Armenti, C. (2004). May babies and posttenure babies: Maternal decisions of women professors. *The Review of Higher Education, 27*(2), 211–231.

Astin, A. W. (1985). *Achieving educational excellence.* San Francisco, CA: Jossey-Bass.

Atherton, T. J., Barthelemy, R. S., Deconinck, W., Falk, M. L., Garmon, S., Long, E., & Reeves, K. (2016). *LGBT climate in physics: Building an inclusive community.* College Park, MD: American Physical Society. Retrieved from https://www .aps.org/programs/lgbt/upload/LGBTClimateinPhysicsReport.pdf

August, L., & Waltman, J. (2004). Culture, climate, and contribution: Career satisfaction among female faculty. *Research in Higher Education, 45*(2), 177–192.

Austin, A. E., & Rice, R. E. (1998). Making tenure viable: Listening to early career faculty. *The American Behavioral Scientist, 41*(5), 736–754.

Baez, B. (2000). Race-related service and faculty of color: Conceptualizing critical agency in academe. *Higher Education, 39*(3), 363–391. doi:10.1023/A:1003972214943

Bain, K. (2004). *What the best college teachers do.* Cambridge, MA: Harvard University Press.

Baldwin, R. G., & Blackburn, R. T. (1981). The academic career as a developmental process: Implications for higher education. *The Journal of Higher Education, 52*(6), 598–614.

Barr, R. B., & Tagg, J. (1995). From teaching to learning: A new paradigm for undergraduate education. *Change Magazine, 27*(6), 12–25.

Bates, R. J. (1984). Toward a critical practice of educational administration. In T. J. Sergiovanni & J. E. Corbally (Eds.), *Leadership and organizational culture: New perspectives on administrative theory and practice* (pp. 260–273). Urbana, IL: University of Illinois Press.

Bavishi, A., Madera, J. M., & Hebl, M. R. (2010). The effect of professor ethnicity and gender on student evaluations: Judged before met. *Journal of Diversity in Higher Education, 3*(4), 245–256. doi:10.1037/a0020763

Baxter Magolda, M. B. (2001). *Making their own way: Narratives for transforming higher education to promote self-authorship.* Sterling, VA: Stylus Publishing.

Bergquist, W. H., & Pawlak, K. (2008). *Engaging the six cultures of the academy* (2nd ed.). San Francisco, CA: Jossey-Bass.

Berrett, D. (2014, November 13). Professors' place in the classroom is shifting to the side. *The Chronicle of Higher Education.* Retrieved from http://www.chronicle.com/article/Professors-Place-in-the/149975

Bess, J. L. (1992). Collegiality: Toward a clarification of meaning and function. *Higher Education: Handbook of Theory and Research, 8,* 1–36.

Bianchi, S. M., Sayer, L. C., Milkie, M. A., & Robinson, J. P. (2012). Housework: Who did, does or will do it, and how much does it matter? *Social Forces, 91*(1), 55–63. doi:10.1093/sf/sos120

Blumer, H. (1980). The convergent methodological perspectives of social behaviorism and symbolic interactionism. *American Sociological Review, 45*(3), 409–419.

Bode, R. (1999). Mentoring and collegiality. In R. J. Menges (Ed.), *Faculty in new jobs: A guide to settling in, becoming established, and building institutional support.* (pp. 118–144). San Francisco, CA: Jossey-Bass.

Bogler, R., & Kremer-Hayon, L. (1999). The socialization of faculty member to university culture and norms. *Journal of Further and Higher Education, 23*(1), 31–40.

Boice, R. (1992). *The new faculty member: Supporting and fostering professional development.* San Francisco, CA: Jossey-Bass.

Boice, R. (1993). New faculty involvement for women and minorities. *Research in Higher Education, 34*(3), 291–341. doi:10.1007/BF00991847

Boice, R. (2000). *Advice for new faculty members: Nihil nimus.* Boston, MA: Allyn and Bacon.

Boyle, P., & Boice, R. (1998). Systematic mentoring for new faculty teachers and graduate teaching assistants. *Innovative Higher Education, 22*(3), 157–179.

Brems, C., Baldwin, M. R., Davis, L., & Namyniuk, L. (1994). The imposter syndrome as related to teaching evaluations and advising relationships of university faculty members. *The Journal of Higher Education, 65*(2), 183–193.

Buddle, C. (2012, October 25). The work-life balance: How many hours do professors work [Web log post]. Retrieved from https://arthropodecology.com/2012/10/25/the-work-life-balance-how-many-hours-do-professors-work/

Cale, G. (2015). An important caveat about self care [Web log post]. Retrieved from https://conditionallyaccepted.com/2015/06/23/selfcare-soothing/

Carnegie Classification of Institutions of Higher Education. (2016, December 6). Distribution of institutions and enrollments by classification category. In *Basic Classification.* Retrieved from http://carnegieclassifications.iu.edu/lookup/standard.php

Cawyer, C. S., & Friedrich, G. W. (1998). Organizational socialization: Processes for new communication faculty. *Communication Education, 47*, 235–245.

Charters, W. W. (1942). How much do professors work? *The Journal of Higher Education, 13*(6), 298–301.

Chickering, A. W., & Gamson, Z. F. (1987). Seven principles for good practice in undergraduate education. *AAHE Bulletin,* March, 3–7.

Clance, P. R., & Imes, S. A. (1978). The imposter phenomenon in high-achieving women: Dynamics and therapeutic intervention. *Psychotherapy: Theory, Research & Practice, 15*(3), 241–247. doi:10.1037/h0086006

Clark, B. R. (1972). The organizational saga in higher education. *Administrative Science Quarterly, 17*, 178–184.

Clark, B. R. (1987). *The academic life: Small worlds, different worlds.* Princeton, NJ: Carnegie Foundation for the Advancement of Teaching.

Clark, B. R. (1997). Small worlds, different worlds: The uniquenesses and troubles of American academic professions. *Daedalus, 126*(4), 21–42. doi:10.2307/20027457

Clark, M., Vardeman, K., & Barba, S. (2014). Perceived inadequacy: A study of the imposter phenomenon among college and research librarians. *College & Research Libraries,* May, 255–271.

COACHE. (2010). *Selected results from the COACHE tenure-track faculty job satisfaction survey.* Cambridge, MA: The President and Fellows of Harvard College. Retrieved from https://www.adapp-advance.msu.edu/sites/default/files/files_adapp-advance/resource/COACHE_AnalysisByAcademicAreaAndGender_2010.pdf

Colbeck, C. L. (1998). Merging into a seamless blend: How faculty integrate teaching and research. *The Journal of Higher Education, 69*(6), 647–671.

Connell, M. A., & Savage, F. G. (2001). The role of collegiality in higher education tenure, promotion, and termination decisions. *Journal of College and University Law, 27*(4), 833–858.

Cornell University Center for Teaching Excellence. (2017, April 3). Writing a syllabus. Retrieved from https://www.cte.cornell.edu/teaching-ideas/designing-your-course/writing-a-syllabus.html

Crutchfield, R. M. (2012). *"If I don't fight for it, I have nothing": Experiences of homeless youth scaling the collegiate mountain.* Unpublished doctoral dissertation. California State University of Long Beach, Long Beach, CA.

Curzan, A. (2015, August 20). "Serious academics" at play. *The Chronicle of Higher Education.* Retrieved from http://www.chronicle.com/blogs/linguafranca/2015/08/20/serious-academics-at-play/

Denard, T. J., Lunsford, J. G., & Rodrigues, H. A. (2015). Early career academic staff support: Evaluating mentoring networks. *Journal of Higher Education Policy and Management, 37*(3), 320-329.

Dmochowski, J. E. (2015, August 19). 10 things this instructor loves. *The Chronicle of Higher Education.* Retrieved from http://www.chronicle.com/article/10-Things-This-Instructor/232483/

Duffy, M. (2015, November 25). You do not need to work 80 hours a week to succeed in academia [Web log post]. Retrieved from http://sasconfidential .com/2015/11/25/80-hours/

Eagan, M. K., Stolzenberg, E. B., Lozano, J., Aragon, M. C., Suchard, M. R., & Hurtado, S. (2014). *Undergraduate teaching faculty: The 2013–2014 HERI faculty survey*. Los Angeles, CA: Higher Education Research Institute at UCLA.

Ernst, C. (2012, October 23). Yes or no [Web log post]. Retrieved from https:// thebuggeek.com/2012/10/23/yes-or-no/

Farmer, L., Ortiz, A. M., Boyd-Batstone, P., Stallones, J., O'Connor, D., & Pandya, J. (2014). *Mentoring tenure track probationary faculty*. College of Education, California State University of Long Beach, Long Beach, CA.

Finkelstein, M. J., Conley, V. M., & Schuster, J. H. (2016). *The faculty factor: Reassessing the American academy in a turbulent era*. Baltimore, MD: Johns Hopkins University Press.

Finkelstein, M. J., & Schuster, J. H. (2011). *A new higher education: The "next model" takes shape* (Advancing Higher Education, April 2011). New York, NY: TIAA-CREF Institute. Retrieved from https://www.tiaa-crefinstitute.org/public/ institute/research/advancing_higher_education/ahe_nextmodel04112.html

Flaherty, C. (2013, June 14). Tenure's fourth rail. *Inside Higher Ed*. Retrieved from https://www.insidehighered.com/news/2013/06/14/collegiality-experts-advocate-its-role-personnel-decisions

Gaff, J. G., Pruitt-Logan, A. S., & Weibl, R. A. (2000). *Building the faculty we need: Colleges and universities working together*. Washington DC: Association of American Colleges and Universities.

Gappa, J. M., Austin, A. E., & Trice, A. G. (2007). *Rethinking faculty work: Higher education's strategic imperative*. San Francisco, CA: Jossey-Bass.

Gaugler, J. E. (2004). On the tenure track in gerontology: I wish I had known then what I know now. *Educational Gerontology, 30,* 517–536. doi:10.1080/03601270490445122

Golde, C. M., & Dore, T. M. (2001). *At cross purposes: What the experiences of today's doctoral students reveal about doctoral education*. Philadelphia, PA: The Pew Charitable Trusts.

Grant, L., Kennelly, I., & Ward, K. B. (2000). Revisiting the gender, marriage, and parenthood puzzle in scientific careers. *Women's Studies Quarterly, 28*(1/2), 62–85.

Gravett, S., & Petersen, N. (2007). "You just try to find your own way": The experience of newcomers to academia. *International Journal of Lifelong Education, 26*(2), 193–207. doi:10.1080/02601370701219509

Greenberg, M. (1993, October 20). Accounting for faculty members' time. *The Chronicle of Higher Education*. Retrieved from http://www.chronicle.com/article/ accounting-for-faculty/93796

Hall, R. M., & Sandler, B. R. (1982). *The classroom climate: A chilly one for women?* Washington, DC: Association of American Colleges. Retrieved from http://files .eric.ed.gov/fulltext/ED215628.pdf

Hargittai, E. (2015). Making the most of the syllabus. *Inside Higher Education*. Retrieved from https://www.insidehighered.com/advice/2015/08/17/essay-how-prepare-syllabus-college-course

Harlow, R. (2003). "Race doesn't matter, but . . .": The effect of race on professors' experiences and emotion management in the undergraduate college classroom. *Social Psychology Quarterly, 66*(4), 348–363.

Harris, M. S. (2015, August 3). The "revise and resubmit." *Inside Higher Ed*. Retrieved from https://www.insidehighered.com/advice/2015/08/03/essay-how-academics-should-approach-revise-and-resubmit-responses-journals

Haviland, D., Alleman, N. F., & Cliburn Allen, C. (2017). "Separate but not quite equal": Collegiality experiences of full-time non-tenure-track faculty members. *Journal of Higher Education. 88*(4), 505–528.
doi: 10.1080/00221546.2016.1272321

Helms, R. M. (2010). *New challenges, new priorities: The experience of Generation X faculty*. Cambridge, MA: The Collaborative on Academic Careers in Higher Education.

Hollenshead, C., Waltman, J., August, L., Miller, J., Smith, G., & Bell, A. (2007). *Making the best of both worlds: Findings from a national institution-level survey of non-tenure-track faculty*. Ann Arbor, MI: The Center for the Education of Women. Retrieved from http://www.cew.umich.edu/sites/default/files/CEW Final Report PP34.pdf

Hurtado, S., Milem, J. F., Clayton-Pedersen, A. R., & Allen, W. R. (1998). Enhancing campus climate for racial/ethnic diversity: Education policy and practice. *The Review of Higher Education, 21*(3), 279–302.

Hutchins, H. M. (2015). Outing the imposter: A study exploring imposter phenomenon among higher education faculty. *New Horizons in Adult Education & Human Resource Development, 27*(2), 3–12.

Jayakumar, U., Howard, T. C., Allen, W. R., & Han, J. C. (2009). Racial privilege in the professoriate: An exploration of campus climate, retention, and satisfaction. *The Journal of Higher Education, 80*(5), 538–563. doi:10.1353/jhe.0.0063

Jenkins, R. (2015, June 22). Conquering mountains of essays: How to effectively and fairly grade a lot of papers without making yourself miserable. *The Chronicle of Higher Education*. Retrieved from http://www.chronicle.com/article/Conquering-Mountains-of-Essays/231063/

Jones, A. (2008). Preparing new faculty members for their teaching role. In N. V. N. Chism (Ed.), *Faculty at the margins* (Vol. 143, pp. 93–100). San Francisco, CA: New Directions for Higher Education. doi: 10.1002/he.317

Kegan, R. (1994). *In over our heads: The mental demands of modern life*. Cambridge, MA: Harvard University Press.

Kelsky, K. (2015, July 13). Ignore the haters and toot your own horn. *Vitae: The Chronicle of Higher Education*. Retrieved from https://chroniclevitae.com/news/1065-ignore-the-haters-and-toot-your-own-horn

Kezar, A., & Maxey, D. (2013, May/June). The changing academic workforce. *Trusteeship*, 1–12. Retrieved from http://agb.org/trusteeship/2013/5/changing-academic-workforce

Kezar, A., Maxey, D., & Eaton, J. S. (2014, January). *An examination of the changing faculty: Ensuring institutional quality and achieving desired student learning outcomes.* CHEA Occasional Paper for the Institute for Research and Study of Accreditation and Quality Assurance, the Council for Higher Education Accreditation (CHEA), Washington, DC.

Kezar, A., & Sam, C. (2010). *Understanding the new majority of non-tenure-track faculty in higher education: Demographics, experiences, and plans of action* (ASHE Report Series, Vol. 36). San Francisco, CA: Jossey-Bass.

Kezar, A., & Sam, C. (2011). Understanding non-tenure-track faculty: New assumptions and theories for conceptualizing behavior. *American Behavioral Scientist, 55*(11), 1419–1442. doi:10.1177/0002764211408879

Kiewra, K. A. (2008). Advice for developing scholars. *Educational Psychology Review, 20,* 79–86.

King, P. M., & Baxter Magolda, M. B. (2005). A developmental model of intercultural maturity. *Journal of College Student Development, 46*(6), 571–592.

Kirk, M. (2013, May 6). 10 tips to earn tenure. *Inside Higher Ed.* Retrieved from https://www.insidehighered.com/advice/2013/05/06/essay-how-earn-tenure

Kuh, G. D., & Whitt, E. J. (1988). *The invisible tapestry: Culture in American colleges and universities.* ASHE-ERIC Higher Education Report. Washington, DC: Association for the Study of Higher Education (ASHE-ERIC).

LaFrance, M., & Corbett, S. J. (2014, July 14). A 21st-century attendance policy. *The Chronicle of Higher Education.* Retrieved from http://www.chronicle.com/article/A-21st-Century-Attendance/147693/

Lakshmi, P. (Host). (2017). *Comida Final* [Television series episode]. In D. Cutforth & J. Lipsitz (Executive producers), Top Chef. New York, NY: Bravo.

Lamott, A. (1994). *Bird by bird: Some instructions on writing and life.* New York, NY: Pantheon Books.

Lang, J. M. (2015a, February 23). The 3 essential functions of your syllabus, part 1. *The Chronicle of Higher Education.* Retrieved from http://www.chronicle.com/article/The-3-Essential-Functions-of/190243/

Lang, J. M. (2015b, March 30). The 3 essential functions of your syllabus, part 2. *The Chronicle of Higher Education.* Retrieved from http://www.chronicle.com/article/The-3-Essential-Functions-of/228909/

Lang, J. M. (2016, January 11). Small changes in teaching: The first 5 minutes of class. *The Chronicle of Higher Education.* Retrieved from http://www.chronicle.com/article/Small-Changes-in-Teaching-The/234869

Lasch, C. (2002). *Plain style: A guide to written English.* Philadelphia, PA: University of Pennsylvania Press.

Light, P. (1994). "Not like us": Removing the barriers to recruiting minority faculty. *Journal of Policy Analysis and Management, 13*(1), 164–180.

Lindholm, J. A. (2003). Perceived organizational fit: Nurturing the minds, hearts, and personal ambitions of university faculty. *Review of Higher Education, 27*(1), 125–149. doi:10.1353/rhe.2003.0040

Lindholm, J. A. (2004). Pathways to the professoriate: The role of self, others, and environment in shaping academic career aspirations. *The Journal of Higher Education, 75*(6), 603–635.

Link, A. N., Swann, C. A., & Bozeman, B. (2008). A time allocation study of university faculty. *Economics of Education Review, 27*(4), 363–374.

Looser, D. (2015, November 20). Me and my shadow CV. [Web log post]. Retrieved from https://sasconfidential.com/2015/11/20/shadow-cv/

Lupton, D. (2012, November 28). 30 tips for successful academic research and writing [Web log post]. Retrieved from http://blogs.lse.ac.uk/impactofsocialsciences/2012/11/28/lupton-30-tips-writing/

Mallon, W. T. (2016). The anatomy and physiology of medical school faculty career models. In A. J. Kezar & D. Maxey (Eds.), *Envisioning the faculty for the twenty-first century: Moving to a mission-oriented and learner-centered model* (pp. 81–100). New Brunswick, NJ: Rutgers University Press.

Mason, S. R. (2015, August 5). Late again? *The Chronicle of Higher Education.* Retrieved from http://www.chronicle.com/article/Late-Again-/232115

Matveev, A. G. (2007). *Faculty enacting their daily work-life: A contextual analysis of the academic role in a comprehensive university.* Unpublished doctoral dissertation. The College of William and Mary, Williamsburg, VA.

Merton, R. K. (1968). The Matthew effect in science. *Science, 159*(3810), 7.

Milem, J. F., Berger, J. B., & Dey, E. L. (2000). Faculty time allocation: A study of change over twenty years. *Journal of Higher Education, 71*(4), 454–475.

Milem, J. F., Chang, M. J., & Antonio, A. L. (2005). *Making diversity work on campus: A research-based perspective* (One in a series of three papers commissioned as part of the Making Excellence Inclusive initiative). Washington, DC: Association of American Colleges and Universities (AAC&U).

Misra, J., Lundquist, J., Holmes, E., & Agiomavritis, S. (2011, January–February). The ivory ceiling of service work. *The American Association of University Professors.* Retrieved from https://www.aaup.org/article/ivory-ceiling-service-work#.WLR0j1UrK72

Mortensen, T. G. (2012, Winter). *State funding: A race to the bottom.* The American Council on Education. Retrieved from http://www.acenet.edu/the-presidency/columns-and-features/Pages/state-funding-a-race-to-the-bottom.aspx

Murray, J. P. (2000). *New faculty's perceptions of the academic work life.* Paper presented at the Association for the Study of Higher Education, Sacramento, CA.

NCES. (2010). Table 264: Full-time instructional faculty in degree-granting institutions, by race/ethnicity, sex, and academic rank: Fall 2005, fall 2007, and fall 2009. In *US Department of Education National Center for Educational Statistics.* Washington, DC: US Department of Education. Retrieved from https://nces.ed.gov/programs/digest/d11/tables/dt11_264.asp

NCES. (2013a). Number of full-time instructional staff employed by degree-granting postsecondary institutions by Carnegie Classification 2000 academic rank for fall 2013 (results limited by: sector of institution). In *US Department of Education*

National Center for Educational Statistics. Washington, DC: US Department of Education.

NCES. (2013b). Table 302.60: Percentage of 18- to 24-year-olds enrolled in degree-granting institutions, by level of institution and sex and race/ethnicity of student: 1967 through 2012. In *US Department of Education National Center for Educational Statistics.* Washington, DC: US Department of Education. Retrieved from http://nces.ed.gov/programs/digest/d13/tables/dt13_302.60.asp

NCES. (2013c). Table 306.10. Total fall enrollment in degree-granting postsecondary institutions, by level of enrollment, sex, attendance status, and race/ethnicity of student: Selected years, 1976 through 2012. In *US Department of Education National Center for Educational Statistics.* Washington, DC: US Department of Education. Retrieved from http://nces.ed.gov/programs/digest/d13/tables/dt13_306.10.asp

NCES. (2014). Table 303.40. Total fall enrollment in degree-granting postsecondary institutions, by attendance status, sex, and age: Selected years, 1970 through 2023. In *US Department of Education National Center for Educational Statistics.* Washington, DC: US Department of Education. Retrieved from http://nces.ed.gov/programs/digest/d13/tables/dt13_303.40.asp

NCES. (2015a). Table 315.10. Number of faculty in degree-granting postsecondary institutions, by employment status, sex, control, and level of institution: Selected years, 2003 through 2013. In *US Department of Education National Center for Educational Statistics.* Washington DC: US Department of Education.

NCES. (2015b). Table 315.20. Full-time faculty in degree-granting postsecondary institutions, by race/ethnicity, sex, and academic rank: Fall 2009, fall 2011, and fall 2013. In *US Department of Education National Center for Educational Statistics.* Washington DC: US Department of Education.

Nel, P. (2015, August 19). Advice for aspiring academics. *Inside Higher Ed.* Retrieved from https://www.insidehighered.com/advice/2015/08/19/essay-advice-academics-starting-their-careers

Nelson, M. (2015, June 2). Setting boundaries on your workload. *Vitae: The Chronicle of Higher Education.* Retrieved from https://chroniclevitae.com/news/1022-setting-boundaries-on-your-workload

Neumann, A. (2006). Professing passion: Emotion in the scholarship of professors at research universities. *43*(3), 381–424.

Olsen, D., & Sorcinelli, M. D. (1992). The pretenure years: A longitudinal perspective. In M. D. Sorcinelli & A. E. Austin (Eds.), *Developing new and junior faculty* (Vol. 50, pp. 15–25). San Francisco, CA: Jossey-Bass.

O'Meara, K. (2007). Striving for what? Exploring the pursuit of prestige. In J. C. Smart (Ed.), *Higher education: Handbook of theory and research* (pp. 121–179). Dordrecht, NL: Springer.

O'Meara, K. (2011). Inside the panopticon: Studying academic reward systems. In J. C. Smart & M. B. Paulsen (Eds.), *Higher education: Handbook of theory and research* (pp. 161–220). Dordrecht, NL: Springer Science+Business Media B.V.

O'Meara, K., Bennett, J. C., & Neihaus, E. (2016). Left unsaid: The role of work expectations and psychological contracts in faculty careers and departure. *The Review of Higher Education, 39*(2), 27. doi: 10.1353/rhe.2016.0007

O'Meara, K., Lounder, A., & Campbell, C. M. (2014). To heaven or hell: Sensemaking about why faculty leave. *The Journal of Higher Education, 85*(5), 603–632.

O'Meara, K., Terosky, A. L., & Neumann, A. (2008). *Faculty careers and work lives: A professional growth perspective* (Vol. 34). Hoboken, NJ: Wiley Periodicals.

O'Neal, C., Meizlish, D., & Kaplan, M. (2007) Writing a statement of teaching philosophy for the academic job search. *Center for Research on Learning and Teaching (CRLT) Occasional Papers,* No. 23. Ann Arbor, MI: The University of Michigan.

Ortiz, A. M., Filimon, I., & Cole-Jackson, M. (2015). Preparing student affairs educators. In E. J. Whitt & J. H. Schuh (Eds.), *New directions for student services* (Vol. 151, pp. 79–88). San Francisco, CA: Wiley.

Peterson, M. W., & Spencer, M. G. (1990). Understanding academic culture and climate. *New Directions for Institutional Research, 1990*(68), 3–18. doi:10.1002/ir.37019906803

Pittman, C. T. (2010). Race and gender oppression in the classroom: The experiences of women faculty of color with White male students. *Teaching Sociology, 38*(3), 183–196. doi:10.1177/0092055x10370120

Ray, V. (2016, October 21). The unbearable Whiteness of mesearch. *Inside Higher Ed.* Retrieved from https://www.insidehighered.com/advice/2016/10/21/me-studies-are-not-just-conducted-people-color-essay

Reybold, L. E. (2005). Surrendering the dream: Early career conflict and faculty dissatisfaction thresholds. *Journal of Career Development, 32*(2), 107–121. doi:10.1177/0894845305279163

Rice, R. E., Sorcinelli, M., & Austin, A. (2000). Heeding new voices: Academic careers for a new generation. In *New pathways: Faculty careers and employment for the 21st century: A working paper series from the Forum on Faculty Roles and Rewards.* Washington, DC: American Association for Higher Education.

Rockquemore, K. A. (2013, August 12). How to be a great mentor: A mentoring manifesto. *Inside Higher Ed.* Retrieved from https://www.insidehighered.com/advice/2013/08/12/essay-how-be-good-faculty-mentor-junior-professors

Rockquemore, K. A. (2015a, June 17). Should I stay or should I go? *Inside Higher Ed.* Retrieved from https://www.insidehighered.com/advice/2015/06/17/advice-frustrated-academic-after-first-year-tenure-track#.VYFgi2BERb4.twitter

Rockquemore, K. A. (2015b, July 1). Academic guilt. *Inside Higher Ed.* Retrieved from https://www.insidehighered.com/advice/2015/07/01/essay-academics-who-face-guilt-whenever-they-arent-working

Rockquemore, K. A., & Laszloffy, T. (2008). *The Black academic's guide to winning tenure—without losing your soul.* Boulder, CO: Lynne Rienner Publishers.

Royles, D. (2014a, September 3). Tenure-track wisdom, part 1. *Vitae: The Chronicle of Higher Education.* Retrieved from https://chroniclevitae.com/news/685-tenure-track-wisdom-part-1

Royles, D. (2014b, October 1). Tenure-track wisdom, part 2: Laura Krystal Porterfield. *Vitae: The Chronicle of Higher Education.* Retrieved from https://chroniclevitae.com/news/729-tenure-track-wisdom-part-2

Royles, D. (2015, March 19). Starting an online writing group. *Vitae: The Chronicle of Higher Education.* Retrieved from https://chroniclevitae.com/news/946-starting-an-online-writing-group

Sandler, B. R. (1986). *The campus climate revisited: Chilly for women faculty, administrators, and graduate students.* Washington, DC: Association of American Colleges.

Sands, R. G., Parsons, L. A., & Duane, J. (1991). Faculty mentoring faculty in a public university. *Journal of Higher Education, 62*(2), 174–193.

Sangaramoorthy, T. (2015, April 8). A hockey mom seeks tenure. *The Chronicle of Higher Education.* Retrieved from http://www.chronicle.com/article/A-Hockey-Mom-Seeks-Tenure/229193/

Schmidt, P. (2009, April 17). Generation gaps are evident in professors' views of their jobs. *The Chronicle of Higher Education.* Retrieved from http://www.chronicle.com/article/Generation-Gaps-Are-Evident-in/47189

Schmidt, P. (2013, June 10). New test to measure faculty collegiality produces some dissension itself. *The Chronicle of Higher Education.* Retrieved from http://www.chronicle.com/article/New-Test-to-Measure-Faculty/139695

Schuster, J. H., & Finkelstein, M. J. (2006). *The American faculty: The restructuring of academic work and careers.* Baltimore, MD: The Johns Hopkins University Press.

Scimago Journal & Country Rank. (2016). Journal rankings. Retrieved from http://www.scimagojr.com/journalrank.php?area=3300&country=US&category=3304

Seltzer, R. (2015, July 19). To find happiness in academe, women should just say no. *The Chronicle of Higher Education.* Retrieved from http://www.chronicle.com/article/To-Find-Happiness-in-Academe-/231641

ShitAcademicsSay. (2016a, January 4). I'm very busy. On an unrelated topic, I have questionable time management skills and difficulty saying no [Facebook post]. Retrieved from https://www.facebook.com/academicssay/

ShitAcademicsSay. (2016b, October 6). I was just wondering if you had time to grab a coffee and discuss how busy we are [Facebook post]. Retrieved from https://www.facebook.com/academicssay/

Silvia, P. J. (1976). *How to write a lot: A practical guide to productive academic writing.* Washington, DC: American Psychological Association.

Snow, D. A. (2001). Extending and broadening Blumer's conceptualization of symbolic interactionism. *Symbolic Interaction, 24*(3), 367–377.

Solem, M. N., & Foote, K. E. (2006). Concerns, attitudes, and abilities of early-career geography faculty. *Journal of Geography in Higher Education, 30*(2), 199–234. doi:10.1080/03098260600717299

Sorcinelli, M. D. (2000). Principle of good practice. In *New pathways: Faculty careers and employment for the 21st century: A working paper series from the Forum on*

Faculty Roles and Rewards. Washington, DC: American Association for Higher Education.

Stanley, C. A. (2006). Coloring the academic landscape: Faculty of color breaking the silence in predominantly White colleges and universities. *American Educational Research Journal, 43*(4), 701–736. doi:10.3102/00028312043004701

Stanley, C. A., & Lincoln, Y. (2005). Cross-race faculty mentoring. *Change: The Magazine of Higher Learning, 37*(2), 44–50.

Sternberg, R. J. (2015, May 26). Career advice from an oldish not-quite geezer. *The Chronicle of Higher Education.* Retrieved from http://www.chronicle.com/article/Career-Advice-From-an-Oldish/230335/

Strippling, J. (2010, January 22). Tenure case hinges on collegiality. *Inside Higher Ed.* Retrieved from https://www.insidehighered.com/news/2010/01/22/tenure

Sue, D. W., Capodilupo, C. M., Torino, G. C., Bucceri, J. M., Holder, A. M. B., Nadal, K. L., & Esquilin, M. (2007). Racial microaggressions in everyday life: Implications for clinical practice. *American Psychologist, 62*(4), 271–286. doi:http://dx.doi.org.ezproxy.library.csulb.edu/10.1037/0003-066X.62.4.271

Terosky, A. L., & Gonzales, L. D. (2016). Re-envisioned contributions: Experiences of faculty employed at institutional types that differ from their original aspirations. *The Review of Higher Education, 39*(2), 241–268.

Thomas, J. D., Lunsford, L. G., & Rodrigues, H. A. (2015). Early career academic staff support: Evaluating mentoring networks. *Journal of Higher Education Policy and Management, 37*(3), 320–329. doi:10.1080/1360080X.2015.1034426

Thomson Reuters (2017). InCites™ Journal Citation Reports. Retrieved from https://jcr.incites.thomsonreuters.com/JCRJournalHomeAction.action?SID=B1-xxQ0qXkDO-qaruwrnf78Muubn9F4vzyemx2F-18x2dOplm9PVYjEF6ZPQtUZbfUAx3Dx3D-jEjtazkK1OxxRmbEECEgsGQx3Dx3D-iyiHxxh55B2RtQWBj2LEuawx3Dx3D-1i-OubBm4x2FSwJjjKtx2F7lAaQx3Dx3D&SrcApp=IC2LS&Init=Yes

Trower, C. A. (2010). A new generation of faculty: Similar core values in a different world. *Peer Review, 12*(3), 27–30.

Trower, C. A., & Bleak, J. L. (2004). *Race: Statistical report* (The Study of New Scholars). Cambridge, MA: Harvard Graduate School of Education. Retrieved from http://sites.gse.harvard.edu/sites/default/files/coache/files/sns_report_race_0.pdf

Trower, C. A., & Gallagher, A. S. (2008). *Perspectives on what pre-tenure faculty want and what six research universities provide.* Cambridge, MA: Harvard Graduate School of Education. Retrieved from http://coache.gse.harvard.edu/files/gse-coache/files/coache_perspectives.pdf

Turner, C. S. V., & González, J. C. (2015). *Modeling mentoring across race/ethnicity and gender: Practices to cultivate the next generation of diverse faculty.* Sterling, VA: Stylus.

Turner, C. S. V., González, J. C., & Wood, J. L. (2008). Faculty of color in academe: What 20 years of literature tells us. *Journal of Diversity in Higher Education, 1*(3), 139–168. doi:10.1037/a0012837

University of Minnesota, Center for Educational Innovation. (2015a, February 20). Teaching philosophy samples. Retrieved from https://cei.umn.edu/support-services/tutorials/writing-teaching-philosophy/teaching-philosophy-samples

University of Minnesota, Center for Educational Innovation. (2015b, February 20). Writing a teaching philosophy. Retrieved from https://cei.umn.edu/support-services/tutorials/writing-teaching-philosophy

University of Washington, Center for Teaching and Learning. (2017). Course and syllabus design. Retrieved from http://www.washington.edu/teaching/teaching-resources/preparing-to-teach/designing-your-course-and-syllabus/

Vanderbilt University, Center for Teaching. (2017). Syllabus construction. Retrieved from https://cft.vanderbilt.edu/guides-sub-pages/syllabus-design/

VanOosting, J. (2015, January 16). The four ages of a professor. *Inside Higher Ed*. Retrieved from https://www.insidehighered.com/views/2015/01/16/essay-four-ages-professor

Ward, K., & Wolf-Wendel, L. F. (2004). Academic motherhood: Managing complex roles in research universities. *The Review of Higher Education, 27*(2), 233–257.

Ziker, J. (2014, March 31). The long, lonely job of *homo academicus*: Focusing the research lens on the professor's own schedule. *The Blue Review*. Retrieved from http://thebluereview.org/faculty-time-allocation/

ABOUT THE AUTHORS

Don Haviland is a professor in the Educational Leadership Department at Long Beach State University. Haviland's research focuses on pretenure and non-tenure-track faculty, and he facilitates the New Faculty Success Group in the College of Education at Long Beach. He was part of a team that did a national evaluation of the Preparing Future Faculty program and participated in that program himself at Syracuse University. His hobbies include listening to music (jazz, blues, and classic rock), watching baseball, and tasting wine.

Laura Henriques is a professor and former chair of the Science Education Department at Long Beach State University. She has mentored and provided support to new department chairs, tenure-track faculty, and lecturers. She also has worked with faculty as principal investigator on large grants, mentored K–12 teachers assuming leadership positions within professional organizations, and been involved in science education at the state level. Her nonwork hobbies include cooking, making cards, and traveling.

Anna M. Ortiz is a professor and department chair in the Educational Leadership Department at Long Beach State University. Ortiz's research focuses on ethnic identity in college students, multicultural issues in higher education, and professional development of student affairs administrators and faculty. She has led numerous faculty development activities, including early career mentoring groups for the past 10 years, and served as the founding director of the NASPA Faculty Division. She is a certified sommelier, teaching classes and writing about all things related to wine.

INDEX

professional community
  creation of, 211–12
  new, strategies for, 59
  off campus, 54
  service roles in, 31
professional relationships
  accountability in, 119
  boundaries in, 68
  with colleagues, 58–60, 62–67
  core values for, 70–71
  in early career faculty, 53, 58,
    62–63
  with faculty, 56, 58–60
  faculty growth perspective of, 7
  goals for, 70–72
  in institutions, 62–63
  mentoring in, 60–61
  in minoritized faculty, 63–64
  research on, 56
  with students, 67–70
professionals
  association mentoring programs
    for, 213–14
  identity of, 34
  priorities of, 53
professional trust, 57
professors. *See also* faculty; *specific
    types*
  graduate students becoming,
    5–6
  images of, 17–18
  self-authorship life of, 35–36
  service roles of, 29–31
  student interaction with, 37
project description, 126, 132–33
project management
  guidance in, 217–18
  tool for, 111
project outcomes, 133
psychological contracts, 203–4
publication
  demands of, 27, 101

of dissertation, 100, 107–10
feedback from, 116–18
organization of, 112
outlets, 103–9
self-, 107
sharing of, 119
PWIs. *See* predominantly White
  institutions

quick starters, 4–5

race, 39, 92
RateMyProfessor, 93–94
Ray, Victor, 226
reading
  of abstracts, 106
  as good habit, 112
  of literature, 103
  writing on, 106
red tape, 27
regimens, 5
registration
  schedule for, 97
  for semesters, 91
  timelines for, 92
rejection, 39–41
reporting, 133
reputation, 60, 124
research
  of associate professors, 30
  changing roles in, 161
  collaboration for, 120
  costs of, 131
  design of, 109–12
  expectations of, 102
  funding for, 120
  HERI, 25–26
  institutions, 102
  lab, 110
  on mentoring, 213
  during negotiations, 200
  paradigms in, 226

"The second updated edition of *What They Didn't Teach You in Graduate School: 299 Helpful Hints for Success in Your Academic Career* includes 100 new tips and keys to success in obtaining a PhD and covers everything from the underlying rules of academic life to the dissertation process, job hunting, and dealing with students. From those who are students to those who have just landed their first faculty position but still strive for their PhDs, this is packed with clear directions and insights not to be missed!"
—*California Bookwatch*

Sty/us

22883 Quicksilver Drive
Sterling, VA 20166-2102   Subscribe to our e-mail alerts: www.Styluspub.com

Also available from Stylus

THE COACH'S GUIDE FOR WOMEN PROFESSORS
Who Want a Successful Career and a Well-Balanced Life

RENA SELTZER
Foreword By Frances Rosenbluth

The Coach's Guide for Women Professors
Who Want a Successful Career and a Well-Balanced Life
Rena Seltzer

Foreword by Frances Rosenbluth

"This book has something for *all* women in academia. Traditionally, the academy has been governed by unwritten rules that determine academic career success. Through the lived experiences of women faculty, *The Coach's Guide* sheds light on those unwritten rules in order to help women navigate successfully around them. This book offers just the right tools."
—*Gloria D. Thomas, Director, Center for the Education of Women, University of Michigan*

"*The Coach's Guide for Women Professors* will be an amazing asset for female academics. It is packed full of practical and empowering strategies that will pay immediate dividends, as well as being a resource that you will want to return to for clear solutions to challenges that arise. It is an invaluable resource for women (and men) who care about advancing their own careers as well as the careers of women in the academy."
—*Linda C. Babcock, James M. Walton Professor of Economics, Carnegie Mellon University, Author of* Women Don't Ask: Negotiation and the Gender Divide

What They Didn't Teach You in Graduate School
299 Helpful Hints for Success in Your Academic Career

Second Edition
Paul Gray and David E. Drew

Illustrated by Matthew Henry Hall

Foreword by Laurie Richlin and Steadman Upham

"*What They Didn't Teach You in Graduate School* is exactly what it claims to be: A collection of tips and hints that are rarely part of graduate education and yet are essential to survival in academic life, no matter what stage or discipline. Gray and Drew share their experiences teaching, publishing, and navigating institutional bureaucracy in a way that is highly readable and uniquely informative. This book would find a welcome place on any scholar's shelf."
—*Mary Hamner, University of North Carolina at Charlotte*

(Continued on preceding page)